Italian Cookbook

600 Modern & Authentic Recipes
For Amazing American Italian Cooking

Brenda Maroni

Warning-Disclaimer

The purpose of this book is to educate and entertain. The author or publisher does not guarantee that anyone following the techniques, suggestions, tips, ideas, or strategies will become successful. The author and publisher shall have neither liability or responsibility to anyone with respect to any loss or damage caused, or alleged to be caused, directly or indirectly by the information contained in this book.

CONTENTS

SOUPS 30

PASTA 39

PIZZA & SNACKS 50

BEANS, RICE & GRAINS 63

PORK, BEEF & LAMB 106

MEATLESS RECIPES 120

SIDES, SAUCES & SPICES 127

DESSERTS 132

INTRODUCTION

Ciao! Welcome to my Italian cookbook!

It's so loving for me to share my passion for Italian cooking with you. I have something for everyone, whether you're a beginner or an expert. My goal is that this cookbook will help you learn how to make some genuinely unique and very tasty Italian dishes.

You don't have to be Italian to make great Italian food.

Don't get me wrong: I love the complexity and nuance of Italian cooking. It's one of my favorite cuisines, and I've spent years exploring it. But I also know how to bring out those flavors in weeknight-worthy fashion.

Italian food is balanced — flavor, texture, temperature, and more. You can achieve magnificent results by using the right spices, understanding how to coax out flavor through easy techniques like roasting and toasting, and learning how to mix richness with acidity and heat with creaminess or a touch of sweetness.

A bit of History

Italian cuisine is a part of Mediterranean cuisine, one of the most popular in the world. It is a diverse and varied cuisine, with influences from all over Europe, Americas, Africa and Asia. Italian food has a crucial role not only in the Italian culture and history but it also shaped the cooking habits around the world.

The origins of Italian cuisine are found in the regional cuisines of ancient Italy, which were characterized by the different social classes, agricultural conditions and culinary traditions that predominated in various parts of the country.

The history of Italian cuisine is almost as old as that of Italy itself, and it's influenced by the many travelers from and to Italy from around the world. With its wide variety of ingredients and dishes, this cuisine has always been one of the trendiest abroad.

Italian flavors

The best way to start cooking Italian food is by understanding the basic flavor profiles of different ingredients.Once you know what flavors work well together, you can create your own recipes without having to follow a recipe exactly.

The base flavors of Italian cuisine are basil, thyme, rosemary, and olive oil. These are all strong and bold flavors that really let you get creative.

Most of the time, when people think of "Italian food," they think of pasta—but there's so much more to it than that! There are also delicious meats like veal and lamb; seafood like fish and shellfish; fruit like grapes and tomatoes; vegetables like potatoes and squash; cheeses like mozzarella or Parmesan; nuts like hazelnuts or almonds… The possibilities are endless.

Italian Staples

Whether making dinner for two or twenty, having a well-stocked pantry is the key to successful Italian cooking.

In the United States, many of these ingredients are familiar because they're also used in other cuisines. However, some might feel new. Taste them all out and see which ones work best for you!

These staples will ensure you are prepped and ready to cook accessible Italian food favorites any night of the week.

Must-Have Italian pantry essentials for Italian food enthusiasts:

- Extra Virgin Olive Oil
- Canned tomatoes
- Balsamic Vinegar
- Dried Pasta

- Canned beans
- Capers
- Olives
- Cooking wine
- Spices and herbs: Some of the more popular are: basil, oregano, marjoram, thyme, rosemary, bay leaves, sage, or Italian Seasoning (blend of herbs and spices used to flavor many Italian dishes).

How to Make an own Italian Seasoning

You'll never want to buy Italian seasoning again after you make your own! It's so simple, and it tastes so much better than store-bought.

My magic ingredients for ½ cup made only in 5 minutes:

- 1 teaspoon ground bay leaf
- 2 tablespoons dried basil
- 2 tablespoons dried oregano
- 1 tablespoon dried rosemary
- 1 tablespoon dried marjoram
- 1 tablespoon dried thyme
- 1 tablespoon red chili flakes
- 1 teaspoon garlic powder

In a small bowl, combine all ingredients. Place into an air tight container and store in a cool dark place for up to 3 months.

About the Recipes

When craving Italian flavor, you don't want to spend hours in the kitchen. You want something delicious and easy to make.

That's why we developed this cookbook—to help you find quick, easy, and delicious recipes. We've got breakfast recipes, appetizer recipes, lunch recipes, dinner recipes and more. Any time of day you need Italian food, we've got it. And everything is made with authentic Italian ingredients like tomatoes, spinach and artichokes

And finally, something interesting: do you know...

I love Italian food, and we're sure you do, too. Whether you're a huge fan of spaghetti and meatballs or just looking for a little something new to try in your favorite restaurant, there are so many reasons why it's such a fantastic cuisine.

Here are 10 interesting facts about Italian food that I think you'll love!

1. Italy has over 600 different varieties of cheese!
2. Pizza started as a bread-like dish made with tomato sauce and cheese
3. Caesar Cardini, not Julius Caesar, made the first Caesar salad
4. The word "pizza" comes from the Greek word "pita," which means "pie"
5. Pasta means "cooked dough" in Spanish and Arabic (not Italian).
6. Tomato sauce is called "salsa" in Italy
7. Eating pasta before bedtime is suitable for digestion and helps your body absorb nutrients better!
8. In Italy, when someone says "ciao," it means hello or goodbye—not just hi! (Italians say "buongiorno" or "buonasera.")
9. Gelato comes from the Latin word for "ice cream."
10. Italy produces more hazelnuts than any other country in the world, accounting for around 19% of global production.

MORNING RECIPES

1. Pepperoncini & Cheese Frittata

Serves: 6 | Ready in about: 35 minutes

2 tbsp olive oil
12 fresh eggs

¼ cup half-and-half
Salt and black pepper to taste

½ pepperoncini, minced
2 ½ cups shredded mozzarella

Whisk the eggs in a bowl and preheat the oven to 350 F. Add the half-and-half, salt, and black and stir to combine. Warm the olive oil in a skillet over medium heat. Sauté the pepperoncini for 2-3 minutes. Sprinkle evenly with mozzarella cheese. Pour eggs over cheese into the skillet. Place the skillet in the oven and bake for 20–25 minutes until just firm. Let cool the frittata for a few minutes and cut it into wedges. Serve hot.

2. Classic Eggs Florentine with Pancetta

Serves: 2 | Ready in about: 20 minutes

1 English muffin, toasted and halved
¼ cup chopped pancetta

2 tsp hollandaise sauce
1 cup spinach

Salt and black pepper to taste
2 large eggs

Place pancetta over medium heat in a pan and cook for 5 minutes until crispy; reserve. Add the baby spinach and cook for 2-3 minutes in the same pan until the spinach wilts. Fill a pot with 3 inches of water over medium heat and bring to a boil. Add 1 tbsp of vinegar and reduce the heat.

Crack the eggs one at a time into a small dish and gently pour them into the simmering water. Poach the eggs for 2-3 minutes until the whites are set, but the yolks are still soft; remove with a slotted spoon. Divide the spinach between muffin halves and top with pancetta and poached eggs. Spoon the hollandaise sauce on top and serve.

3. Smoked Salmon Frittata

Serves: 4 | Ready in about: 15 minutes

1 ball fresh mozzarella, chopped
2 tsp olive oil
8 fresh eggs

½ cup whole milk
1 spring onion, chopped
¼ cup chopped fresh basil

Salt and black pepper to taste
3 oz smoked salmon, chopped

Whisk the eggs with milk, spring onion, basil, pepper, and salt in a bowl. Preheat your broiler to medium. Heat the olive oil in a skillet over medium heat and pour in the egg mixture. Top with mozzarella cheese and cook for 3–5 minutes until the frittata is set on the bottom, and the egg is almost set but still moist on top. Scatter over the salmon and place the skillet under the preheated broiler for 1-2 minutes or until set and slightly puffed. Cut the frittata into wedges. Enjoy!

4. Garlicky Mushroom Frittata

Serves: 2 | Ready in about: 15 minutes

2 tsp olive oil, divided
4 eggs, beaten

1 cup mushrooms, sliced
1 garlic clove, minced

Salt and black pepper to taste
¼ cup sliced onions

In a frying pan over medium heat, warm the olive oil. Place in garlic, mushrooms, and onions. Cook for 6 minutes, stirring often. Season with salt and pepper. Increase the heat and cook for 3 minutes. Remove to a plate. Add the eggs to the same pan and ensure they are evenly spread. Top with the veggies. Slice into wedges and serve.

5. Berry & Walnut Porridge

Serves: 2 | Ready in about: 10 minutes

1 cup mixed berries
1 ½ cups rolled oats

2 tbsp walnuts, chopped
2 tsp maple syrup

Take the oats and cook them according to the package instructions and share in 2 bowls. Microwave the maple syrup and berries for 30 seconds; stir well. Pour over each bowl. Top with walnuts.

6. Zucchini Scrambled Eggs with Cherry Tomatoes

Serves: 4 | Ready in about: 15 minutes

2 tbsp olive oil
6 cherry tomatoes, halved
½ cup chopped zucchini

½ chopped green bell pepper
8 eggs, beaten
1 shallot, chopped

1 tbsp chopped fresh parsley
1 tbsp chopped fresh basil
Salt and black pepper to taste

In a pan over medium heat, warm the olive oil. Place in zucchini, green bell peppers, salt, black pepper, and shallot. Cook for 4-5 minutes to sweat the shallot. Stir in tomatoes, parsley, and basil. Cook for a minute and top with the beaten eggs. Lower the heat and cook for 6-7 minutes until the eggs are set but not runny. Remove to a platter to serve.

7. Baked Zucchini & Egg Nests

Serves: 4 | Ready in about: 25 minutes

2 tbsp olive oil
4 eggs

1 lb zucchini, shredded
Salt and black pepper to taste

½ red chili pepper, minced
2 tbsp parsley, chopped

Combine zucchini, salt, pepper, and olive oil in a bowl. Preheat the oven to 360 F. Form nest shapes with a spoon onto a greased baking sheet. Crack an egg into each nest and season with salt, pepper, and chili. Bake for 11 minutes. Serve topped with parsley.

8. Scallion Scrambled Eggs with Smoked Salmon

Serves: 4 | Ready in about: 15 minutes

2 tbsp olive oil
4 oz smoked salmon, flaked
½ red onion, finely chopped

8 eggs
Salt and black pepper to taste
½ tsp garlic powder

1 scallion, chopped
2 tbsp green olives, chopped

In a bowl, beat eggs, garlic powder, salt, and pepper. Warm olive oil in a skillet over medium heat. Stir in onion and sauté for 1-2 minutes. Add in olives and salmon and cook for another minute. Pour in the eggs and stir-fry for 5-6 minutes until the eggs are set. Serve topped with scallion.

9. Mushroom & Cherry Tomato Frittata

Serves: 4 | Ready in about: 30 minutes

1 cup brown mushrooms, sliced
2 tbsp olive oil
2 spring onions, chopped

8 cherry tomatoes, halved
6 eggs
½ cup milk

Salt and black pepper to taste
¼ cup grated Parmesan
½ tbsp Italian seasoning mix

Mix eggs, milk, Italian seasoning, salt, and pepper in a bowl. Preheat oven to 370 F. Warm olive oil in a skillet over medium heat until sizzling. Add in mushrooms, spring onions, and tomatoes and sauté for 5 minutes. Pour in the egg mixture and cook for 5 minutes until the eggs are set. Scatter Parmesan cheese and bake in the oven for 6-7 minutes until the cheese melts. Slice before serving.

10. Poppy Seed Bread

Serves: 6 | Ready in about: 25 minutes + rising time

¼ cup olive oil
4 cups whole-wheat flour
3 tbsp oregano, chopped

2 tsp dry yeast
1 cup black olives, sliced
1 cup lukewarm water

½ cup ricotta cheese, crumbled
1 tbsp poppy seeds
1 egg, beaten

In a bowl, mix the flour, water, yeast, and olive oil and knead the dough well. Transfer to a bowl and let sit covered with plastic wrap to rise until doubled in size for 60 minutes. Remove the wrap and fold in oregano, black olives, and ricotta cheese. Place on a floured surface and knead again. Shape the dough into 6 balls and place them in a lined baking sheet. Cover and let rise for another 40 minutes. Preheat the oven to 390 F. Brush the balls with the egg and sprinkle with the poppy seeds. Bake for 25-30 minutes. Serve.

11. Pizza-Style Frittata

Serves: 4 | Ready in about: 20 minutes

2 tbsp butter
8 oz pancetta, chopped
½ onion, finely chopped
1 cup mushrooms, sliced

8 large eggs, beaten
¼ cup heavy cream
1 tsp dried oregano
¼ tsp red pepper flakes

½ cup mozzarella, shredded
8 cherry tomatoes, halved
4 black olives, sliced

In a large skillet over medium heat, melt the butter until almost smoking. Add the pancetta and cook for 4 minutes until browned. Stir in the onion and mushrooms and cook for 3 more minutes, stirring occasionally, until the veggies are tender. In a bowl, beat the eggs, heavy cream, oregano, and red pepper flakes. Pour over the veggies and pancetta. Cook for about 5-6 minutes until the eggs are set. Spread the mozzarella cheese all over and arrange the cherry tomatoes on top. Place under the preheated broiler for 4-5 minutes. Leave to cool slightly and cut into wedges. Top with sliced olives and serve warm.

12. Vegetable Polenta & Fried Eggs

Serves: 4 | Ready in about: 35 minutes

2 tbsp butter
½ tsp sea salt
1 cup polenta
4 eggs

2 spring onions, chopped
1 bell pepper, chopped
1 zucchini, chopped
1 tsp ginger-garlic paste

1 ½ cups vegetable broth
¼ tsp chili flakes, crushed
2 tbsp basil leaves, chopped

In a skillet, melt 1 tbsp of the butter over medium heat. Place in spring onions, ginger-garlic paste, bell pepper, and zucchini and sauté for 5 minutes; set aside. Pour the broth and 1 ½ cups of water into a pot and bring to a boil. Gradually whisk in polenta to avoid chunks, lower the heat, and simmer for 4-5 minutes. Keep whisking until it begins to thicken. Cook covered for 20 minutes, stirring often. Add the zucchini mixture, chili flakes, and salt and stir. Heat the remaining butter in a skillet. Break the eggs and fry them until set and well cooked. Divide the polenta between bowls, top with fried eggs and basil, and serve.

13. Eggplant & Kale Frittata

Serves: 1 | Ready in about: 20 minutes

1 tbsp olive oil
3 large eggs
1 tsp milk

1 cup curly kale, torn
½ eggplant, peeled and diced
¼ red bell pepper, chopped

Salt and black pepper to taste
1 oz crumbled Goat cheese

Whisk the eggs with milk, salt, and pepper until just combined. Preheat your broiler. Heat the olive oil in a small skillet over medium heat. Spread the eggs on the bottom and add the kale on top in an even layer; top with veggies. Season with salt and pepper. Allow the eggs and vegetables to cook 3 to 5 minutes until the bottom half of the eggs are firm and vegetables are tender. Top with the crumbled Goat cheese and place under the broiler for 5 minutes until the eggs are firm in the middle and the cheese has melted. Slice into wedges and serve immediately.

14. Herby Cheese Frittata

Serves: 2 | Ready in about: 20 minutes

1 tbsp olive oil
½ pint cherry tomatoes
2 garlic cloves, minced

5 large eggs, beaten
3 tbsp milk
Salt and black pepper to taste

2 tbsp fresh oregano, minced
2 tbsp fresh basil, minced
2 oz ricotta cheese, crumbled

In a skillet, warm the olive oil over medium heat. Add the cherry tomatoes. Reduce the heat, cover the pan, and let the tomatoes soften. When the tomatoes are mostly softened and broken down, remove the lid, add garlic and continue to sauté. In a bowl, combine the eggs, milk, salt, pepper, and herbs and whisk well to combine. Increase the heat to medium, pour the egg mixture over the tomatoes and garlic, and then sprinkle with ricotta cheese. Cook for 7-8 minutes, flipping once until the eggs are set. Run a spatula around the edge of the pan to make sure they won't stick.

15. Fontina Cheese Frittata with Veggies

Serves: 4 | Ready in about: 30 minutes

2 tbsp olive oil
½ lb cauliflower florets
½ cup skimmed milk

6 eggs
1 red bell pepper, chopped
½ cup fontina cheese, grated

½ tsp red pepper
½ tsp turmeric
Salt and black pepper to taste

In a bowl, beat the eggs with milk. Preheat oven to 360 F. Add in fontina cheese, red pepper, turmeric, salt, and pepper. Mix in bell pepper. Warm the oil in a skillet over medium heat, pour in the egg mixture and cook for 5 minutes; set aside. Blanch the cauliflower florets in a pot for 5 minutes until tender. Spread over the egg mixture. Place the skillet in the oven and bake for 15 minutes or until golden brown. Allow cooling for a few minutes before slicing.

16. Ricotta & Zucchini Egg Muffins

Serves: 4 | Ready in about: 20 minutes

3 tbsp olive oil
½ cup ricotta cheese, crumbled
1 lb zucchini, spiralized

¼ cup sweet onion, chopped
4 large eggs
½ tsp hot paprika

2 tbsp fresh parsley, chopped
Salt and black pepper to taste

Combine the zucchini and sweet onion with olive oil, salt, and black pepper in a bowl. Preheat oven to 350 F. Divide between greased muffin cups. Crack an egg in each one; scatter some salt and hot paprika. Bake for 12 minutes or until set. Serve topped with ricotta cheese and parsley.

17. Ricotta & Spinach Bruschetta

Serves: 2 | Ready in about: 15 minutes

2 sourdough bread slices, toasted
1 avocado
2 tbsp ricotta cheese, crumbled

Salt and black pepper to taste
½ tsp lime juice
1 cup baby spinach

3 radishes, thinly sliced

In a bowl, mash the avocado with lime juice, salt, and pepper until smooth. Spread the mixture on the bread slices. Top with baby spinach and ricotta cheese. Top with radishes and serve.

18. Roasted Peppers & Spinach Frittata

Serves: 4 | Ready in about: 30 minutes

2 tbsp olive oil
1 cup roasted peppers, chopped
½ cup milk

8 eggs
Salt and black pepper to taste
1 tsp oregano, dried

½ cup red onions, chopped
4 cups baby spinach
1 cup goat cheese, crumbled

Beat the eggs with salt, pepper, and oregano in a bowl. Warm the olive oil in a skillet over medium heat and sauté onions for 3 minutes until soft. Mix in spinach, milk, and goat cheese and pour over the eggs. Cook for 2-3 minutes until the base of the frittata is set. Place in preheated 360 F oven and bake for 10-15 minutes until the top is golden. Top with roasted peppers.

19. Anchovy & Scrambled Eggs a la Napolitana

Serves: 4 | Ready in about: 20 minutes

2 tbsp olive oil
1 green bell pepper, chopped
2 anchovy fillets, chopped
8 cherry tomatoes, cubed

2 spring onions, chopped
1 tbsp capers, drained
5 black olives, pitted and sliced
6 eggs, beaten

Salt and black pepper to taste
¼ tsp dried oregano
1 tbsp parsley, chopped

In a skillet over medium heat, warm the olive oil, and cook the bell pepper and spring onions for 3 minutes. Add in anchovies, cherry tomatoes, capers, and black olives and cook for another 2 minutes. Stir in eggs and sprinkle with salt, pepper, and oregano and scramble for 5 minutes. Serve sprinkled with parsley.

20. Salami & Cheese Egg Cupcakes

Serves: 6 | Ready in about: 25 minutes

½ cup roasted red peppers, chopped
1 tbsp olive oil
5 eggs, whisked

4 oz Italian dry salami, sliced
1/3 cup spinach, chopped
¼ cup ricotta cheese, crumbled

Salt and black pepper to taste
1 ½ tbsp basil pesto

Brush 6 ramekin cups with olive oil and line them with dry salami slices. Preheat the oven to 380 F. Top with spinach, ricotta cheese, and roasted peppers. Whisk the eggs with pesto, salt, and pepper in a bowl and pour over the peppers. Bake for 15 minutes and serve warm.

21. Bruschetta with Avocado & Tomatoes

Serves: 4 | Ready in about: 5 minutes

1 tbsp olive oil
1 baguette, sliced
2 sun-dried tomatoes, chopped
1 avocado, chopped

2 tbsp lemon juice
8 cherry tomatoes, chopped
¼ cup red onion, chopped
1 tsp dried oregano

2 tbsp parsley, chopped
4 black olives, chopped
Salt and black pepper to taste

Arrange the bread slices on a greased baking tray and drizzle with olive oil. Preheat oven to 360 F. Bake until golden, about 6-8 minutes. Mash the avocado in a bowl with lemon juice, salt, and pepper. Stir in sun-dried tomatoes, onion, oregano, parsley, and olives. Spread the avocado mixture on toasted bread slices and top with cherry tomatoes. Serve.

22. Parmesan Egg Cupcakes

Serves: 2 | Ready in about: 30 minutes

¼ cup kale, chopped
3 eggs
1 leek, sliced

4 tbsp Parmesan, grated
2 tbsp almond milk
1 red bell pepper, chopped

Salt and black pepper to taste
1 tomato, chopped
2 tbsp mozzarella, grated

Grease a muffin tin with cooking spray. Preheat the oven to 360 F. Whisk the eggs in a bowl. Add in milk, kale, leek, Parmesan cheese, bell pepper, salt, black pepper, tomato, and mozzarella cheese and stir to combine. Divide the mixture between the cases and bake for 20-25 minutes. Let cool completely on a wire rack before serving.

23. Green Frittata

Serves: 4 | Ready in about: 55 minutes

4 oz canned artichokes, chopped
2 tsp olive oil
½ cup whole milk
8 eggs

1 cup spinach, chopped
1 garlic clove, minced
½ cup Parmesan, crumbled
1 tsp oregano, dried

1 Jalapeño pepper, minced
Salt to taste

Warm the olive oil in a skillet over medium heat and sauté garlic and spinach for 3 minutes. Preheat oven to 360 F. Beat the eggs in a bowl. Stir in artichokes, milk, Parmesan cheese, oregano, jalapeño pepper, and salt. Add in spinach mixture and toss to combine. Transfer to a greased baking dish and bake for 20 minutes until golden and bubbling. Slice into wedges and serve.

24. Bell Pepper Frittata

Serves: 2 | Ready in about: 10 minutes

2 tbsp olive oil
2 red bell peppers, chopped

¼ tsp nutmeg
4 eggs, beaten

2 garlic cloves, crushed
1 tsp Italian seasoning

Heat olive oil in a skillet over medium heat. Stir-fry the peppers for 3 minutes or until lightly charred; reserve. Add the garlic to the skillet and sauté for 1 minute. Pour the eggs over the garlic, sprinkle with Italian seasoning and nutmeg, and cook for 2-3 minutes or until set. Using a spatula, loosen the edges and gently slide them onto a plate. Add charred peppers and fold over. Serve hot.

25. Prosciutto & Spinach Crostini

Serves: 1 | Ready in about: 5 minutes

1 tsp olive oil
2 prosciutto slices
2 ciabatta slices, toasted

1 tbsp Dijon mustard
Salt and black pepper to taste
1 tomato, sliced

¼ cup baby spinach

Cover one side of each ciabatta slice with Dijon mustard and top with prosciutto, tomato, spinach, salt, and pepper on each slice. Drizzle with olive oil and serve.

26. Grated Zucchini & Egg Stuffed Tomatoes

Serves: 4 | Ready in about: 40 minutes

1 tbsp olive oil
1 small zucchini, grated

8 tomatoes, insides scooped
8 eggs

Salt and black pepper to taste

Place tomatoes on a greased baking dish. Preheat the oven to 360 F. Mix the zucchini with olive oil, salt, and pepper. Divide the mixture between the tomatoes and crack an egg on each one. Bake for 20-25 minutes. Serve warm.

27. Tomato-Basil Eggs in a Pan

Serves: 2 | Ready in about: 25 minutes

2 tsp olive oil
2 eggs, whisked

2 tomatoes, cubed
1 tbsp basil, chopped

1 green onion, chopped
Salt and black pepper to taste

In a skillet, warm the oil over medium heat and sauté tomatoes, green onion, salt, and pepper for 5 minutes. Stir in eggs and cook for another 10 minutes. Serve topped with basil.

28. Chive & Mozzarella Cheese Cups

Serves: 2 | Ready in about: 20 minutes

2 eggs, whisked
1 tbsp chives, chopped

1 tbsp dill, chopped
Salt and black pepper to taste

3 tbsp mozzarella, grated
1 tomato, chopped

Grease 2 ramekins with cooking spray. Preheat the oven to 400 F. Whisk eggs, tomato, mozzarella cheese, salt, pepper, dill, and chives in a bowl. Share into each ramekin and bake for 10 minutes. Serve warm.

29. Stir-Fried Scrambled Eggs with Pancetta

Serves: 4 | Ready in about: 1 hour 15 minutes

2 tbsp olive oil
4 eggs, whisked
1 red onion, chopped

3 oz pancetta, chopped
2 garlic cloves, minced
2 oz goat cheese, crumbled

1 tbsp basil, chopped
Salt and black pepper to taste

Warm half of the olive oil in a skillet over medium heat and sauté onion, pancetta, and garlic for 3 minutes. Add in goat cheese and whisked eggs and cook for 5-6 minutes, stirring often. Season with salt and pepper. Sprinkle with basil and serve.

30. Power Green Smoothie

Serves: 1 | Ready in about: 10 minutes

1 tbsp extra-virgin olive oil
1 avocado, peeled and pitted
1 cup milk

½ cup watercress
½ cup baby spinach leaves
½ cucumber, peeled and seeded

10 mint leaves, stems removed
½ lemon, juiced

In your blender, mix avocado, milk, baby spinach, watercress, cucumber, olive oil, mint, and lemon juice and blend until smooth and creamy. Add more milk or water to achieve your desired consistency. Serve.

31. Sweet Potato Frittata

Serves: 4 | Ready in about: 25 minutes

2 sweet potatoes, boiled and chopped
2 tbsp olive oil
4 eggs, whisked
1 red onion, chopped

¾ cup ham, chopped
½ cup white beans, cooked
2 tbsp Greek yogurt
Salt and black pepper to taste

10 cherry tomatoes, halved
¾ cup cheddar cheese, grated

In a skillet, warm the olive oil over medium heat and sauté onion for 2 minutes. Stir in sweet potatoes, ham, beans, yogurt, salt, pepper, and tomatoes and cook for another 3 minutes. Pour in eggs and cheese, lock the lid and cook for an additional 10 minutes. Cut before serving.

32. Breakfast Smoothie

Serves: 1 | Ready in about: 10 minutes

1 tbsp olive oil
2 tbsp almond butter
1 cup almond milk

¼ cup blueberries
1 tbsp ground flaxseed
1 tsp honey

½ tsp vanilla extract
¼ tsp ground cinnamon

In your blender, mix the almond milk, blueberries, almond butter, flaxseed, olive oil, stevia vanilla, and cinnamon and pulse until smooth and creamy. Add more milk or water to achieve your desired consistency. Serve at room temperature.

33. Strawberry-Chocolate Smoothie

Serves: 2 | Ready in about: 5 minutes

1 cup buttermilk
2 cups strawberries, hulled

1 cup crushed ice
3 tbsp cocoa powder

3 tbsp honey
2 mint leaves

In a food processor or a blender, pulse buttermilk, strawberries, ice, cocoa powder, mint, and honey until smooth.

34. Date Smoothie

Serves: 1 | Ready in about: 5 minutes

1 apple, peeled and chopped
½ cup milk

4 dates
1 tsp ground cinnamon

In your blender, place the milk, ½ cup of water, dates, cinnamon, and apple. Blitz until smooth. Let chill in the fridge for 30 minutes. Serve in a tall glass.

35. Peach Smoothie

Serves: 2 | Ready in about: 5 minutes

2 cups almond milk
2 cups peaches, chopped

1 cup crushed ice
½ tsp ground ginger

1 tbsp maple syrup

In your food processor or a blender, mix milk, peaches, ice, maple syrup, and ginger until smooth. Serve.

36. Morning Detox Juice

Serves: 1 | Ready in about: 5 minutes

½ grapefruit
½ lemon
3 cups cavolo nero

1 cucumber
¼ cup fresh parsley leaves
¼ pineapple, cut into wedges

½ green apple
1 tsp grated fresh ginger

In a blender or a mixer, place the cavolo nero, parsley, cucumber, pineapple, grapefruit, apple, lemon, and ginger and pulse until smooth. Serve in a tall glass.

37. Prosciutto Sandwiches

Serves: 4 | Ready in about: 10 minutes

1 large, ripe tomato, sliced into 8 rounds
8 whole-wheat bread slices

1 avocado, halved and pitted
Salt and black pepper to taste
8 romaine lettuce leaves

8 thin prosciutto slices
1 tbsp cilantro, chopped

Toast the bread slices and place on a large platter. Scoop the avocado flesh out of the skin into a small bowl. Season with pepper and salt. With a fork, gently mash the avocado until it resembles a creamy spread. Smear 4 bread slices with the avocado mix. Top with a layer of lettuce leaves, tomato slices, and prosciutto slices. Repeat the layers one more time, sprinkle with cilantro, then cover with the remaining bread slices. Serve and enjoy!

38. Caper & Egg Scramble

Serves: 4 | Ready in about: 30 minutes

2 tbsp olive oil
1 small red onion, chopped
1 bell green pepper, chopped
½ tsp red pepper flakes

1 tbsp capers
3 medium tomatoes, chopped
Salt and black pepper to taste
1 tbsp ground cumin

1 tsp ground coriander
4 large eggs, lightly beaten

In a skillet, warm the olive oil over medium heat. Add the onion and cook until soft and translucent, 5-7 minutes. Add in the tomatoes and season to taste. Stir in the capers, cumin, and coriander. Simmer for 10 minutes. Add the eggs, stirring them into the mixture to distribute. Cover the skillet and cook until the eggs are set but still fluffy and tender, 5-6 more minutes. Serve topped with red pepper flakes.

39. Cheesy Muffins with Pear Glaze

Serves: 4 | Ready in about: 45 minutes

16 oz ricotta cheese
2 large eggs
¼ cup flour

1 tbsp sugar
1 tsp vanilla extract
¼ tsp ground nutmeg

1 pear, cored and diced
1 tbsp sugar

Preheat your oven to 400 F. In a large bowl, whisk the ricotta, eggs, flour, sugar, vanilla, and nutmeg. Spoon into 4 greased ramekins. Bake for 20-25 minutes. Transfer to a wire rack to cool before unmolding. Place the pear, sugar, and 2 tbsp of water in a small saucepan over low heat. Simmer for 10 minutes until slightly softened. Remove from the heat, and stir in the honey. Serve the ricotta ramekins glazed with pear sauce.

40. Strawberry-Banana Pancakes

Serves: 4 | Ready in about: 15 minutes

2 tbsp olive oil
1 cup flour
1 cup + 2 tbsp milk
2 eggs, beaten

1/3 cup honey
1 tsp baking soda
¼ tsp salt
1 sliced banana

1 cup sliced strawberries
1 tbsp maple syrup

In a bowl, mix together flour, milk, eggs, honey, baking soda, and salt. Warm the olive oil in a skillet over medium heat and pour in **1/3** cup of the pancake batter. Cook for 2-3 minutes. Add half of the fresh fruit and flip to cook for 2-3 minutes on the other side until cooked through. Top with the remaining fruit, drizzle with maple syrup and serve.

41. Pumpkin & Apple Muffins

Serves: 12 | Ready in about: 30 minutes

½ cup butter, melted
1 ½ cups granulated sugar
½ cup sugar
¾ cup flour

2 tsp pumpkin pie spice
1 tsp baking soda
¼ tsp salt
¼ tsp nutmeg

1 apple, grated
1 (15-oz) can pumpkin puree
½ cup full-fat yogurt
2 large egg whites

In a bowl, mix the sugars, flour, pumpkin pie spice, baking soda, salt, and nutmeg. In a separate bowl, mix apple, pumpkin puree, yogurt, and butter. Preheat the oven to 350 F. Slowly mix the wet ingredients with the dry ingredients. Using a mixer on high, whip the egg whites until stiff and fold them into the batter. Pour the batter into a greased muffin tin, filling each cup halfway. Bake for 25 minutes or until a fork inserted in the center comes out clean. Let cool.

42. Artichoke & Ricotta Frittata

Serves: 2 | Ready in about: 20 minutes

4 oz canned artichoke hearts, quartered
2 tbsp olive oil
4 large eggs
1 tsp dried herbs

Salt and black pepper to taste
1 cup kale, chopped
8 cherry tomatoes, halved

½ cup crumbled ricotta cheese

In a bowl, whisk the eggs, herbs, salt, and pepper and whisk well with a fork. Set aside. Warm the olive oil in a skillet over medium heat. Sauté the kale, artichoke, and cherry tomatoes until just wilted, 1-2 minutes. Preheat oven to 360 F. Pour the egg mixture over and let it cook for 3-4 minutes until the eggs begin to set on the bottom. Sprinkle with ricotta cheese on top. Place the skillet under the preheated broiler for 5 minutes until the frittata is firm in the center and golden brown on top. Invert the frittata onto a plate and slice in half. Serve warm.

43. Blueberry Oatmeal

Serves: 2 | Ready in about: 10 minutes +chilling time

⅔ cup milk
1/3 cup quick rolled oats

¼ cup blueberries
1 tsp honey

½ tsp ground cinnamon
¼ tsp ground cloves

In 2 mason jars, layer the oats, milk, blueberries, honey, cinnamon, and cloves. Cover and store in the refrigerator overnight. Serve cold, and enjoy!

44. Almond & Chia Oatmeal

Serves: 2 | Ready in about: 10 minutes

¼ tsp almond extract
½ cup milk
½ cup rolled oats

2 tbsp almonds, sliced
2 tbsp sugar
1 tsp chia seeds

¼ tsp ground cardamom
¼ tsp ground cinnamon

Mix the milk, oats, almonds, sugar, chia seeds, cardamom, almond extract, and cinnamon in a mason jar and shake well. Keep in the refrigerator for 4 hours. Serve.

45. Weekend Pancakes in Berry Sauce

Serves: 4 | Ready in about: 20 minutes

Pancakes
6 tbsp olive oil
1 cup flour
1 tsp baking powder
Berry Sauce
1 cup mixed berries
3 tbsp sugar

¼ tsp salt
2 large eggs
1 lemon, zested and juiced

1 tbsp lemon juice
½ tsp vanilla extract

½ tsp vanilla extract
½ tsp dark rum

In a large bowl, mix the flour, baking powder, and salt and whisk to break up any clumps. Add 4 tablespoons of olive oil, eggs, lemon zest and juice, rum, and vanilla extract and whisk to combine well. Brush a frying pan with butter over medium heat and cook the pancakes for 5-7 minutes, flipping once until bubbles begin to form. To make the sauce, pour the mixed berries, lemon juice, vanilla, and sugar into a small saucepan over medium heat. Cook for 3-4 minutes until bubbly, adding a little water if the mixture is too thick. Mash the berries with a fork and stir until smooth. Pour over the pancakes and serve.

46. Peppery Egg Scramble

Serves: 4 | Ready in about: 20 minutes

½ cup fresh mozzarella cheese, crumbled

2 tsp olive oil

1 cup bell peppers, chopped

2 garlic cloves, minced

6 large eggs, beaten

Salt to taste

2 tbsp fresh cilantro, chopped

In a large skillet, warm the olive oil over medium heat. Add the peppers and sauté for 5 minutes, stirring occasionally. Add the garlic and cook for 1 minute. Stir in the eggs and salt and cook for 2-3 minutes until the eggs begin to set on the bottom. Top with mozzarella cheese and cook the eggs for about 2 more minutes, stirring slowly, until the eggs are soft-set and custardy. Sprinkle with cilantro and serve.

47. Basil Mascarpone-Strawberry Toast

Serves: 2 | Ready in about: 15 minutes

4 fresh basil leaves, sliced

4 whole-grain bread slices, toasted

½ cup mascarpone cheese

1 tbsp honey

1 cup strawberries, sliced

In a bowl, combine the mascarpone and honey. Spread the mixture evenly over each slice of bread. Top with sliced strawberries and basil.

48. Tomato Eggs

Serves: 6 | Ready in about: 25 minutes

2 tbsp olive oil

1 onion, chopped

2 garlic cloves, minced

2 (14-oz) cans tomatoes, diced

6 large eggs

½ cup fresh chives, chopped

Warm the oil in a large skillet over medium heat. Add the onion and garlic and cook for 3 minutes, stirring occasionally. Pour in the tomatoes with their juices o and cook for 3 minutes until bubbling. Crack one egg into a small custard cup. With a large spoon, make six indentations in the tomato mixture. Gently pour the first cracked egg into one indentation and repeat, cracking the remaining eggs, one at a time, into the custard cup and pouring one into each indentation. Cover the skillet and cook for 6-8 minutes. Top with chives and serve.

49. Spinach & Egg Pie

Serves: 8 | Ready in about: 30 minutes

2 puff pastry doughs, at room temperature

2 tbsp olive oil

1 onion, chopped

1 lb spinach, chopped

Salt and black pepper to taste

¼ tsp ground nutmeg

4 large eggs

1 cup grated Pecorino cheese

4 hard-boiled eggs, halved

Preheat your oven to 350 F. Warm the oil in a large skillet over medium heat. Sauté onion for 5 minutes until translucent. Add the spinach and cook for 5 minutes until wilted. Add the garlic salt, pepper, and nutmeg. Set aside to cool. Whisk 3 eggs in a small bowl. Pour them over the cooled spinach mixture and sprinkle with ½ cup Pecorino cheese.

Roll out one of the pastry doughs on a greased baking sheet. Spread the spinach mix on top, leaving 2 inches around each edge. Top with hard-boiled egg halves, then cover with the second pastry dough. Pinch the edges closed. Beat the remaining egg in a small bowl. Brush the egg wash over the top of the pie. Bake for 15-20 minutes until golden.

50. Raisin Spinach with Pine Nuts

Serves: 4 | Ready in about: 10 minutes

2 tbsp olive oil

4 cups fresh baby spinach

1 garlic clove, minced

2 tbsp raisins, soaked

2 tbsp toasted pine nuts

Salt and black pepper to taste

Warm the olive oil in a pan over medium heat and sauté spinach and garlic for 3 minutes until the spinach wilts. Mix in raisins, pine nuts, salt, and pepper and cook for 3 minutes.

SALADS

51. Classic Tuscan Panzanella Salad

Serves: 4 | Ready in about: 25 minutes

2 cups mixed cherry tomatoes, quartered
4 bread slices, crusts removed, cubed
4 tbsp extra-virgin olive oil
1 cucumber, sliced
½ red onion, thinly sliced

¼ cup chopped fresh basil
½ tsp dried oregano
1 tbsp capers
1 garlic clove, minced

¼ cup red wine vinegar
2 anchovy fillets, chopped
Salt and black pepper to taste

Preheat your oven to 320 F. Pour the bread cubes into a baking dish and drizzle with 2 tbsp of olive oil. Bake for 6-8 minutes, shaking occasionally until browned and crisp. Let cool. Toss the cooled bread, cherry tomatoes, cucumber, red onion, basil, anchovies, and capers in a serving dish. In another bowl, whisk the remaining olive oil, oregano, red wine vinegar, and garlic. Adjust the seasoning with salt and pepper. Drizzle the dressing over the salad and toss to coat.

52. Tomato & Burrata Tuna Salad

2 tbsp extra-virgin olive oil
2 tbsp canned tuna, flaked
4 heirloom tomato slices

Salt and black pepper to taste
4 burrata cheese slices
8 fresh basil leaves, sliced

1 tbsp balsamic vinegar

Place the tomato slices on a plate. Top with burrata slices and tuna. Sprinkle with basil. Drizzle with olive oil and balsamic vinegar and serve.

53. Tuna & Bean Salad

Serves: 4 | Ready in about: 10 minutes

2 (5-oz) cans can tuna packed in olive oil, drained and flaked
4 cups spring mix greens
1 (15-oz) can cannellini beans
2/3 cup ricotta cheese, crumbled
6 sun-dried tomatoes, sliced

10 Kalamata olives, sliced
2 thinly sliced green onions
¼ medium red onion, sliced
3 tbsp extra-virgin olive oil

½ tsp dried cilantro
3 leaves fresh basil, chopped
1 lemon, zested and juiced
Salt and black pepper to taste

In a large bowl, place the greens, cannellini beans, tuna, ricotta cheese, tomatoes, olives, green onions, red onion, olive oil, cilantro, basil, lemon juice and zest. Season with salt and pepper and mix to coat. Serve and enjoy!

54. Corn & Spinach Salad

Serves: 4 | Ready in about: 10 minutes

10 oz baby spinach
1 red bell pepper, sliced

2 cups corn
1 lemon, zested and juiced

Salt and black pepper to taste

In a large bowl, combine bell pepper, corn, lemon juice, lemon zest, baby spinach, salt, and pepper. Serve immediately.

55. Pesto Chicken Salad with Parmesan

Serves: 4 | Ready in about: 15 minutes

2 cups chopped cooked chicken breasts
1 cup canned artichoke hearts, chopped
2 tbsp extra-virgin olive oil
2 tomatoes, chopped
2 heads romaine lettuce, torn

2 cucumbers, chopped
½ red onion, finely chopped
3 oz Parmesan cheese, shaved
4 oz pesto
1 lemon, zested

2 garlic cloves, minced
2 tbsp chopped fresh basil
2 tbsp chopped scallions
Salt and black pepper to taste

In a bowl, combine the lettuce, artichoke, chicken, tomatoes, cucumbers, and red onion, and mix well. In another bowl, mix pesto, olive oil, lemon zest, garlic, basil, salt, and pepper and stir to combine. Drizzle the pesto dressing over the salad and top with scallions and Parmesan cheese shavings to serve.

56. Healthy Caesar Salad

Serves: 6 | Ready in about: 10 minutes

½ cup buttermilk
4 tbsp light mayonnaise
1 tbsp yellow mustard
2 tbsp lemon juice

2 cloves garlic, chopped
¼ cup Parmesan, grated
¼ tsp cayenne pepper
Salt and black pepper to taste

1 head romaine lettuce, torn
1 cup croutons
¼ cup Parmesan, shaved

In a large mixing bowl, vigorously whisk the buttermilk, mayonnaise, mustard, lemon juice, and garlic until all is well incorporated. Stir in Parmesan cheese, cayenne pepper, salt, and pepper. Place the lettuce in a large salad bowl and toss with dressing. Arrange the croutons on top. Garnish with Parmesan shaves and serve.

57. Ravioli Salad

Serves: 6 | Ready in about: 15 minutes

1 cup smoked mozzarella cheese, cubed
¼ tsp lemon zest
1 cup basil pesto

½ cup mayonnaise
2 red bell peppers, chopped

18 oz cheese ravioli

In a pot, bring to a boil salted water over high heat. Add the ravioli and cook, uncovered, for 4-5 minutes, stirring occasionally; drain and place them in a salad bowl to cool slightly. Blend the lemon zest, pesto, and mayonnaise in a large bowl and stir in mozzarella cheese and bell peppers. Pour the mixture over the ravioli and toss to coat. Serve.

58. Spelt Salad with Chicken

Serves: 4 | Ready in about: 35 minutes

4 tbsp olive oil
½ lb chicken breasts
1 tbsp dill, chopped
2 lemons, zested

Juice of 2 lemons
3 tbsp parsley, chopped
Salt and black pepper to taste
1 cup spelt grains

1 red lettuce head, torn
1 red onion, sliced
10 cherry tomatoes, halved
1 cucumber, sliced

In a medium-sized bowl, mix dill, lemon zest, lemon juice, 2 tbsp olive oil, parsley, salt, and pepper. Add in chicken breasts, toss to coat, cover, and refrigerate for 30 minutes. Place spelt grains in a pot and cover with water. Stir in salt and pepper. Put over medium heat and bring to a boil. Cook for 45 minutes and drain.

Transfer to a bowl and let it cool. Preheat the grill. Remove the chicken and grill for 12 minutes on all sides. Transfer to a bowl to cool before slicing. Once the spelt is cooled, add in the remaining olive oil, lettuce, onion, tomatoes, and cucumber and toss to coat. Top the salad with sliced chicken and serve.

59. Nutty Tuna Salad

Serves: 6 | Ready in about: 10 minutes

1 (5-oz) can tuna in olive oil, drained and flaked
1 endive head, chopped
1 shallot, sliced
3 tbsp chives, chopped

3 tbsp mayonnaise
1 tsp Dijon mustard
1/2 lemon, juiced and zested

Salt and black pepper to taste
¼ cup toasted pine nuts

In a medium-sized salad bowl, toss endive, tuna, shallot, and chives. Whisk the mayonnaise, mustard, lemon zest, lemon juice, salt, and pepper in a bowl. Spoon the mayonnaise mixture over the tuna salad and top with pine nuts.

60. Olive Three-Bean Salad

Serves: 6 | Ready in about: 15 minutes

1 lb green beans, trimmed
1 red onion, thinly sliced
2 tbsp marjoram, chopped
¼ cup black olives, chopped

½ cup canned cannellini beans
½ cup canned chickpeas
2 tbsp extra-virgin olive oil
½ cup balsamic vinegar

½ tsp dried oregano
Salt and black pepper to taste

Steam the green beans for about 2 minutes or until just tender. Drain and place them in an ice-water bath. Drain thoroughly and pat them dry with paper towels. Put them in a large bowl and toss with the remaining ingredients.

61. Mustardy Turkey Salad

Serves: 4 | Ready in about: 15 minutes

2 cups chopped cooked turkey breasts
1 cup canned artichoke hearts, chopped
2 hard-boiled eggs, chopped
½ cup green olives, sliced

1 red bell pepper, chopped
8 cherry tomatoes, quartered
2 tbsp yellow mustard
½ cup extra-virgin olive oil

3 tbsp lemon juice
1green onion, chopped
Salt and black pepper to taste
¼ tsp red pepper flakes

In a large bowl, whisk the mustard, oil, lemon juice, salt, pepper, and red pepper flakes. Add the chicken, eggs, green olives, bell pepper, artichoke hearts, green onion, and cherry tomatoes and toss to coat. Serve.

62. Gorgonzola Fuit Salad

Serves: 4 | Ready in about: 10 minutes

2 tbsp gorgonzola cheese, crumbled
¼ cup extra-virgin olive oil
4 apples, peeled and sliced
2 kiwis, peeled and chopped

1 tbsp lemon juice
½ cup curly endive, chopped
½ cup sliced strawberries
½ cup walnuts, chopped

¼ cup balsamic vinegar
2 tbsp sesame seeds
Salt and black pepper to taste

In a bowl, combine apples with lemon juice. Stir in strawberries, kiwis, endive, gorgonzola cheese, and walnuts. In another bowl, mix balsamic vinegar, olive oil, salt, and pepper. Pour over the salad and toss to combine. Share into bowls and top with sesame seeds. Serve.

63. Caesar Salad with Ricotta Cheese

Serves: 2 | Ready in about: 5 minutes +chilling time

2 grilled chicken breasts, sliced
2 tbsp olive oil
¼ cup balsamic vinegar
½ cup sliced red onion

1 tsp lemon juice
10 cherry tomatoes, halved
1 iceberg lettuce head, torn
Salt and black pepper to taste

½ cup ricotta cheese, crumbled
8 pitted black olives, halved

In a bowl, mix vinegar and lemon juice. Slowly pour in olive oil and mix until blended. Sprinkle with salt and pepper. Combine well. Stir in chicken, tomatoes, onion, and olives. Cover and transfer to the fridge for 2 hours. Share the lettuce into 2 salad bowls and scoop each with half of the chicken mixture. Serve topped with ricotta cheese.

64. Caprese Salad with Tuna

Serves: 4 | Ready in about: 15 minutes

2 tbsp extra-virgin olive oil
2 oz tuna in water, flaked
3 large tomatoes, sliced

¼ cup basil leaves, torn
4 oz fresh mozzarella, sliced
¼ cup balsamic vinegar

Sea salt to taste
10 black olives

On a serving plate, arrange the tomato and mozzarella slices. Season with salt, scatter basil all over, and drizzle with vinegar and olive oil. Top with tuna and olives and serve.

65. Fish Salad

Serves: 4 | Ready in about: 5 minutes

3 tbsp olive oil
4 oz smoked mackerel, flaked
10 radishes, sliced

5 oz baby arugula
1 cup corn
2 tbsp lemon juice

Sea salt to taste
2 tbsp fresh parsley, chopped

Arrange the arugula on a serving plate. Top with corn, mackerel, and radishes. Mix olive oil, lemon juice, and salt in a bowl and pour the dressing over the salad. Top with parsley.

66. Potato & Egg Salad

Serves: 6 | Ready in about: 15 minutes

¼ cup olive oil
2 lb potatoes, peeled and sliced
4 spring onions, chopped

½ cup fennel, sliced
2 eggs
2 tbsp fresh lemon juice

1 tbsp capers
½ tbsp Dijon mustard
Salt and black pepper to taste

To a pot, add the eggs and cover them with salted water. Bring to a boil and turn the heat off. Let sit covered in hot water for 10 minutes, then cool before peeling and cutting into slices. In another pot, place the potatoes and cover them with enough water. Bring to a boil, then lower the heat and simmer for 8-10 minutes until tender. In a serving bowl, whisk the olive oil with lemon juice, mustard, salt, and pepper. Add in the potatoes, eggs, capers, spring onions, and fennel slices and toss to combine. Serve.

67. Cheesy Spinach & Bean Salad

Serves: 4 | Ready in about: 35 minutes

4 tbsp olive oil
1 garlic clove, minced
½ tsp cumin
½ tsp chili flakes
2 tbsp red wine vinegar

1 tbsp fresh lemon juice
1 tbsp fresh dill
Salt to taste
1 (14.5-oz) can black beans
2 cups fresh baby spinach

¼ lb goat cheese, crumbled
½ cup spring onions, sliced
1 jalapeño pepper, chopped
2 bell peppers, chopped

In a bowl, combine the garlic, cumin, chili flakes, olive oil, vinegar, lemon juice, dill, and salt. Put it in the fridge. Mix the black beans, baby spinach, spring onions, jalapeño pepper, and bell pepper in another bowl. Remove the dressing from the refrigerator and pour over the salad; toss to coat. Top with the goat cheese and serve.

68. Shrimp Salad with Avocado

Serves: 4 | Ready in about: 10 minutes +cooling time

1 lb shrimp, peeled and deveined
2 tbsp olive oil
1 tbsp lemon juice

1 yellow bell pepper, sliced
1 Romano lettuce, torn
1 avocado, chopped

Salt to taste
12 cherry tomatoes, halved

Preheat your grill pan over high heat. Drizzle the shrimp with some olive oil and arrange them on the preheated grill pan. Sear for 5 minutes on both sides until pink and cooked through. Let cool completely. On a serving plate, arrange the lettuce and top with bell pepper, shrimp, avocado, and cherry tomatoes. In a bowl, add the lemon juice, salt, and olive oil and whisk to combine. Drizzle the dressing over the salad and serve immediately.

69. Lentil Salad with Tomatoes

2 tomatoes, chopped
1 green bell pepper, chopped
14 oz canned lentils, drained

2 spring onions, chopped
1 red bell pepper, chopped
2 tbsp cilantro, chopped

2 tsp balsamic vinegar

In a large bowl, mix lentils, spring onions, tomatoes, bell peppers, cilantro, and vinegar in a bowl. Serve immediately.

70. Sundried Tomato Salad with Eggs & Spinach

Serves: 4 | Ready in about: 10 minutes

2 tbsp olive oil
10 oz baby spinach
6 eggs, at room temperature

Juice of 1 lime
1 cup ricotta cheese, crumbled
Salt and black pepper to taste

2 tbsp mustard
8 sundried tomatoes, chopped
1 cup walnuts, chopped

In a large pot, bring to a boil salted water over medium heat. Add in the eggs and cook for 10 minutes. Remove to a bowl with ice-cold water and let them cool; peel and chop. Put the baby spinach on a large serving plate. Place olive oil, eggs, lime juice, ricotta cheese, salt, pepper, mustard, sun-dried tomatoes, and walnuts and toss to combine in a bowl. Pour the mixture over the spinach and serve.

71. Seafood Salad

Serves: 4 | Ready in about: 50 minutes

2 tbsp olive oil
2 cups olives, sliced
1 octopus, tentacles separated
2 oz calamari rings

3 garlic cloves, minced
1 white onion, chopped
¾ cup chicken stock
2 cups watercress, sliced

1 cup parsley, chopped
Salt and black pepper to taste
1 tbsp red wine vinegar

In a large pot, place octopus, stock, calamari rings, salt, and pepper over medium heat and bring to a simmer. Cook for 40 minutes. Strain seafood and let cool completely. Chop tentacles into pieces. Remove to a serving bowl along with the calamari rings. Stir in garlic, onion, watercress, olives, parsley, red wine vinegar, and olive oil and toss to coat.

72. Almond & Red Cabbage Coleslaw

Serves: 4 | Ready in about: 10 minutes

2 tbsp olive oil
1 red cabbage head, shredded
2 tbsp cilantro, chopped

½ cup almonds, chopped
1 tomato, cubed
Salt and black pepper to taste

1 tbsp white wine vinegar

In a large bowl, combine red cabbage, cilantro, almonds, olive oil, tomato, salt, pepper, and vinegar. Serve cold.

73. Balsamic Potato Salad

Serves: 2 | Ready in about: 30 minutes

2 tbsp olive oil
3 potatoes, peeled and cubed

2 tbsp capers
1 red onion, chopped

1 tbsp balsamic vinegar
Salt and black pepper to taste

Place the potatoes in a pot over medium heat with enough water and bring to a boil; cook for 20 minutes. Drain and remove to a bowl. Stir in red onion, olive oil, capers, vinegar, salt, and pepper. Serve chilled.

74. Rice & Carrot Salad

Serves: 4 | Ready in about: 10 minutes

2 tbsp olive oil
1 Iceberg lettuce head, torn
2 carrots, grated

1 cup brown rice, cooked
1 red onion, sliced
½ cup mint, chopped

1 lime, juiced
½ cup corn
Salt and black pepper to taste

Mix the rice, olive oil, onion, lettuce, carrot, mint, lime juice, corn, salt, and pepper in a bowl. Serve right away.

75. Anchovy Cucumber Salad

Serves: 4 | Ready in about: 10 minutes

2 tbsp extra virgin olive oil
1 tbsp lemon juice
4 canned anchovy fillets

6 black olives
½ head Romaine lettuce, torn
Salt and black pepper to taste

1 cucumber, cubed
3 tomatoes, cubed
2 spring onions, chopped

Whisk olive oil, lemon juice, salt, and pepper in a bowl. Add the cucumber, tomatoes, and spring onions and toss to coat. Top with anchovies and black olives, and serve.

76. Colorful Salad

Serves: 4 | Ready in about: 10 minutes

¼ cup olive oil
1 cup black olives, halved
10 cherry tomatoes, halved

1 red onion, chopped
2 tbsp parsley, chopped
2 tbsp balsamic vinegar

2 tsp dried Italian herbs
Salt and black pepper to taste

Mix the black olives, cherry tomatoes, red onion, parsley, vinegar, olive oil, Italian herbs, salt, and pepper in a bowl and toss to combine. Serve right away.

77. Caper & Arugula Salad

Serves: 4 | Ready in about: 10 minutes

1 tbsp olive oil
10 green olives, sliced
4 cups baby arugula

1 tbsp capers, drained
1 tbsp balsamic vinegar
1 tsp lemon zest, grated

1 tbsp lemon juice
1 tsp parsley, chopped
Salt and black pepper to taste

Mix the capers, olives, vinegar, lemon zest, lemon juice, oil, parsley, salt, pepper, and arugula in a bowl. Serve.

78. Cilantro Carrot & Tomato Salad

Serves: 4 | Ready in about: 10 minutes

2 tbsp olive oil
4 tomatoes, chopped
1 carrot, grated

¼ cup lime juice
1 garlic clove, minced
Salt and black pepper to taste

1 lettuce head, chopped
2 green onions, chopped
½ cup cilantro, chopped

Toss the lime juice, garlic, salt, pepper, olive oil, carrot, lettuce, onions, tomatoes, and cilantro in a bowl. Serve cold.

79. Seed & Radicchio Salad

Serves: 4 | Ready in about: 10 minutes

3 tbsp olive oil
1 cup radicchio, shredded
1 lettuce head, torn

1 cup raisins
2 tbsp lemon juice
¼ cup chives, chopped

Salt and black pepper to taste
1 tbsp sunflower seeds, toasted

Mix the olive oil, raisins, lemon juice, chives, radicchio, salt, pepper, lettuce, and sunflower seeds in a bowl. Serve.

80. Spinach & Cherry Tomato Salad

Serves: 4 | Ready in about: 15 minutes

¼ cup olive oil
4 cups baby spinach leaves

10 cherry tomatoes, halved
Salt and black pepper to taste

¼ cup pumpkin seeds
½ lemon, juiced

Toast the seeds in a dry sauté pan over medium heat for 2 minutes, shaking often. Let cool. In a small jar, add the olive oil, lemon juice, salt, and pepper. Place the baby spinach on a salad platter and top with cherry tomatoes. Drizzle with the vinaigrette and sprinkle with toasted pumpkin seeds. Serve immediately.

81. Radish Salad with Olives

Serves: 4 | Ready in about: 10 minutes

2 tbsp olive oil
1 Romaine lettuce, shredded
1 lb red radishes, sliced

1 tbsp lemon zest
Salt and black pepper to taste
2 tbsp parsley, chopped

1 small red onion, sliced
10 black olives, sliced

Mix the lemon zest, salt, pepper, parsley, olive oil, radishes, onion, olives, and lettuce in a bowl. Serve right away.

82. Ricotta & Fruit Summer Salad

Serves: 6 | Ready in about: 10 minutes

1 cantaloupe melon, quartered and seeded
2 tbsp extra-virgin olive oil
½ small seedless watermelon
1 cup grape tomatoes

2 cups ricotta cheese, crumbled
1/3 cup mint leaves, torn into small pieces

1 tbsp balsamic vinegar
Salt and black pepper to taste

Scoop balls out of the melon using a melon baller. Put the balls in a shallow bowl. Repeat the process with the watermelon. Add the watermelon balls to the cantaloupe bowl. Add the tomatoes, ricotta cheese, mint, olive oil, vinegar, pepper, and salt, and gently mix until everything is incorporated. Serve and enjoy!

83. Lettuce & Tuna Salad

Serves: 2 | Ready in about: 10 minutes

2 tbsp olive oil
½ iceberg lettuce, torn
¼ Endive head, chopped

1 tomato, cut into wedges
5 oz canned tuna, flaked
4 black olives, sliced

1 tbsp lemon juice
Salt and black pepper to taste

In a large bowl, mix olive oil, lemon juice, salt, and pepper. Add in lettuce, endive, and tuna and toss to coat. Top with black olives and tomato wedges, and serve.

84. Cabbage & Carrot

Serves: 4 | Ready in about: 10 minutes

2 tbsp olive oil
1 green cabbage head, torn

1 tbsp lemon juice
1 carrot, grated

Salt and black pepper to taste
¼ cup parsley, chopped

In a bowl, mix olive oil, lemon juice, carrot, parsley, salt, pepper, and cabbage. Serve right away.

85. Asparagus Salad

Serves: 4 | Ready in about: 10 minutes

4 tbsp olive oil
1 lb asparagus

1 garlic clove, minced
Salt and black pepper to taste

1 tbsp balsamic vinegar
1 tbsp lemon zest

In a greased skillet, roast the asparagus over medium heat for 5-6 minutes, turning once. Season to taste. Toss with garlic, olive oil, lemon zest, and vinegar. Serve.

86. Pear & Endive Salad

Serves: 4 | Ready in about: 5 minutes

2 tbsp olive oil
1 tbsp balsamic vinegar
2 garlic cloves, minced
1 tsp yellow mustard

1 tbsp lemon juice
Sea salt and pepper to taste
12 black olives, chopped
1 tbsp parsley, chopped

7 cups baby spinach
2 endives, shredded
2 pears, sliced lengthwise
2 fennel bulbs, shredded

Place the spinach, endives, pears, fennel, parsley, olives, salt, pepper, lemon juice, olive oil, mustard, garlic, and balsamic vinegar in a bowl and toss to combine. Serve right away.

87. Garden Salad

Serves: 4 | Ready in about: 10 minutes

¼ cup extra-virgin olive oil
2 green onions, sliced
½ tsp fresh lemon zest

3 tbsp balsamic vinegar
Salt to taste
2 cups baby spinach

1 cup watercress
1 cup arugula
1 celery stick, sliced

In a bowl, whisk together the lemon zest, balsamic vinegar, olive oil, and salt. Put the remaining ingredients in a large bowl. Pour the dressing over the salad and lightly toss to coat. Serve and enjoy!

88. Fig & Prosciutto Salad

Serves: 2 | Ready in about: 15 minutes

2 tbsp crumbled Gorgonzola cheese
2 tbsp olive oil
3 cups Romaine lettuce, torn

4 figs, sliced
3 thin prosciutto slices
¼ cup pecan halves, toasted

1 tbsp balsamic vinegar

Toss the lettuce and figs in a large bowl. Drizzle with olive oil. Slice the prosciutto lengthwise into 1-inch strips. Add the prosciutto, pecans, and Gorgonzola cheese to the bowl. Toss the salad lightly. Drizzle with balsamic vinegar.

89. Salmon & Curly Endive Salad

Serves: 4 | Ready in about: 5 minutes

4 oz smoked salmon, flaked
2 heads curly endive, torn
2 tsp yellow mustard

¼ cup lemon juice
½ cup Greek yogurt
Salt and black pepper to taste

1 cucumber, sliced
2 tbsp chives, chopped

Toss curly endive, salmon, mustard, lemon juice, yogurt, salt, pepper, cucumber, and chives in a large bowl. Serve.

90. Pecan Cheese Salad with Orange Dressing

Serves: 2 | Ready in about: 10 minutes

Dressing
1 tbsp olive oil
2 tbsp orange juice
Salad
2 cups packed baby kale
½ small fennel bulb, sliced

1 tbsp cider vinegar
1 tbsp honey

3 tbsp toasted pecans, chopped
2 oz ricotta cheese, crumbled

Salt and black pepper to taste

Mix orange juice, olive oil, vinegar, and honey in a small bowl. Season with salt and pepper and set aside. Divide the baby kale, orange segments, fennel, pecans, and ricotta cheese evenly between two plates. Drizzle with the dressing.

91. Pecorino & Kale Salad

Serves: 6 | Ready in about: 15 minutes

6 tbsp grated Pecorino Romano cheese
¼ cup extra-virgin olive oil
6 cups kale, chopped
2 tbsp lemon juice

Salt to taste
2 cups arugula
1/3 cup shelled pistachios

20 radishes, sliced

In a bowl, whisk the olive oil, lemon juice, and salt. Add the kale and gently massage the leaves with your hands for about 15 seconds until all are thoroughly coated. Let the kale sit for 5 minutes. Add in the arugula, radishes, and pistachios and toss. Sprinkle with Pecorino and serve.

92. Bell Pepper & MushroomSalad

Serves: 4 | Ready in about: 15 minutes

2 tbsp olive oil
½ lb mushrooms, sliced
3 garlic cloves, minced

Salt and black pepper to taste
1 tomato, diced
1 red bell pepper, sliced

3 tbsp lime juice
½ cup chicken stock
2 tbsp cilantro, chopped

Warm olive oil in a skillet over medium heat and sauté mushrooms for 4 minutes. Stir in garlic, salt, pepper, tomato, bell pepper, lime juice, and chicken stock and sauté for another 4 minutes. Top with cilantro and serve right away.

93. Flank Steak Salad with Spinach

Serves: 4 | Ready in about: 20 minutes

1 tsp extra-virgin olive oil
1 lb flank steak
1 tbsp garlic powder
Salt and black pepper to taste

4 cups baby spinach
10 cherry tomatoes, halved
10 white mushrooms, sliced
1 small red onion, sliced

½ red bell pepper, sliced
2 tbsp parsley, chopped

Preheat your oven to 390 F. Rub the flank steak with olive oil, garlic powder, salt, and pepper and bake in the oven for 5 minutes on each side. Leave the meat to sit on a cutting board for 10 minutes. In a large bowl, combine the spinach, tomatoes, mushrooms, onion, bell pepper, and parsley and toss well. Slice the steak on the diagonal and place it on top of the salad. Serve.

94. Pea Salad with Rice

Serves: 2 | Ready in about: 30 minutes

1 tbsp olive oil
Salt and black pepper to taste
½ cup baby spinach

½ cup green peas, blanched
1 garlic clove, minced
½ cup white rice, rinsed

6 cherry tomatoes, halved
1 tbsp parsley, chopped
2 tbsp Italian salad dressing

Bring a large pot of salted water to a boil over medium heat. Pour in the rice, cover, and simmer on low heat for 15-18 minutes or until the rice is al dente. Drain and let cool. In a large bowl, whisk the olive oil, garlic, salt, and black pepper. Toss the green peas, baby spinach, and rice together. Pour the dressing all over and gently stir to combine. Decorate with cherry tomatoes and parsley and serve. Enjoy!

95. Sweet Potato & Eggplant Salad

Serves: 4 | Ready in about: 25 minutes

1 tbsp olive oil
4 cups arugula
2 baby eggplants, cubed

2 sweet potatoes, cubed
1 red onion, cut into wedges
1 tsp hot paprika

2 tsp cumin, ground
Salt and black pepper to taste
¼ cup lime juice

Warm olive oil in a skillet over medium heat and cook eggplants and potatoes for 5 minutes. Stir in onion, paprika, cumin, salt, pepper, and lime juice and cook for another 10 minutes. Mix in arugula and serve.

96. Pork Chop & Arugula Salad

Serves: 4 | Ready in about: 50 minutes

1 lb pork chops
2 cups goat cheese, crumbled
2 garlic cloves, minced

2 tsp lemon zest
½ tsp thyme, chopped
2 cups arugula

1 tbsp lemon juice

Preheat your oven to 390 F. Rub the pork chops with garlic, lemon zest, thyme, and lemon juice and arrange them on a greased baking pan. Roast for 30 minutes. Sprinkle with goat cheese and bake for another 10 minutes. Place the arugula on a platter and top with the pork chops to serve.

97. Walnut & Baby Spinach Salad

Serves: 4 | Ready in about: 5 minutes

2 oz sharp white cheddar cheese, cubed
3 tbsp olive oil
8 cups baby spinach

1 Granny Smith apple, diced
1 medium red apple, diced

½ cup toasted pecans
1 tbsp apple cider vinegar

Toss the spinach, apples, pecans, and cubed cheese in a bowl. Lightly drizzle olive oil and vinegar over the top. Serve.

98. Summer Arugula & Fruit Salad

Serves: 4 | Ready in about: 5 minutes

6 figs, quartered
2 cups arugula
1 cup strawberries, halved

1 tbsp hemp seeds
1 cucumber, sliced
1 tbsp lime juice

1 tbsp tahini paste

Arrange the arugula on a serving plate. Top with strawberries, figs, and cucumber. In another bowl, whisk tahini, hemp seeds, and lime juice and pour over the salad. Serve.

SOUPS

99. Green Bean & Zucchini Soup

Serves: 4 | Ready in about: 30 minutes

1 ¼ lb green beans, cut into bite-sized chunks
2 tbsp olive oil
1 onion, chopped
1 celery stalk, chopped
1 carrot, chopped
2 garlic cloves, minced

1 zucchini, chopped
5 cups vegetable broth
2 tomatoes, chopped
Salt and black pepper to taste
½ tsp cayenne pepper

1 tsp oregano
½ tsp dried dill
½ cup black olives, sliced

Warm the olive in a pot over medium heat. Sauté the onion, celery, and carrot for about 4 minutes or until the vegetables are just tender. Add in the garlic and zucchini and continue to sauté for 1 minute or until aromatic. Pour in the broth, green beans, tomatoes, salt, black pepper, cayenne pepper, oregano, and dried dill; bring to a boil. Reduce the heat to a simmer and let it cook for about 15 minutes. Serve in individual bowls with sliced olives.

100. Chickpea Soup with Sausages

Serves: 4 | Ready in about: 35 minutes

2 tbsp olive oil
8 oz Italian sausage, sliced
1 (14-oz) can chickpeas
4 cups chopped spinach

1 onion, chopped
1 carrot, chopped
1 red bell pepper, chopped
3 garlic cloves, minced

6 cups chicken broth
1 tsp dried oregano
Salt and black pepper to taste
½ tsp red pepper flakes

Warm the olive oil in a pot over medium heat. Sear the sausage for 5 minutes until browned. Set aside. Add carrot, onion, garlic, and bell pepper to the pot and sauté for 5 minutes until soft. Pour in broth, chickpeas, spinach, oregano, salt, pepper, and red flakes; let simmer for 5 minutes until the spinach softens. Bring the sausage back to the pot and cook for another minute. Serve warm.

101. Instant Pot Italian Sausage & Tomato Soup

Serves: 4 | Ready in about: 25 minutes

28 oz fire-roasted diced tomatoes
1 tbsp olive oil
2 shallots, chopped
3 cloves garlic, minced

Salt and black pepper to taste
4 cups beef broth
½ cup fresh ripe tomatoes
1 tbsp red wine vinegar

3 Italian sausages, chopped
½ cup thinly chopped basil

Warm the olive oil on Sauté in your Instant Pot. Cook the sausage until crispy, stirring occasionally, about 5 minutes. Remove to a plate. Add the garlic and shallots to the pot and sauté for 3 minutes until soft. Season with salt and pepper. Stir in red wine vinegar, broth, diced tomatoes, and ripe tomatoes. Seal the lid and cook on High Pressure for 8 minutes. Release the pressure quickly. Pour the soup into a blender and process until smooth. Divide into bowls, top with chorizo, and decorate with basil.

102. Parmesan Soup with Roasted Vegetables

Serves: 4 | Ready in about: 45 minutes

3 tbsp olive oil
2 carrots, sliced
3 sweet potatoes, sliced

1 celery stalk, sliced
1 tsp chopped dill
4 cups vegetable broth

Salt and black pepper to taste
1 tbsp Parmesan, grated

Preheat your oven to 400°F. Mix carrots, sweet potatoes, and celery in a bowl. Drizzle with olive oil and toss. Sprinkle with dill, salt, and pepper. Arrange the vegetable on a lined with parchment paper sheet and bake for 30 minutes or until the veggies are tender and golden brown. Let cool slightly. Place the veggies and some broth in a food processor and pulse until smooth; work in batches. Transfer to a pot over low heat and add in the remaining broth. Cook just until heated through. Serve topped with Parmesan cheese.

103. Cauliflower Soup with Pancetta Crisps

Serves: 4 | Ready in about: 50 minutes

2 tbsp olive oil
4 oz pancetta, cubed
5 oz cauliflower florets

1 yellow onion, chopped
Salt and black pepper to taste
4 cups chicken stock

1 tsp mustard powder
2 garlic cloves, minced
½ cup mozzarella, shredded

Over medium heat, place a saucepan and add in the pancetta. Cook until crispy, about 4 minutes, and set aside. Add olive oil, onion, and garlic to the pot and cook for 3 minutes. Pour in chicken stock, cauliflower, mustard powder, salt, and pepper and cook for 20 minutes. Using an immersion blender, purée the soup and stir in the mozzarella cheese. Serve immediately topped with pancetta croutons.

104. Tomato Soup with Roasted Peppers

Serves: 4 | Ready in about: 30 minutes

1 cup roasted bell peppers, chopped
2 tbsp olive oil
3 tomatoes, cored and halved
2 cloves garlic, minced
1 yellow onion, quartered

1 celery stalk, chopped
1 carrot, shredded
½ tsp ground cumin
½ tsp chili pepper
4 cups vegetable broth

½ tsp red pepper flakes
2 tbsp fresh basil, chopped
Salt and black pepper to taste
¼ cup crème fraîche

Preheat your oven to 380 F. Arrange the tomatoes and peppers on a roasting pan. Drizzle olive oil over the vegetables. Roast for 20 minutes until charred. Remove, let cool, and peel them. Heat olive oil in a pot over medium heat and sauté onion, garlic, celery, and carrots for 3-5 minutes until tender. Stir in chili pepper and cumin for 1-2 minutes. Pour in roasted bell peppers and tomatoes, stir, then add in the vegetable broth. Season with salt and pepper. Bring to a boil and reduce the heat; simmer for 10 minutes. Using an immersion blender, purée the soup until smooth. Sprinkle with pepper flakes and basil. Serve topped with crème fraîche.

105. Sausage Zuppa Frutti di Mare

Serves: 4 | Ready in about: 30 minutes

2 tbsp olive oil
2 tbsp butter
½ lb shrimp, deveined
3 Italian sausages, sliced
1 red onion, chopped
1 ½ cups clams

1 carrot, chopped
1 celery stalk, chopped
2 garlic cloves, minced
1 (14.5-oz) canned tomatoes
1 tsp dried basil
1 tsp dried dill

4 cups chicken broth
4 tbsp cornflour
2 tbsp lemon juice
2 tbsp fresh cilantro, chopped
Salt and black pepper to taste

In a pot, melt the butter over medium heat and brown the sausage; set aside. Heat the olive oil in the same pot and add in cornflour; cook for 4 minutes. Add in the onion, garlic, carrot, and celery and stir-fry them for 3 minutes. Stir in tomatoes, basil, dill, and chicken broth. Bring to a boil. Lower the heat and simmer for 5 minutes. Mix in the reserved sausages, salt, black pepper, clams, and shrimp and simmer for 10 minutes. Discard any unopened clams. Share into bowls and sprinkle with lemon juice. Serve warm garnished with fresh cilantro.

106. Root Veggie Soup

Serves: 4 | Ready in about: 40 minutes

3 cups chopped butternut squash
2 tbsp olive oil
1 carrot, chopped
1 leek, chopped

2 garlic cloves, minced
1 celery stalk, chopped
1 parsnip, chopped
1 potato, chopped

4 cups vegetable broth
1 tsp dried thyme
Salt and black pepper to taste

Warm the olive oil in a pot over medium heat and sauté leek, garlic, parsnip, carrot, and celery for 5-6 minutes until the veggies start to brown. Throw in squash, potato, broth, thyme, salt, and pepper. Bring to a boil, then decrease the heat and simmer for 20-30 minutes until the veggies soften. Transfer to a food processor and blend until you get a smooth and homogeneous consistency.

107. Lemon Chicken Soup with Barley

Serves: 4 | Ready in about: 40 minutes

2 tbsp olive oil
1 lb boneless chicken thighs
¼ cup pearl barley
1 red onion, chopped

2 cloves garlic, minced
4 cups chicken broth
¼ tsp oregano
½ lemon, juiced

¼ tsp parsley
¼ cup scallions, chopped
Salt and black pepper to taste

Heat olive oil in a pot over medium heat and sweat the onion and garlic for 2-3 minutes until tender. Place in chicken thighs and cook for 5-6 minutes, stirring often. Pour in chicken broth and barley and bring to a boil. Then lower the heat and simmer for 5 minutes. Remove the chicken and shred it with two forks. Return to the pot and add in lemon, oregano, and parsley. Simmer for 20-22 more minutes. Stir in shredded chicken and adjust the seasoning. Divide between 4 bowls and top with chopped scallions.

108. Halibut & Potato Soup

Serves: 4 | Ready in about: 25 minutes

3 gold potatoes, peeled and cubed
4 oz halibut fillets, boneless and cubed
2 tbsp olive oil

2 carrots, chopped
1 red onion, chopped
Salt and white pepper to taste

4 cups fish stock
½ cup heavy cream
1 tbsp dill, chopped

Warm olive oil in a skillet over medium heat and cook the onion for 3 minutes. Put in potatoes, salt, pepper, carrots, and stock and bring to a boil. Cook for 5-6 minutes. Stir in halibut, cream, and dill and simmer for another 5 minutes.

109. Fennel Chicken Soup with Mushrooms

Serves: 4 | Ready in about: 30 minutes

2 tbsp olive oil
1 (14-oz) can diced tomatoes
½ lb chicken breasts, cubed
4 cups chicken broth
2 carrots, chopped

1 onion, chopped
1 red bell pepper, chopped
1 fennel bulb, chopped
2 garlic cloves, minced
½ tsp paprika

1 cup mushrooms, sliced
1 tbsp Italian seasoning
Salt and black pepper to taste

Warm the olive oil in a pot over medium heat. Place in chicken and brown for 5 minutes. Set aside. Add the onion, carrots, bell pepper, and fennel and sauté for 5 minutes until softened. Throw in garlic and paprika and cook for 30 seconds. Mix in tomatoes, mushrooms, Italian seasoning, broth, chicken, salt, and pepper. Bring to a boil, decrease the heat, and simmer for 20 minutes. Serve.

110. Yummy Chicken Soup with Vegetables

Serves: 4 | Ready in about: 35 minutes

2 tsp olive oil
1 cup mushrooms, chopped
1 large carrot, chopped
1 yellow onion, chopped

1 celery stalk, chopped
2 yellow squash, chopped
2 chicken breasts, cubed
½ cup chopped fresh parsley

4 cups chicken stock
Salt and black pepper to taste

Warm olive oil in a skillet over medium heat. Place in carrot, onion, mushrooms, and celery and cook for 5 minutes. Stir in chicken and cook for 10 more minutes. Mix in squash, salt, and black pepper. Cook for 5 minutes, then lower the heat and pour in the stock. Cook covered for 10 more minutes. Divide between bowls and scatter with parsley.

111. Thyme Bean Soup

Serves: 4 | Ready in about: 50 minutes

2 tbsp olive oil
6 cups veggie stock
1 cup celery, chopped
1 cup carrots, chopped

1 yellow onion, chopped
2 garlic cloves, minced
½ cup navy beans, soaked
2 tbsp chopped parsley

½ tsp paprika
1 tsp thyme
Salt and black pepper to taste

Warm the olive oil in a saucepan and sauté onion, garlic, carrots, and celery for 5 minutes, stirring occasionally. Stir in paprika, thyme, salt, and pepper for 1 minute. Pour in broth and navy beans. Bring to a boil, then reduce the heat and simmer for 40 minutes. Sprinkle with parsley and serve.

112.   Spinach & Rice Soup

Serves: 6 | Ready in about: 65 minutes

3 tbsp olive oil
1 large onion, chopped
2 cloves garlic, minced

2 lb spinach leaves, chopped
6 cups chicken broth
½ cup arborio rice

Salt and black pepper to taste
2 oz shaved Parmesan cheese

Warm the olive oil in a large pot oven over medium heat and add the onion and garlic. Cook until the onions are soft and translucent, about 5 minutes. Add the spinach and stir. Cover the pot and cook the spinach until wilted, about 3 more minutes. With a slotted spoon, remove the spinach and onions from the pot, leaving the liquid.

Transfer the spinach mixture to your food processor and process until smooth, then return to the pot. Add the chicken broth and bring to a boil. Add the rice, reduce heat, and simmer until the rice is tender, about 20 minutes. Adjust the taste. Serve topped with Parmesan shavings.

113.   Rice & Turkey Egg Soup

Serves: 4 | Ready in about: 40 minutes

2 tbsp olive oil
1 lb turkey breasts, cubed
½ cup Arborio rice
1 onion, chopped

1 celery stalk, chopped
1 carrot, sliced
1 egg
2 tbsp yogurt

1 tsp dried tarragon
1 tsp lemon zest
2 tbsp fresh parsley, chopped
Salt and black pepper to taste

Heat the olive oil in a pot over medium heat and sauté the onion, celery, turkey, and carrot for 6-7 minutes, stirring occasionally. Stir in the rice for 1-2 minutes, pour in 4 cups of water, and season with salt and pepper. Bring the soup to a boil. Lower the heat and simmer for 20 minutes. In a bowl, beat the egg with yogurt until well combined. Remove 1 cup of the hot soup broth with a spoon and add slowly to the egg mixture, stirring constantly. Pour the whisked mixture into the pot and stir in salt, black pepper, tarragon, and lemon zest. Garnish with parsley and serve.

114.   Rich Green Bean & Rice Chicken Soup

Serves: 4 | Ready in about: 45 minutes

2 tbsp olive oil
4 cups chicken stock
½ lb chicken breasts strips
1 celery stalk, chopped
2 garlic cloves, minced

1 yellow onion, chopped
½ cup white rice
1 egg, whisked
½ lemon, juiced
1 cup green beans, chopped

1 cup carrots, chopped
½ cup dill, chopped
Salt and black pepper to taste

Warm the olive oil in a pot over medium heat and sauté onion, garlic, celery, carrots, and chicken for 6-7 minutes. Pour in stock and rice. Bring to a boil and simmer for 10 minutes. Stir in green beans, salt, and pepper and cook for 15 minutes. Whisk the egg and lemon juice and pour into the pot. Stir and cook for 2 minutes. Serve topped with dill.

115.   Hot Lentil Soup

Serves: 4 | Ready in about: 30 minutes

2 tbsp olive oil
1 cup lentils, rinsed
1 onion, chopped
2 carrots, chopped

1 potato, cubed
1 tomato, chopped
4 garlic cloves, minced
4 cups vegetable broth

½ tsp chili powder
Salt and black pepper to taste
2 tbsp fresh parsley, chopped

Warm the olive oil in a pot over medium heat. Add in onion, garlic, and carrots and sauté for 5-6 minutes until tender. Mix in lentils, broth, salt, pepper, chili powder, potato, and tomato. Bring to a boil, lower the heat and simmer for 15-18 minutes, stirring often. Top with parsley and serve.

116. Bean & Potato Soup

Serves: 4 | Ready in about: 50 minutes

2 tbsp olive oil
2 shallots, chopped
1 potato, chopped
5 celery sticks, chopped

1 carrot, chopped
½ tsp dried oregano
1 bay leaf
30 oz canned white beans

2 tbsp tomato paste
4 cups chicken stock

Warm the olive oil in a pot over medium heat and cook shallots, celery, carrot, bay leaf, and oregano for 5 minutes. Stir in beans, tomato paste, potato, and chicken stock and bring to a boil. Cook for 20 minutes. Remove the bay leaf. Serve.

117. Cavolo Nero Soup with Chickpeas

Serves: 4 | Ready in about: 35 minutes

2 tbsp olive oil
1 lb cavolo nero, torn
1 cup canned chickpeas
Salt and black pepper to taste

1 celery stalk, chopped
1 onion, chopped
1 carrot, chopped
14 oz canned tomatoes, diced

2 tbsp rosemary, chopped
4 cups vegetable stock

Warm the olive oil in a pot over medium heat and cook onion, celery, and carrot for 5 minutes. Stir in cavolo nero, salt, pepper, tomatoes, rosemary, chickpeas, and vegetable stock and simmer for 20 minutes. Serve warm.

118. Chicken Soup with Kale & Vermicelli

Serves: 4 | Ready in about: 25 minutes

2 tbsp olive oil
1 carrot, chopped
1 leek, chopped
½ cup vermicelli

4 cups chicken stock
2 cups kale, chopped
2 chicken breasts, cubed
1 cup orzo

¼ cup lemon juice
2 tbsp parsley, chopped
Salt and black pepper to taste

Warm olive oil in a pot over medium heat and sauté leek and chicken for 6 minutes. Stir in carrot and chicken stock and bring to a boil. Cook for 10 minutes. Add in vermicelli, kale, orzo, and lemon juice and continue cooking for another 5 minutes. Adjust the seasoning with salt and pepper and sprinkle with parsley. Ladle into soup bowls; serve.

119. Delicious Green Soup

Serves: 4 | Ready in about: 20 minutes

1 tbsp olive oil
1 white onion, chopped
½ cup Greek yogurt

1 celery stalk, chopped
4 cups vegetable stock
2 cups green peas

2 tbsp mint leaves, chopped
1 cup spinach
Salt and black pepper to taste

Warm the olive oil in a pot over medium heat and cook onion and celery for 4 minutes. Add in stock, green peas, spinach, salt, and pepper and bring to a boil. Simmer for 4 minutes. Take off the heat and let cool the soup for a few minutes. Blend the soup with an immersion blender until smooth. Apportion the soup among bowls and garnish with a swirl of Greek yogurt. Sprinkle with chopped mint and serve.

120. Basil-Tomato Pecorino Soup

Serves: 4 | Ready in about: 45 minutes

½ cup Pecorino cheese, grated
2 tbsp olive oil
2 lb tomatoes, halved

2 garlic cloves, minced
1 onion, chopped
Salt and black pepper to taste

4 cups chicken stock
½ tsp red pepper flakes
½ cup basil, chopped

Preheat your oven to 380 F. Place the tomatoes in a baking tray, drizzle with olive oil, and season with salt and pepper. Roast in the oven for 20 minutes. When ready, peel them. Warm the remaining olive oil in a pot over medium heat and sauté onion for 3 minutes. Put in roasted tomatoes, garlic, chicken stock, and red pepper flakes and bring to a boil. Simmer for 15 minutes. Using an immersion blender, purée the soup and stir in Pecorino cheese. Top with basil.

121. Roasted Eggplant & Tomato Soup

Serves: 6 | Ready in about: 60 minutes

2 tbsp olive oil
3 eggplants, sliced lengthwise
Salt to taste
1 red onion, chopped

2 tbsp garlic, minced
1 tsp dried thyme
Salt and black pepper to taste
2 ripe tomatoes, halved

5 cups chicken broth
¼ cup heavy cream
2 tbsp fresh basil, chopped

Preheat your oven to 400 F. Place the eggplants on a greased sheet pan and drizzle with some olive oil. Roast for 45 minutes. Remove from oven and allow to cool. When cool, remove all of the insides, discarding the skins. Warm the remaining olive oil in a large skillet over medium heat. Add the onions and garlic and cook for 5 minutes until soft and translucent. Add the thyme and season with salt and pepper. Put the eggplant, tomatoes, and onion in your food processor and process until smooth. Pour the chicken broth into a pot and bring to a boil. Reduce heat to a simmer and add the eggplant mixture. Stir until well combined and fold in the heavy cream. Serve topped with basil.

122. Veggie Lentil Soup

Serves: 4 | Ready in about: 55 minutes

2 tbsp olive oil
1 yellow onion, chopped
2 celery stalks, chopped
1 carrot, sliced
2 tbsp parsley, chopped

2 garlic cloves, minced
2 tbsp ginger, grated
1 tsp turmeric powder
2 tsp sweet paprika
1 tsp cinnamon powder

½ cup red lentils
1 cup spinach, torn
14 oz canned tomatoes, diced
4 cups chicken stock
Salt and black pepper to taste

Warm olive oil in a pot over medium heat and sauté onion, ginger, garlic, celery, and carrot for 5 minutes. Stir in turmeric powder, sweet paprika, cinnamon powder, red lentils, tomatoes, chicken stock, salt, and pepper and bring to a boil. Simmer for 15 minutes. Stir in spinach for 5 minutes until the spinach is wilted. Sprinkle with parsley; serve.

123. Pork Meatball Soup

Serves: 4 | Ready in about: 35 minutes

2 tbsp olive oil
½ cup white rice
½ lb ground pork
Salt and black pepper to taste

2 garlic cloves, minced
1 onion, chopped
½ tsp dried thyme
4 cups beef stock

½ tsp saffron powder
14 oz canned tomatoes, diced
1 tbsp parsley, chopped

In a large bowl, mix ground pork, rice, salt, and pepper with your hands. Shape the mixture into ½-inch balls; set aside. Warm the olive oil in a pot over medium heat and cook the onion and garlic for 5 minutes. Pour in beef stock, thyme, saffron powder, and tomatoes and bring to a boil. Add in the pork balls and cook for 20 minutes. Adjust the seasoning with salt and pepper. Serve sprinkled with parsley.

124. Prawn Soup

Serves: 4 | Ready in about: 15 minutes

1 lb prawns, peeled and deveined
3 tbsp olive oil
1 cucumber, chopped
3 cups tomato juice

3 roasted red peppers, chopped
2 tbsp balsamic vinegar
1 garlic clove, minced
Salt and black pepper to taste

½ tsp cumin
1 tsp thyme, chopped

In a food processor or a blender, blitz tomato juice, cucumber, red peppers, 2 tbsp of olive oil, vinegar, cumin, salt, pepper, and garlic until smooth. Remove to a bowl and transfer to the fridge for 10 minutes. Warm the remaining oil in a pot over medium heat and sauté prawns, salt, pepper, and thyme for 4 minutes on all sides; then let them cool. Ladle the soup into individual bowls and serve topped with prawns.

125.   Traditional Zuppa Toscana

Serves: 4 | Ready in about: 25 minutes

2 tbsp olive oil
1 yellow onion, chopped
4 garlic cloves, minced
1 celery stalk, chopped
1 carrot, chopped

15 oz canned tomatoes, diced
1 zucchini, chopped
6 cups vegetable stock
2 tbsp tomato paste
15 oz canned white beans

5 oz Tuscan kale
1 tbsp basil, chopped
Salt and black pepper to taste

Warm olive oil in a pot over medium heat. Cook garlic and onion for 3 minutes. Stir in celery, carrot, tomatoes, zucchini, stock, tomato paste, white beans, kale, salt, and pepper and bring to a simmer. Cook for 10 minutes. Top with basil.

126.   Turkey & Cabbage Soup

Serves: 4 | Ready in about: 40 minutes

2 tbsp olive oil
½ lb turkey breast, cubed
2 leeks, sliced
4 spring onions, chopped

2 cups green cabbage, grated
4 celery sticks, chopped
4 cups vegetable stock
½ tsp sweet paprika

½ tsp ground nutmeg
Salt and black pepper to taste

Warm the olive oil in a pot over medium heat and brown turkey for 4 minutes, stirring occasionally. Add in leeks, spring onions, and celery and cook for another minute. Stir in cabbage, vegetable stock, sweet paprika, nutmeg, salt, and pepper and bring to a boil. Cook for 30 minutes. Serve.

127.   Lamb Egg Soup

Serves: 4 | Ready in about: 50 minutes

2 tbsp olive oil
½ lb lamb meat, cubed
3 eggs, whisked

4 cups beef broth
5 spring onions, chopped
2 tbsp mint, chopped

2 lemons, juiced
Salt and black pepper to taste
1 cup baby spinach

Warm olive oil in a pot over medium heat and cook lamb for 10 minutes, stirring occasionally. Add in spring onions and cook for another 3 minutes. Pour in beef broth, salt, and pepper and simmer for 30 minutes. Whisk eggs with lemon juice and some soup, pour into the pot, and spinach and cook for an additional 5 minutes. Sprinkle with mint and serve.

128.   Minty Chicken & Pasta Soup

Serves: 4 | Ready in about: 40 minutes

2 tbsp olive oil
1 onion, chopped
2 garlic cloves, minced
1 celery stalk, chopped

1 carrot, chopped
4 cups chicken stock
Salt and black pepper to taste
¼ cup lemon juice

1 chicken breast, cubed
½ cup stelline pasta
6 mint leaves, chopped

Warm the olive oil in a pot over medium heat and sauté onion, garlic, celery, and carrot for 5 minutes until tender. Add in the chicken and cook for another 4-5 minutes, stirring occasionally. Pour in chicken stock and bring to a boil; cook for 10 minutes. Add in the stelline pasta and let simmer for 10 minutes. Stir in lemon juice and adjust the seasoning with salt and pepper. Sprinkle with mint and serve immediately.

129.   Cream Soup with Leek & Hazelnuts

Serves: 4 | Ready in about: 25 minutes

2 tbsp olive oil
1 tbsp ground hazelnuts
4 leeks (white part), sliced

1 onion, chopped
2 garlic cloves, minced
4 cups chicken stock

¼ cup heavy cream
2 tbsp chopped chives

Warm the olive oil in a medium saucepan. Add the leeks, garlic, and onion and sauté over low heat until tender, 3-5 minutes. Add ½ cup of chicken stock, then puree the mixture in a blender until smooth.

Return the chicken stock mixture to the saucepan. Add the remaining chicken stock and simmer for 10 minutes. Stir in the heavy cream until combined. Pour into bowls and garnish with hazelnuts and chives. Serve and enjoy!

130.   Orzo Soup with Mushrooms & Spinach

Serves: 4 | Ready in about: 20 minutes

2 tbsp butter
3 cups spinach
½ cup orzo
4 cups chicken broth

1 cup ricotta cheese, crumbled
Salt and black pepper to taste
½ tsp dried oregano
1 onion, chopped

2 garlic cloves, minced
1 cup mushrooms, sliced

Melt the butter in a pot over medium heat and sauté onion, garlic, and mushrooms for 5 minutes until tender. Add in chicken broth, orzo, salt, pepper, and oregano. Bring to a boil and reduce the heat to a low. Continue simmering for 10 minutes, partially covered. Stir in spinach and continue to cook until the spinach wilts, about 3-4 minutes. Ladle into individual bowls and serve garnished with ricotta cheese.

131.   Shrimp & Leek Soup

Serves: 6 | Ready in about: 40 minutes

1 lb shrimp, peeled and deveined
3 tbsp olive oil
1 celery stalk, chopped
1 leek, sliced

1 fennel bulb, chopped
2 garlic cloves, minced
Salt and black pepper to taste
1 tbsp coriander seeds

6 cups vegetable broth
2 tbsp buttermilk
1 lemon, juiced

Warm the olive oil in a large pot oven over medium heat. Add the celery, leek, and fennel, and cook for about 5 minutes until tender. Add the garlic and season with salt and pepper. Add the coriander seeds and stir. Pour in the broth, bring to a boil, and then reduce to a simmer and cook for 20 more minutes. Add the shrimp to the soup and cook until just pink, about 3 minutes. Stir in buttermilk and lemon juice. Serve.

132.   Cavolo Nero & Bean Soup

Serves: 4 | Ready in about: 30 minutes

2 tbsp olive oil
1 onion, chopped
2 cloves garlic, minced
10 oz cavolo nero, torn

8 oz stelline pasta
6 cups vegetable broth
2 cups diced canned tomatoes
1 cup canned white beans

Salt and black pepper to taste
2 tbsp Parmesan, grated

Warm the olive oil in a large soup pot over medium heat. Add the onions and cook for 5 minutes, or until soft and translucent. Add the garlic and cook for 1 more minute. Pour in the broth and bring to boil. Lower the heat to low, add the tomatoes, pasta, and beans, and simmer for 5 minutes. Add the cavolo nero and stir. Cook for another 5 minutes. Season with salt and pepper. To serve, ladle into bowls and sprinkle with grated Parmesan cheese.

133.   Ham & Green Lentil Soup

Serves: 4 | Ready in about: 30 minutes

2 tbsp olive oil
½ lb ham, cubed
1 onion, chopped
2 tsp parsley, dried
1 potato, chopped

3 garlic cloves, chopped
Salt and black pepper to taste
1 carrot, chopped
½ tsp paprika
½ cup green lentils, rinsed

4 cups vegetable stock
3 tbsp tomato paste
2 tomatoes, chopped

Warm the olive oil in a pot over medium heat and cook ham, onion, carrot, and garlic for 4 minutes. Stir in tomato paste, paprika, and tomatoes for 2-3 minutes. Pour in lentils, vegetable stock, and potato and bring to a boil. Cook for 18-20 minutes. Adjust the seasoning with salt and pepper and sprinkle with parsley. Serve warm.

134. Zuppa di Fagioli

Serves: 4 | Ready in about: 10 minutes

2 tbsp Pecorino cheese, grated
2 tbsp olive oil
1 carrot, peeled and diced

1 onion, chopped
2 cloves garlic, chopped
4 cups chicken broth

½ cup white beans, soaked
Salt and black pepper to taste
4 whole-wheat bread slices

Warm olive oil in a large stockpot over medium heat. Add the carrot and onion and sauté until the onion is translucent. Stir-fry the garlic for 1 more minute. Pour in the broth, beans, salt, and pepper, and cover. Bring to a boil and simmer for 2 hours or until the beans are tender. Adjust the taste and top with Pecorino cheese. Serve with toasted bread.

135. Celery-Carrot Soup with Beans

Serves: 6 | Ready in about: 35 minutes

3 tbsp olive oil
1 onion, finely chopped
3 garlic cloves, minced
2 cups carrots, diced

2 cups celery, diced
1 medium potato, cubed
2 oz cubed pancetta
2 (15-oz) cans white beans, rinsed

6 cups vegetable broth
Salt and black pepper to taste

Heat the olive oil in a stockpot over medium heat. Add the pancetta, onion, and garlic and cook for 3-4 minutes, stirring often. Add the carrots and celery and cook for another 3-5 minutes until tender. Add the beans, potato, broth, salt, and pepper. Stir and simmer for about 20 minutes, stirring occasionally. Serve warm.

136. Veggie Soup

Serves: 4 | Ready in about: 40 minutes

2 tbsp olive oil
2 potatoes, peeled and cubed
1 celery stalk, chopped
1 zucchini, chopped

½ head broccoli, chopped
1 onion, chopped
1 carrot, cubed
1 tsp dried rosemary

½ tsp cayenne pepper
4 cups vegetable stock
Salt and black pepper to taste
1 tbsp chives, chopped

Warm the olive oil in a pot over medium heat and sauté onion, celery, and carrot for 5 minutes. Add in rosemary, cayenne pepper, potatoes, and zucchini and sauté for 5 minutes. Pour in the vegetable stock and bring to a simmer. Cook for 20 minutes. Adjust the seasoning and add in the broccoli; cook for 5-8 minutes. Sprinkle with chives.

137. Farro & White Bean Soup

Serves: 4 | Ready in about: 2 hours 10 minutes

1 (14-oz) can diced tomatoes with juice
2 tbsp olive oil
1 onion, diced
1 celery stalk, diced

2 garlic cloves, minced
6 cups chicken broth
1 cup white beans, soaked

1 cup farro
½ tsp rosemary
Salt and black pepper to taste

Warm the olive oil in a pot over medium heat. Sauté the onion, celery, and garlic until tender. Add the broth, beans, tomatoes, farro, and seasonings, and bring to a simmer. Cook for 2 hours or until the beans and farro are tender.

138. Chicken Bean Soup

Serves: 6 | Ready in about: 40 minutes

3 tbsp olive oil
3 garlic cloves, minced
1 onion, chopped
3 tomatoes, chopped

4 cups chicken stock
1 lb chicken breasts, cubed
1 red chili pepper, chopped
1 tbsp fennel seeds, crushed

14 oz canned white beans
1 lime, zested and juiced
Salt and black pepper to taste
2 tbsp parsley, chopped

Warm olive oil in a pot over medium heat. Cook the onion and garlic, adding a splash of water, for 10 minutes until aromatic. Add in the chicken and chili pepper and sit-fry for another 6-8 minutes. Put in tomatoes, chicken stock, beans, lime zest, lime juice, salt, pepper, and fennel seeds and bring to a boil; cook for 30 minutes. Serve topped with parsley.

PASTA

139. Olive & Ricotta Rigatoni

Serves: 4 | Ready in about: 25 minutes

2 tbsp extra-virgin olive oil
1 lb rigatoni
½ lb Ricotta cheese, crumbled

¾ cup black olives, chopped
10 sun-dried tomatoes, sliced
1 tbsp dried oregano

Black pepper to taste

In a pot, bring to a boil salted water over high heat. Add the rigatoni and cook according to package directions; drain. Heat the olive oil in a large saucepan over medium heat. Add the rigatoni, ricotta, olives, and sun-dried tomatoes. Toss mixture to combine and cook 2–3 minutes or until cheese just starts to melt. Season with oregano and pepper.

140. Cannellini Beans with Tortellini & Meatballs

Serves: 4 | Ready in about: 30 minutes

2 tbsp parsley, chopped
12 oz fresh tortellini
3 tbsp olive oil

5 cloves garlic, minced
½ lb meatballs
1 (19-oz) can cannellini beans

1 (14-oz) can roasted tomatoes
Salt and black pepper to taste

In a pot, bring to a boil salted water over high heat. Add the tortellini and cook according to package directions. Drain and set aside. Warm the olive oil in a large skillet over medium heat and sauté the garlic for 1 minute. Stir in meatballs and brown for 4–5 minutes on all sides. Add the tomatoes and cannellini and continue to cook for 5 minutes or until heated through. Adjust seasoning with salt and pepper. Stir in tortellini. Sprinkle with parsley to serve.

141. Mozzarella Rigatoni with Peppers

Serves: 4 | Ready in about: 30 minutes +marinating time

1 lb fresh mozzarella cheese, cubed
3 tbsp olive oil
¼ cup chopped fresh chives
¼ cup basil, chopped
½ tsp red pepper flakes

1 tsp apple cider vinegar
Salt and black pepper to taste
3 garlic cloves, minced
2 cups sliced onions
3 cups bell peppers, sliced

2 cups tomato sauce
8 oz rigatoni
1 tbsp butter
¼ cup grated Parmesan cheese

In a pot, bring to a boil salted water over high heat. Add the rigatoni and cook according to package directions. Drain and set aside, reserving 1 cup of the cooking water. Combine the mozzarella, 1 tablespoon of olive oil, chives, basil, pepper flakes, apple cider vinegar, salt, and pepper. Let the cheese marinate for 30 minutes at room temperature. Warm the remaining olive oil in a skillet over medium heat. Stir-fry the garlic for 10 seconds and add the onions and peppers. Cook for 3-4 minutes, stirring occasionally until the onions are translucent. Pour in the tomato sauce, and reduce the heat to a simmer. Add the rigatoni and reserved cooking water and toss to coat. Heat off and adjust the seasoning with salt and pepper. Toss with marinated mozzarella and butter. Sprinkle with Parmesan cheese and serve.

142. Parmesan Arrabbiata Penne Rigate

Serves: 4 | Ready in about: 30 minutes

2 tbsp olive oil
1 onion, chopped
6 cloves garlic, minced
½ red chili, chopped

2 cups canned tomatoes, diced
½ tsp sugar
Salt and black pepper to taste
1 lb penne rigate

1 cup shredded mozzarella
1 cup fresh basil, chopped
½ cup grated Parmesan cheese

Bring a pot of salted water to a boil, add the penne, and cook for 7-9 minutes until al dente. Reserve ¼ cup pasta cooking water and drain pasta. Set aside. Warm the olive oil in a saucepan over medium heat. Sauté the onion and garlic for 3-5 minutes or until softened. Add tomatoes with their liquid, black pepper, sugar, and salt. Cook 20 minutes or until the sauce thickens. Add the pasta and reserved cooking water and stir for 2-3 minutes. Add mozzarella cheese and red chili and cook until the cheese melts, 3-4 minutes. Top with Parmesan and basil and serve.

143. Microwave Lasagna

Serves: 2 | Ready in about: 30 minutes

½ tbsp chopped basil
½ lb ground beef, crumbled
1 cup tomatoes, diced

1 ½ cups marinara sauce
1 ½ cups mozzarella, grated
1 ½ cups ricotta cheese

12 oven-ready lasagna noodles

Microwave the ground beef in a microwave-safe bowl for 5 minutes. Stir and microwave for 4 more minutes until the beef is cooked through. Remove and mix the ground beef with tomatoes and marinara sauce. Stir in cheeses. Place 4 lasagna noodles in a large bowl. Spread 1/3 of the meat mixture over the noodle layer. Repeat until you run out of ingredients. Cover the bowl with parchment paper. Microwave for about 8 minutes until cheeses are cooked. Let lasagna stand for 10 minutes. Top with basil. Serve.

144. Asparagus & Parmesan Linguine

Serves: 2 | Ready in about: 30 minutes

2 tsp olive oil
1 bunch of asparagus spears
1 yellow onion, thinly sliced
¼ cup white wine

¼ cup vegetable stock
2 cups heavy cream
¼ tsp garlic powder
8 oz linguine

¼ cup Parmesan cheese
1 lemon, juiced
Salt and black pepper to taste
2 tbsp chives, chopped

In a pot, bring to a boil salted water over high heat. Add the linguine and cook according to package directions. Drain and transfer to a bowl. Slice the asparagus into bite-sized pieces. Warm the olive oil in a skillet over medium heat. Add onion and cook 3 minutes until softened. Add asparagus and wine and cook until wine is mostly evaporated, then add the stock. Stir in cream and garlic powder and bring to a boil and simmer until the sauce is slightly thick, 2-3 minutes. Add the linguine and stir until everything is heated through. Remove from the heat and season with lemon juice, salt, and pepper. Top with parmesan cheese and chives and serve.

145. Shrimp with Tie Pasta

Serves: 4 | Ready in about: 25 minutes

1 lb shrimp, peeled and deveined
1 tbsp olive oil
2 tbsp unsalted butter
Salt and black pepper to taste

6 garlic cloves, minced
½ cup dry white wine
1 ½ cups heavy cream
½ cup grated Asiago cheese

2 tbsp chopped fresh parsley
16 oz bow tie pasta
Salt to taste

In a large pot of boiling salted water, cook the tie pasta for 8-10 minutes until al dente. Drain and set aside. Heat the olive oil in a large skillet, season the shrimp with salt and black pepper, and cook in the oil on both sides until pink and opaque, 2 minutes. Set aside. Melt the butter in the skillet and sauté the garlic until fragrant. Stir in the white wine and cook until reduced by half, scraping the bottom of the pan to deglaze. Reduce the heat to low and stir in the heavy cream. Allow simmering for 1 minute and stir in the Asiago cheese to melt. Return the shrimp to the sauce and sprinkle the parsley on top. Adjust the taste with salt and black pepper, if needed. Top the pasta with sauce and serve.

146. Fall Vegetable & Rigatoni Bake

Serves: 6 | Ready in about: 45 minutes

2 tbsp grated Pecorino-Romano cheese
2 tbsp olive oil
1 lb pumpkin, chopped
1 zucchini, chopped

1 onion, chopped
1 lb rigatoni
Salt and black pepper to taste

½ tsp garlic powder
½ cup dry white wine

Preheat oven to 420 F. Combine zucchini, pumpkin, onion, and olive oil in a bowl. Transfer to a lined aluminum foil sheet and season with salt, pepper, and garlic powder. Bake for 30 minutes until tender. In a pot of boiling water, cook rigatoni for 8-10 minutes until al dente. Drain and set aside. In a food processor, place ½ cup of the roasted veggies and wine and pulse until smooth. Transfer to a skillet over medium heat. Stir in rigatoni and cook until heated through. Top with the remaining vegetables and Pecorino cheese to serve.

147. Salmon Fettuccine in White Sauce

Serves: 4 | Ready in about: 35 minutes

5 tbsp butter
16 oz fettuccine
4 salmon fillets, cubed
Salt and black pepper to taste

3 garlic cloves, minced
1 ¼ cups heavy cream
½ cup dry white wine
1 tsp grated lemon zest

1 cup baby spinach
Lemon wedges for garnishing

In a large pot of boiling water, cook the fettuccine pasta for 8-10 minutes until al dente. Drain and set aside. Melt half of the butter in a large skillet; season the salmon with salt, black pepper, and cook in the butter until golden brown on all sides and flaky within, 8 minutes. Transfer to a plate and set aside. Add the remaining butter to the skillet to melt and stir in the garlic. Cook until fragrant, 1 minute. Mix in heavy cream, white wine, lemon zest, salt, and pepper. Allow boiling over low heat for 5 minutes. Stir in spinach, allow wilting for 2 minutes and stir in fettuccine and salmon until well-coated in the sauce. Garnish with lemon wedges.

148. Linguine with Brussels Sprouts

Serves: 4 | Ready in about: 35 minutes

8 oz whole-wheat linguine
⅔ cup + 2 tbsp olive oil
1 medium sweet onion, diced
2 garlic cloves, minced

1 tsp red chili flakes
1 lb Brussels sprouts, shredded
½ cup chicken stock
⅔ cup dry white wine

½ cup grated Parmesan cheese
1 lemon, juiced
2 tbsp parsley, chopped

Cook the pasta in boiling salted water according to package directions. Reserve 1 cup of the pasta water. Drain the linguine and mix with 2 tablespoons of olive oil; set aside. Warm the remaining olive oil in a skillet over medium heat. Sauté the onion for 3 minutes, until softened. Add the garlic and cook for 1 minute, until fragrant. Stir in the Brussels sprouts and cook covered for 15 minutes. Pour in chicken stock and cook for 3-4 more minutes until the sprouts are fork-tender. Add white wine and cook for 5-7 minutes, until reduced. Add the pasta to the skillet and the pasta water. Serve with Parmesan cheese, chili flakes, and lemon juice.

149. Classic Beef Lasagna

Serves: 4 | Ready in about: 70 minutes

2 tbsp olive oil
1 lb lasagne sheets
1 lb ground beef

1 white onion, chopped
1 tsp Italian seasoning
Salt and black pepper to taste

1 cup marinara sauce
½ cup grated Parmesan cheese

Preheat your oven to 350 F. Warm olive oil in a skillet and add the beef and onion. Cook until the beef is brown, 7-8 minutes. Season with Italian seasoning, salt, and pepper. Cook for 1 minute and mix in the marinara sauce. Simmer for 3 minutes. Spread a layer of the beef mixture in a lightly greased baking sheet and make a first single layer on the beef mixture. Top with a single layer of lasagna sheets. Repeat the layering two more times using the remaining ingredients in the same quantities. Sprinkle with Parmesan cheese. Bake in the oven until the cheese melts and is bubbly with the sauce, 20 minutes. Remove the lasagna, allow cooling for 2 minutes and dish onto serving plates.

150. Tasty Linguine a la Carbonara

Serves: 4 | Ready in about: 30 minutes

1 ¼ cups heavy whipping cream
16 oz linguine
4 bacon slices, chopped

¼ cup mayonnaise
Salt and black pepper to taste
4 egg yolks

1 cup grated Parmesan cheese

In a large pot of boiling water, cook the linguine pasta for 8-10 minutes until al dente. Drain and set aside. Add the bacon to a skillet and cook over medium heat until crispy, 5 minutes. Set aside. Pour heavy cream into a pot and allow simmering for 5 minutes. Whisk in mayonnaise and season with salt and pepper. Cook for 1 minute and spoon 2 tbsp of the mixture into a medium bowl. Allow cooling and mix in the egg yolks. Pour the mixture into the pot and mix quickly. Stir in Parmesan cheese and fold in the pasta. Cook for 1 minute until the pasta is heated through.

151. Farfalle with Ricotta Cheese

Serves: 4 | Ready in about: 25 minutes

¼ cup extra-virgin olive oil
½ cup crumbled ricotta cheese
2 tbsp black olives, halved

4 cups fresh baby spinach, chopped
2 tbsp scallions, chopped
16 oz farfalle pasta

¼ cup red wine vinegar
2 tsp lemon juice
Salt and black pepper to taste

Cook the pasta according to pack instructions, drain and let it to cool. Mix the scallions, spinach, and cooled pasta in a bowl. Top with ricotta and olives. Combine the vinegar, olive oil, lemon juice, salt, and pepper in another bowl. Pour over the pasta mixture and toss to combine. Serve chilled.

152. Pecorino Leftover Pasta & Mushroom Frittata

Serves: 4 | Ready in about: 25 minutes

2 tbsp olive oil
4 oz leftover spaghetti, cooked
8 large eggs, beaten

¼ cup heavy cream
½ tsp Italian seasoning
½ tsp garlic salt

1/8 tsp garlic pepper
1 cup chopped mushrooms
1 cup Pecorino cheese, grated

Preheat your broiler. Warm olive oil in a large skillet over medium heat. Add mushrooms and cook for 3–4 minutes, until almost tender. In a large bowl, beat the eggs with cream, Italian seasoning, garlic salt, and garlic pepper. Stir in the leftover spaghetti. Pour the egg mixture over the mushrooms and level with a spatula. Cook for 5–7 minutes until the eggs are almost set. Sprinkle with cheese and place under broiler for 3–5 minutes, until the cheese melts. Serve.

153. Caper & Sardine Tagliatelle

Serves: 4 | Ready in about: 20 minutes

1 tbsp olive oil
8 oz tagliatelle
¼ cup chopped onion
2 garlic cloves, minced

1 tsp tomato paste
16 canned sardines in olive oil
1 tbsp capers
½ cup grated Parmesan cheese

Salt and black pepper to taste
1 tbsp chopped parsley
1 tsp chopped oregano

In a pot, boil water over medium heat and place in the pasta. Cook for 8-10 minutes for al dente. Drain and set aside; reserve ½ cup of the cooking liquid. Warm the olive oil in a pan over medium heat. Place in onion, garlic, and oregano and cook for 5 minutes until soft. Stir in salt, tomato paste, pepper, and ½ cup of reserved liquid for 1 minute. Mix in cooked pasta, capers, and sardines and toss to coat. Serve topped with Parmesan cheese and parsley.

154. Fusilli with Broccoli

Serves: 4 | Ready in about: 25 minutes

¼ cup olive oil
4 Roma tomatoes, diced
1 cup broccoli florets
1 lb fusilli

2 tsp tomato paste
2 garlic cloves, minced
1 tbsp chopped fresh oregano
½ tsp salt

1 cup vegetable broth
6 fresh basil leaves
¼ cup grated Parmesan cheese
¼ cup pine nuts

Place the fusilli pasta in a pot with salted boiling water and cook for 8-10 minutes until al dente. Drain and set aside. In a pan over medium heat, sauté tomato paste, tomatoes, broth, oregano, garlic, and salt for 10 minutes. In a food processor, place basil, broccoli, Parmesan, olive oil, and pine nuts; pulse until smooth. Pour into the tomato mixture. Stir in pasta, cook until heated through and the pasta is well coated. Serve.

155. Walnut Pasta with Dill Sauce

Serves: 4 | Ready in about: 10 minutes

3 tbsp extra-virgin olive oil
8 oz whole-wheat pasta

¼ cup walnuts, chopped
3 garlic cloves, finely minced

½ cup fresh dill, chopped
¼ cup grated Parmesan cheese

Cook the pasta according to pack instructions, drain and let it cool. Place the olive oil, dill, garlic, Parmesan, and walnuts in a food processor and blend for 15 seconds or until paste forms. Pour over the cooled pasta and toss to combine.

156. Pesto Penne with Broccoli Casserole

Serves: 4 | Ready in about: 40 minutes

1 lb broccoli florets
16 oz penne pasta
1 cup vegetable stock

Salt and black pepper
2 tbsp basil pesto
2 cups mozzarella, shredded

3 tbsp Parmesan cheese, grated
2 green onions, chopped

In a large bowl, bring to a boil salted water over medium heat and add in the pasta. Cook for 7-9 minutes until al dente. Drain and set aside. Preheat the oven to 380 F. Place pasta, vegetable stock, salt, pepper, pesto, broccoli, and green onions in a greased baking pan and combine. Scatter with mozzarella and Parmesan and bake for 30 minutes.

157. Mint Tortellini with Peas

Serves: 4 | Ready in about: 30 minutes

1 (14-oz) package frozen cheese tortellini
2 tbsp olive oil
3 garlic cloves, minced

½ cup vegetable broth
2 cups frozen baby peas

1 lemon, zested
2 tbsp mint leaves, chopped

In a pot, bring to a boil salted water over high heat. Add the tortellini and cook according to package directions. Drain and transfer to a bowl. Warm the oil in a large saucepan over medium and sauté the garlic for 2 minutes until golden. Pour in broth and peas and bring to a simmer. Add in the tortellini and cook for 5 minutes until the mixture is slightly thickened. Stir in lemon zest, top with mint, and serve.

158. Fast Pesto Pasta

Serves: 4 | Ready in about: 20 minutes

1 lb linguine
2 tomatoes, chopped

10 oz basil pesto
½ cup pine nuts, toasted

½ cup Parmesan cheese, grated
1 lemon, zested

In a pot, bring to a boil salted water over high heat. Add the linguine and cook according to package directions, 9-11 minutes. Drain and transfer to a serving bowl. Add the tomatoes, pesto, and lemon zest and toss gently to coat the pasta. Sprinkle with Parmesan cheese and pine nuts and serve.

159. Pork & Green Bean Fettuccine

Serves: 4 | Ready in about: 40 minutes

1 tbsp olive oil
16 oz fettuccine
4 pork loin, cut into strips
Salt and black pepper to taste

½ cup green beans, chopped
1 lemon, zested and juiced
¼ cup chicken broth
1 cup crème fraiche

6 basil leaves, chopped
1 cup shaved Parmesan cheese

In a large pot of boiling water, cook the fettuccine pasta for 8-10 minutes until al dente. Drain and set aside. Heat olive oil in a skillet, season the pork with salt, pepper, and cook for 10 minutes. Mix in green beans and cook for 5 minutes. Stir in lemon zest, lemon juice, and chicken broth. Cook for 5 more minutes or until the liquid reduces by a quarter. Add crème fraiche and mix well. Pour in pasta and basil and cook for 1 minute. Top with Parmesan cheese.

160. Beef Fusilli

Serves: 4 | Ready in about: 30 minutes

1 cup grated Pecorino Romano cheese
1 lb thick-cut New York strip steaks,
cut into 1-inch cubes

4 tbsp butter
16 oz fusilli pasta
Salt and black pepper to taste

4 garlic cloves, minced
2 tbsp chopped fresh parsley

In a large pot of boiling water, cook the fusilli pasta for 8-10 minutes until al dente. Drain and set aside. Melt the butter in a large skillet, season the steaks with salt, black pepper and cook in the butter until brown, and cooked through, 10 minutes. Stir in the garlic and cook until fragrant, 1 minute. Mix in the parsley and fusilli pasta; toss well and season with salt and black pepper. Dish the food, top with the Pecorino Romano cheese and serve immediately.

161. Beef Ragu

Serves: 4 | Ready in about: 20 minutes

2 tbsp butter
16 oz tagliatelle pasta
1 lb ground beef

Salt and black pepper to taste
¼ cup tomato sauce
1 green bell pepper, chopped

1 red bell pepper, chopped
1 small red onion, chopped
1 cup grated Parmesan cheese

In a pot of boiling water, cook the tagliatelle pasta for 8-10 minutes until al dente. Drain and set aside. Heat half of the butter in a medium skillet and cook the beef until brown, 5 minutes. Season with salt and black pepper. Stir in the tomato sauce and cook for 10 minutes or until the sauce reduces by a quarter. Stir in the bell peppers and onion; cook for 1 minute and turn the heat off. Adjust the taste with salt and black pepper and mix in the tagliatelle. Dish the food onto serving plates. Garnish with Parmesan.

162. Pecorino Chicken Linguine a la Toscana

Serves: 4 | Ready in about: 35 minutes

1 cup sundried tomatoes, chopped
¾ cup grated Pecorino Romano
2 tbsp olive oil
16 oz linguine

4 chicken breasts
1 white onion, chopped
1 red bell pepper, chopped
5 garlic cloves, minced

¾ cup chicken broth
1 ½ cups heavy cream
1 cup baby kale, chopped
Salt and black pepper to taste

In a pot of boiling water, cook the linguine pasta for 8-10 minutes until al dente. Drain and set aside. Heat the olive oil in a large skillet, season the chicken with salt, black pepper, and cook in the oil until golden brown on the outside and cooked within, 7 to 8 minutes. Transfer the chicken to a plate and cut into 4 slices each. Set aside. Add the onion, sundried tomatoes, bell pepper to the skillet and sauté until softened, 5 minutes. Mix in the garlic and cook until fragrant, 1 minute. Deglaze the skillet with the chicken broth and mix in the heavy cream. Simmer for 2 minutes and stir in the Pecorino Romano cheese until melted, 2 minutes. Once the cheese melts, stir in the kale to wilt and adjust the taste with salt and black pepper. Mix in the linguine and chicken until well coated in the sauce. Serve warm.

163. Chicken with Kale & Pappardelle

Serves: 4 | Ready in about: 30 minutes+chilling time

1 cup grated Parmigiano-Reggiano
4 chicken thighs, cut into pieces
3 tbsp olive oil
16 oz pappardelle pasta

Salt and black pepper to taste
1 yellow onion, chopped
4 garlic cloves, minced
12 cherry tomatoes, halved

½ cup chicken broth
2 cups baby kale, chopped
2 tbsp pine nuts for topping

In a large pot of boiling water, cook the pappardelle pasta for 8-10 minutes until al dente. Drain and set aside. Heat the olive oil in a medium pot. Season the chicken with salt and pepper and sear in the oil until golden brown on the outside. Transfer to a plate and set aside. Add the onion and garlic to the oil and cook until softened and fragrant, 3 minutes. Mix in tomatoes and chicken broth and cook over low heat until the tomatoes soften and the liquid reduces by half. Season with salt and pepper. Return the chicken to the pot and stir in kale. Allow wilting for 2 minutes. Spoon the pappardelle onto serving plates, top with kale sauce and Parmigianino-Reggiano cheese. Garnish with pine nuts.

164. Chicken Pasta

Serves: 4 | Ready in about: 35 minutes

16 oz whole-wheat pasta
2 tbsp olive oil
2 chicken breasts, cubed
1 yellow onion, minced

3 garlic cloves, minced
1 tsp Italian seasoning
¼ tsp red chili flakes
¼ tsp cayenne pepper

1 cup marinara sauce
2 tbsp grated mozzarella
2 tbsp grated Parmesan cheese
Salt and black pepper to taste

In a pot of boiling water, cook the whole-wheat pasta according to the package directions. Drain and set aside. Heat the olive oil in a pot, season the chicken with salt, pepper, and cook in the oil until golden brown on both sides.

Transfer to a plate, cut into cubes and set aside. Add the onion and garlic to the pan and cook until softened and fragrant, 3 minutes. Season with Italian seasoning, garlic powder, chili flakes, and cayenne pepper. Cook for 1 minute. Stir in marinara sauce and simmer for 5 minutes. Reduce heat to low and return the chicken to the sauce and pasta, mozzarella and Parmesan. Stir until the cheese melts. Serve and enjoy!

165.   Cauliflower & Macaroni Gratin

Serves: 4 | Ready in about: 45 minutes

16 oz elbow pasta
20 oz cauliflower florets
1 cup heavy cream

1 cup grated mozzarella
1 tsp dried thyme
1 tsp smoked paprika

Salt to taste
½ tsp red chili flakes

In a pot of boiling water, cook the macaroni for 8-10 minutes until al dente. Drain and set aside. Preheat your oven to 350 F. Grease a baking dish with cooking spray. Bring 4 cups of water to a boil in a pot and blanch the cauliflower for 4 minutes. Drain through a colander. In a large bowl, mix the cauliflower, macaroni, heavy cream, half of the mozzarella cheese, thyme, paprika, salt, and red chili flakes until well-combined. Transfer the mixture to the baking dish and top with the remaining cheese. Bake for 30 minutes. Allow cooling for 2 minutes and serve afterwards.

166.   Basil Spaghetti

Serves: 6 | Ready in about: 30 minutes

½ cup extra-virgin olive oil
Zest and juice from 1 lemon
1 garlic clove, minced

Salt and black pepper to taste
2 oz ricotta cheese, chopped
1 lb spaghetti

6 tbsp shredded fresh basil

In a large bowl, whisk oil, grated lemon zest, juice, garlic, salt, and pepper. Stir in ricotta cheese and mix well. Meanwhile, bring a pot filled with salted water to a boil. Cook the pasta until al dente. Reserve ½ cup of the cooking liquid, then drain pasta and return it to the pot. Add oil mixture and basil and toss to combine. Season to taste and adjust consistency with reserved cooking water as needed. Serve warm.

167.   Mushroom & Tomato Spaghetti

Serves: 4 | Ready in about: 30 minutes

¼ cup olive oil
16 oz spaghetti, cut in half
2 cups mushrooms, chopped
1 bell pepper, chopped

½ cup yellow onion, chopped
3 garlic cloves, minced
½ tsp five-spice powder
2 tbsp fresh parsley, chopped

1 tbsp tomato paste
2 ripe tomatoes, chopped
½ cup Parmesan cheese, grated
Salt and black pepper to taste

Heat the olive oil in a skillet over medium heat. Add in mushrooms, bell pepper, onion, and garlic and stir-fry for 4-5 minutes until tender. Mix in salt, black pepper, five-spice powder, tomato paste, and tomatoes; stir well and cook for 10-12 minutes. In a pot with salted boiling water, add the pasta and cook until al dente, about 8-10 minutes, stirring occasionally. Drain and stir in the vegetable mixture. Serve topped with Parmesan cheese and fresh parsley.

168.   Zucchini Farfalle

Serves: 4 | Ready in about: 45 minutes

3 tbsp olive oil
2 garlic cloves, minced
4 medium zucchini, diced

Salt and black pepper to taste
½ cup milk
¼ tsp ground nutmeg

8 oz bow ties
½ cup Romano cheese, grated
1 tbsp lemon juice

Heat olive oil in a large skillet over medium heat. Stir-fry garlic for 1 minute. Add zucchini, pepper, and salt, stir and cook for 15 minutes, stirring once or twice. In a microwave-safe bowl, warm the milk in the microwave on high for 30 seconds. Stir the milk and nutmeg into the skillet and cook for another 5 minutes, stirring occasionally. Meanwhile, in a large pot, cook the pasta according to the package directions. Drain the pasta in a colander, saving ¼ cup of the pasta liquid. Add the pasta and liquid to the skillet. Mix everything together and remove from the heat. Stir in the grated cheese and lemon juice and serve immediately.

169.   Creamy Chicken Farfalle

Serves: 4 | Ready in about: 40 minutes

1 tbsp olive oil
16 oz farfalle
4 chicken breasts, cut into strips
Salt and black pepper to taste

1 yellow onion, finely sliced
1 yellow bell pepper, sliced
1 garlic clove, minced
1 tbsp wholegrain mustard

5 tbsp heavy cream
1 cup minced mustard greens
1 tbsp chopped parsley

In a large pot of boiling water, cook the farfalle pasta for 8-10 minutes until al dente. Drain and set aside. Heat the olive oil in a large skillet, season the chicken with salt, black pepper, and cook in the oil until golden brown, 10 minutes. Set aside. Stir in the onion, bell pepper and cook until softened, 5 minutes. Mix in the garlic and cook until fragrant, 30 seconds. Mix in the mustard and heavy cream; simmer for 2 minutes and mix in the chicken and mustard greens. Allow wilting for 2 minutes and adjust the taste with salt and black pepper. Stir in the farfalle pasta, allow warming for 1 minute and dish the food onto serving plates. Garnish with the parsley and serve warm.

170.   Beef Rotini with Asparagus

Serves: 4 | Ready in about: 40 minutes

1 lb asparagus, cut into 1-inch pieces
3 tbsp olive oil
16 oz rotini pasta

1 lb ground beef
2 large shallots, chopped
3 garlic cloves, minced

Salt and black pepper to taste
1 cup grated Parmesan cheese

In a large pot of boiling water, cook the rotini pasta for 8-10 minutes until al dente. Drain and set aside. Heat a large non-stick skillet over medium heat and add the beef. Cook while breaking the lumps that form until brown, 10 minutes. Use a slotted spoon to transfer the beef to a plate and discard the drippings. Heat olive oil in a skillet and sauté asparagus until tender, 7 minutes. Stir in shallots and garlic and cook for 2 minutes. Season with salt and pepper. Stir in the beef and rotini pasta and toss until well combined. Adjust the taste with salt and black pepper as desired. Dish the food between serving plates and garnish with Parmesan.

171.   Mussel Spaghetti

Serves: 4 | Ready in about: 20 minutes

1 lb mussels, debearded and rinsed
2 tbsp olive oil
16 oz spaghetti, broken in half
1 cup white wine

3 shallots, finely chopped
6 garlic cloves, minced
2 tsp red chili flakes
½ cup fish stock

1 ½ cups heavy cream
2 tbsp chopped fresh parsley
Salt and black pepper to taste

In a large pot, boil water over medium heat and place in the pasta. Cook for 8-10 minutes for al dente. Drain and set aside. Pour in mussels and wine, cover, and cook for 4 minutes. Occasionally stir until the mussels have opened. Strain the mussels and reserve the cooking liquid. Allow cooling, discard any mussels with closed shells, and remove the meat out of ¾ of the mussel shells. Set aside the remaining mussels in the shells. Heat olive oil in a skillet and sauté shallots, garlic, and chili flakes for 3 minutes. Mix in reduced wine and fish stock. Allow boiling and whisk in the heavy cream. Taste and adjust the seasoning with salt and pepper; top with parsley. Pour in the pasta, mussels and toss in the sauce.

172.   Pasta Primavera

Serves: 4 | Ready in about: 25 minutes

½ cup grated Pecorino Romano
2 cups cauliflower florets, chopped
¼ cup olive oil
16 oz tortiglioni

½ cup chopped green onions
1 red bell pepper, sliced
4 garlic cloves, minced
1 cup grape tomatoes, halved

2 tsp dried Italian seasoning
½ lemon, juiced

In a large pot of boiling water, cook the tortiglioni pasta for 8-10 minutes until al dente. Drain and set aside. Heat olive oil in a skillet and sauté onion, cauliflower, and bell pepper for 7 minutes. Mix in garlic and cook until fragrant, 30 seconds. Stir in the tomatoes and Italian seasoning; cook until the tomatoes soften, 5 minutes. Mix in the lemon juice and tortiglioni. Garnish with cheese.

173. Asparagus & Mozzarella Pasta

Serves: 4 | Ready in about: 40 minutes

1 ½ lb asparagus, cut into 1-inch
2 tbsp olive oil
8 oz orecchiette

2 cups cherry tomatoes, halved
Salt and black pepper to taste
2 cups fresh mozzarella, chopped

⅓ cup torn basil leaves
2 tbsp balsamic vinegar

Preheat oven to 390 F. In a large pot, cook the pasta according to the directions. Drain, reserving ¼ cup of cooking water. In the meantime, in a large bowl, toss in asparagus, cherry tomatoes, oil, pepper, and salt. Spread the mixture onto a rimmed baking sheet and bake for 15 minutes, stirring twice throughout cooking. Remove the veggies from the oven, and add the cooked pasta to the baking sheet. Mix with a few tbsp of pasta water to smooth the sauce and veggies. Slowly mix in the mozzarella and basil. Drizzle with the balsamic vinegar and serve in bowls.

174. Fusilli in Chickpea Sauce

Serves: 4 | Ready in about: 35 minutes

1 (15-oz) can chickpeas, drained, liquid reserved
¼ cup olive oil
½ large shallot, chopped
5 garlic cloves, thinly sliced

1 cup whole-grain fusilli
Salt and black pepper to taste
¼ cup Parmesan, shaved

2 tsp dried parsley
1 tsp dried oregano
A pinch of red pepper flakes

Heat olive oil in a skillet over medium heat and sauté the shallot and garlic for 3-5 minutes until the garlic is golden. Add ¾ of the chickpeas and 2 tbsp of the water from the can; bring to a simmer. Remove from the heat, transfer to a blender, and pulse until smooth. Add the remaining chickpeas and some more of the reserved liquid if it's too thick. Bring a large pot of salted water to a boil and cook pasta until al dente, 7-8 minutes. Reserve ½ cup of the pasta liquid, drain the pasta and return it to the pot. Add the chickpea sauce to the hot pasta and keep adding ¼ cup of the pasta liquid until your desired consistency is reached. Place the pasta pot over medium heat and mix occasionally until the sauce thickens. Season with salt and pepper. Sprinkle with freshly grated Parmesan, parsley, oregano, and pepper flakes!

175. Famous Bolognese Penne Bake

Serves: 6 | Ready in about: 55 minutes

1 lb penne pasta
1 lb ground beef

A pinch of two salt
1 (25-oz) basil-tomato sauce

1 lb baby spinach, washed
3 cups mozzarella, shredded

Bring a large pot of salted water to a boil, add the pasta, and cook until al dente. Reserve 1 cup of the pasta water; drain the pasta. Preheat the oven to 350F. In a skillet over medium heat, stir-fry the ground beef along with a pinch of salt until browned, 5 minutes. Stir in basil-tomato sauce and 2 cups of pasta water and let simmer for 5 minutes. Add a handful of spinach, one at a time, into the sauce, and cook for 3 minutes. In a large baking dish, add the pasta and pour the sauce over it. Stir in 1 ½ cups of mozzarella cheese, cover the dish with aluminum foil and bake for 20 minutes. After 20 minutes, remove the foil, top with the remaining mozzarella, and bake for another 8-12 minutes until golden brown.

176. Olive & Spinach Penne

Serves: 4 | Ready in about: 30 minutes

1 tbsp olive oil
8 oz uncooked penne
2 garlic cloves, minced
¼ tsp paprika

2 cups parsley, chopped
4 cups baby spinach
¼ tsp ground nutmeg
Salt and black pepper to taste

⅓ cup green olives, sliced
⅓ cup Parmesan cheese, grated

Cook the penne pasta according to the package directions in a large pot until almost al dente. Drain the pasta, and save ¼ cup of the cooking water. Meanwhile, heat the oil in a skillet over medium heat. Add the garlic and paprika, and cook for 30 seconds, stirring constantly. Stir in the parsley for 1 minute. Add the spinach, nutmeg, pepper, and salt, and keep stirring for 3 minutes until the spinach wilts. Add the pasta and the reserved water to the skillet. Stir in the olives, and cook for about 2 minutes until most of the pasta water has been absorbed. Sprinkle with Parmesan and serve.

177.   Penne in Tomato Sauce

Serves: 6 | Ready in about: 60 minutes

¼ cup olive oil
1 shallot, sliced thin
2 lb cherry tomatoes, halved
3 garlic cloves, sliced thin

1 tbsp balsamic vinegar
1 tbsp sugar
Salt and black pepper to taste
¼ tsp red pepper flakes

1 lb penne
¼ cup oregano, chopped
Grated Pecorino cheese

Preheat the oven to 350 F. In a bowl, drizzle shallot with some olive oil and mix well. In a separate bowl, gently add the tomatoes, remaining oil, garlic, vinegar, sugar, red pepper flakes, salt, and pepper. Spread tomato mixture in an even layer in a rimmed baking sheet, spread shallot over the tomatoes, and roast until edges of the shallot begin to brown and tomato skins are slightly shriveled, 33-38 minutes; do not stir. Let cool for 5 to 10 minutes.

Meanwhile, fill a pot with water and bring to a boil. Add the pasta and a pinch of salt and cook until al dente. Reserve ½ cup of cooking liquid, drain pasta and return it to the pot. Using a spatula, scrape tomato mixture onto the pasta. Add oregano and toss to combine. Season to taste and adjust consistency with the reserved water. Top with Pecorino cheese.

178.   Pinot Genovese Mussel Linguine

Serves: 4 | Ready in about: 40 minutes

1 lb mussels, scrubbed and debearded
1 tbsp olive oil
½ cup Pinot Grigio wine

2 garlic cloves, minced
½ tsp red pepper flakes
½ lemon, zested and juiced

1 lb linguine
Salt and black pepper to taste
2 tbsp parsley, finely chopped

In a saucepan, bring mussels and wine to a boil, cover, and cook, shaking pan occasionally, until mussels open, 5-7 minutes. As they open, remove them with a slotted spoon into a bowl. Discard all closed mussels. Drain steaming liquid through fine-mesh strainer into a bowl, avoiding any gritty sediment that has settled on the bottom of the pan. Wipe the pan clean. Warm the olive oil in the pan and stir-fry garlic and pepper flake until the garlic turns golden, 3 minutes. Stir in reserved mussel liquid and lemon zest and juice, bring to a simmer and cook for 3-4 minutes. Stir in mussels and cook until heated through, 3 minutes. Bring a large pot filled with salted water to a boil. Add pasta and cook until al dente. Reserve ½ cup of cooking liquid, drain pasta and return it to pot. Add the sauce and parsley and toss to combine and season to taste. Adjust consistency with the reserved cooking liquid as needed and serve.

179.   Saffron Chicken with Ziti

Serves: 4 | Ready in about: 35 minutes

3 tbsp butter
16 oz ziti
4 chicken breasts, cut into strips
½ tsp ground saffron threads
1 yellow onion, chopped

2 garlic cloves, minced
1 tbsp almond flour
1 pinch cardamom powder
1 pinch cinnamon powder
1 cup heavy cream

1 cup chicken stock
¼ cup chopped scallions
3 tbsp chopped parsley
Salt and black pepper to taste

In a large pot of boiling water, cook the ziti pasta for 8-10 minutes until al dente. Drain and set aside. Melt the butter in a large skillet, season the chicken with salt, black pepper, and cook in the oil until golden brown on the outside, 5 minutes. Stir in the saffron, onion, garlic and cook until the onion softens and the garlic and saffron are fragrant, 3 minutes. Stir in the almond flour, cardamom powder, and cinnamon powder, and cook for 1 minute to exude some fragrance. Add the heavy cream, chicken stock and cook for 2 to 3 minutes. Adjust the taste with salt, pepper and mix in the ziti and scallions. Allow warming for 1-2 minutes and turn the heat off. Garnish with parsley.

180.   Veggie & Pasta Bake

Serves: 4 | Ready in about: 45 minutes

1 cup sliced white button mushrooms
1 tbsp olive oil
16 oz penne
1 cup chopped bell peppers

1 yellow squash, chopped
1 red onion, sliced
Salt and black pepper to taste
¼ tsp red chili flakes

1 cup marinara sauce
1 cup grated Pecorino cheese
¼ cup chopped fresh basil

In a large pot of boiling water, cook the penne pasta for 8-10 minutes until al dente. Drain and set aside. Heat the olive oil in a pan and sauté the bell peppers, squash, onion, and mushrooms. Cook until softened, 5 minutes. Season with salt, pepper, and red chili flakes. Mix in marinara sauce and cook for 5 minutes. Transfer to a baking dish and stir in the penne. Spread the Pecorino cheese on top. Bake in the oven until the cheeses melt and golden brown on top, 15 minutes. Allow cooling for 2 minutes and dish onto serving plates. Serve warm topped with basil.

181.   Sunday Ziti Marinara Bake

Serves: 4 | Ready in about: 60 minutes

2 tbsp olive oil
¼ onion, diced
3 cloves garlic, chopped
1 (28-oz) can tomatoes, diced

Sprig of fresh thyme
½ bunch fresh basil
Salt and pepper to taste
1 lb ziti

1 cup cottage cheese
1 cup grated Mozzarella cheese
¾ cup grated Pecorino cheese

In a saucepan, warm the olive oil over medium heat. Stir-fry onion and garlic until lightly browned, 3 minutes. Add the tomatoes and herbs and bring to a boil, then simmer for 7 minutes, covered. Set aside. Discard the herb sprigs and stir in salt and pepper to taste. Preheat the oven to 375F. Prepare the pasta according to package directions. Drain and mix the pasta in a bowl along with half of the prepared marinara sauce, cottage cheese, and half the Mozzarella and Pecorino cheeses. Transfer the mixture to a baking dish, and top with the remaining marinara sauce and cheese. Bake for 25 to 35 minutes, or until bubbly and golden brown. Serve warm.

182.   Cheesy Pasta with Red Sauce

Serves: 6 | Ready in about: 60 minutes

¼ cup olive oil
1 shallot, sliced thin
2 lb cherry tomatoes, halved
3 large garlic cloves, sliced

1 tbsp red wine vinegar
3 oz ricotta cheese, crumbled
1 tsp sugar
Salt and black pepper to taste

¼ tsp red pepper flakes
1 lb penne
4 oz baby arugula

Preheat the oven to 350 F. Toss shallot with 1 tsp of oil in a bowl. In a separate bowl, toss tomatoes with remaining oil, garlic, vinegar, sugar, salt, pepper, and flakes. Spread tomato mixture in even layer in rimmed baking sheet, scatter shallot over tomatoes, and roast until edges of shallot begin to brown and tomato skins are slightly charred, 35-40 minutes; do not stir. Let cool for 5 to 10 minutes.

Meanwhile, bring a pot filled with salted water to a boil and add pasta. Cook, stirring often until al dente. Reserve ½ cup cooking water, then drain pasta and return it to pot. Add arugula to pasta and toss until wilted. Using a spatula, scrape tomato mixture onto pasta and toss to combine. Season to taste and adjust consistency with reserved cooking water as needed. Serve, passing ricotta cheese separately.

183.   Farfalle with Zucchini & Tomatoes

Serves: 6 | Ready in about: 30 minutes

2 lb zucchini, halved lengthwise cut into ½ inch
2 tbsp Pecorino-Romano, grated
5 tbsp extra-virgin olive oil
Salt and black pepper to taste
3 garlic cloves, minced

½ tsp red pepper flakes
1 lb farfalle
12 oz grape tomatoes, halved
½ cup fresh basil, chopped

¼ cup pine nuts, toasted
2 tbsp balsamic vinegar

Sprinkle the zucchini with 1 tablespoon salt and let drain in a colander for 30 minutes; pat dry. Heat 1 tbsp of oil in a large skillet. Add half of the zucchini and cook until golden brown and slightly charred, 5-7 minutes, reducing the heat if the skillet begins to scorch; transfer to plate. Repeat with 1 tbsp of oil and remaining zucchini; set aside.

Heat 1 tbsp of oil in the same skillet and stir-fry garlic and pepper flakes for 30 seconds. Add in squash and stir-fry for 40 seconds. Meanwhile, bring a large pot filled with water to a boil. Add pasta, a pinch of salt and cook until al dente. Reserve ½ cup of cooking liquid, drain pasta and return it to pot. Add the zucchini mixture, tomatoes, basil, pine nuts, vinegar, and remaining oil and toss to combine. Season to taste and adjust consistency with the reserved cooking liquid as needed. Serve with freshly grated Pecorino-Romano cheese.

PIZZA & SNACKS

184. Simple Pizza Margherita

Serves: 4 | Ready in about: 30 minutes

1 (15-ounce) can diced San Marzano tomatoes with juices

16 oz pizza dough

Salt to taste

1 tsp oregano

2 tbsp extra-virgin olive oil

10 mozzarella cheese slices

12 fresh basil leaves

6 whole black olives

Preheat your oven to 440 F. Place the dough on a floured surface and roll it out thinly. Place it on a lightly floured pizza pan and drizzle with some olive oil. Puree the tomatoes, a splash of olive oil and a sprinkle of salt until smooth. Spread the tomato sauce over the base, leaving a 1-inch border and sprinkle with oregano. Arrange the mozzarella cheese slices on top and bake for 8-10 minutes until the crust is golden. Top with basil and olives, and serve.

185. Mini Meatball Pizza

Serves: 4 | Ready in about: 25 minutes

1 pizza crust

1 ½ cups pizza sauce

½ tsp dried oregano

8 oz bite-sized meatballs

1 cup bell peppers, sliced

2 cups mozzarella, shredded

Preheat oven to 410 F. Spread the pizza crust evenly with pizza sauce and sprinkle with oregano. Arrange the meatballs on the pizza sauce. Sprinkle with bell peppers and mozzarella cheese. Bake for about 20 minutes or until the crust is golden brown and the cheese melts. Serve immediately.

186. Sun-Dried Tomato & Artichoke Pizza

Serves: 4 | Ready in about: 80 minutes

2 tbsp olive oil

1 cup canned passata

2 cups flour

1 pinch of sugar

1 tsp active dry yeast

¾ tsp salt

1 ½ cups artichoke hearts

¼ cup grated Asiago cheese

½ onion, minced

3 garlic cloves, minced

1 tbsp dried oregano

6 sundried tomatoes, chopped

½ tsp red pepper flakes

5-6 basil leaves, torn

Sift flour and salt in a bowl and stir in yeast. Mix 1 cup of lukewarm water, olive oil, and sugar in another bowl. Add the wet mixture to the dry mixture and whisk until you obtain a soft dough. Place the dough on a lightly floured work surface and knead it thoroughly for 4-5 minutes until elastic. Transfer the dough to a greased bowl. Cover with cling film and leave to rise for 50-60 minutes in a warm place until doubled in size. Roll out the dough to a thickness of around 12 inches. Preheat oven to 400 F. Warm oil in a saucepan over medium heat and sauté onion and garlic for 3-4 minutes. Mix in tomatoes and oregano and bring to a boil. Decrease the heat and simmer for another 5 minutes. Transfer the pizza crust to a baking sheet. Spread the sauce all over and top with artichoke hearts and sun-dried tomatoes. Scatter the cheese and bake for 15 minutes until golden. Top with red pepper flakes and basil, and serve.

187. Double Cheese Pizza

Serves: 4 | Ready in about: 35 minutes

For the crust:

1 tbsp olive oil

½ cup almond flour

¼ tsp salt

2 tbsp ground psyllium husk

For the topping

½ cup pizza sauce

4 oz mozzarella, sliced

1 cup grated mozzarella

3 tbsp grated Parmesan cheese

2 tsp Italian seasoning

Preheat oven to 400 F. Line a baking sheet with parchment paper. In a medium bowl, mix the almond flour, salt, psyllium powder, olive oil, and 1 cup of lukewarm water until dough forms. Spread the mixture on the pizza pan and bake in the oven until crusty, 10 minutes. When ready, remove the crust and spread the pizza sauce on top. Add the sliced mozzarella, grated mozzarella, Parmesan, and Italian seasoning. Bake for 18 minutes or until the cheeses melt.

188.   Basil Mushroom & Black Olive Pizza

Serves: 4 | Ready in about: 45 minutes

For the crust

2 tbsp olive oil	1 cup lukewarm water	1 tsp active dry yeast
2 cups flour	1 pinch of sugar	¾ tsp salt

For the topping

2 medium cremini mushrooms, sliced	1 tsp sugar	Salt and black pepper to taste
1 tsp olive oil	1 bay leaf	½ cup grated mozzarella
1 garlic clove, minced	1 tsp dried oregano	½ cup grated Parmesan cheese
½ cup tomato sauce	1tsp dried basil	6 black olives, sliced

Sift flour and salt in a bowl and stir in yeast. Mix lukewarm water, olive oil, and sugar in another bowl. Add the wet mixture to the dry mixture and whisk until you obtain a soft dough. Place the dough on a lightly floured work surface and knead it thoroughly for 4-5 minutes until elastic. Transfer the dough to a greased bowl. Cover with cling film and leave to rise for 50-60 minutes in a warm place until doubled in size. Roll out the dough to a thickness of around 12 inches. Preheat the oven to 400 F. Line a pizza pan with parchment paper. Heat the olive oil in a medium skillet and sauté the mushrooms until softened, 5 minutes. Stir in the garlic and cook until fragrant, 30 seconds. Mix in the tomato sauce, sugar, bay leaf, oregano, basil, salt, and black pepper. Cook for 2 minutes and turn the heat off. Spread the sauce on the crust, top with the mozzarella and Parmesan cheeses, and then the olives. Bake in the oven until the cheeses melt, 15 minutes. Serve warm.

189.   Pesto Turkey Pizza

Serves: 4 | Ready in about: 35 minutes

Pizza Crust

3 tbsp olive oil	¼ tsp salt
3 cups flour	3 large eggs

Topping

½ lb turkey ham, chopped	1 ½ cups basil pesto	4 fresh basil leaves, chopped
2 tbsp cashew nuts	1 cup mozzarella, grated	¼ tsp red pepper flakes
1 green bell pepper, sliced	2 tbsp Parmesan cheese, grated	

In a bowl, mix flour, olive oil, salt, and egg until a dough forms. Mold the dough into a ball and place it in between two full parchment papers on a flat surface. Roll it out into a circle of a ¼ -inch thickness. After, slide the pizza dough into the pizza pan and remove the parchment paper. Place the pizza pan in the oven and bake the dough for 20 minutes at 350 F. Once the pizza bread is ready, remove it from the oven, fold and seal the extra inch of dough at its edges to make a crust around it. Apply 2/3 of the pesto on it and sprinkle half of the mozzarella cheese too. Toss the chopped turkey meat in the remaining pesto and spread it on top of the pizza. Sprinkle with the remaining mozzarella, bell peppers, and cashew nuts and put the pizza back in the oven to bake for 9 minutes. When it is ready, remove from the oven to cool slightly, garnish with the basil leaves and sprinkle with parmesan cheese and red pepper flakes. Slice and serve.

190.   Lamb Arancini

Serves: 4 | Ready in about: 25 minutes

3 tbsp olive oil	Salt and black pepper to taste	¼ cup shallots, chopped
1 lb ground lamb	1 cup rice	½ tsp allspice
½ tsp cumin, ground	2 cups vegetable broth	2 eggs, lightly beaten
1 garlic clove, minced	¼ cup parsley, chopped	1 cup breadcrumbs

Place the rice in the vegetable broth and cook for about 15 minutes. Remove from the heat and leave to cool uncovered. In a large bowl, mix the cooled rice, ground lamb, cumin, garlic, salt, pepper, parsley, shallots, and allspice until combined. Form medium balls out of the mixture. Dip the arancini in the beaten eggs and toss in the breadcrumbs. Warm the olive oil in a skillet over medium heat and fry meatballs for 14 minutes on all sides until golden brown. Remove to paper towels to absorb excess oil. Serve warm.

191. Caprese Pizza

Serves: 4 | Ready in about: 40 minutes

2 tbsp olive oil
2 ¼ cups chickpea flour
Salt and black pepper to taste

1 tsp onion powder
1 tomato, sliced
¼ tsp dried oregano

2 oz mozzarella cheese, sliced
¼ cup tomato sauce
2 tbsp fresh basil, chopped

Preheat oven to 350 F. Combine the chickpea flour, salt, pepper, 1 ¼ cups of water, olive oil, and onion powder in a bowl. Mix well to form a soft dough, then knead a bit until elastic. Let sit covered in a greased bowl to rise for 25 minutes in a warm place. Remove the dough to a floured surface and roll out it with a rolling pin into a thin circle. Transfer to a floured baking tray and bake in the oven for 10 minutes. Evenly spread the tomato sauce over the pizza base. Sprinkle with oregano and arrange the mozzarella cheese and tomato slices on top. Bake for 10 minutes. Top with basil and serve sliced.

192. Oregano Pepperoni Fat Head Pizza

Serves: 4 | Ready in about: 35 minutes

2 tbsp olive oil
2 cups flour
1 cup lukewarm water

1 pinch of sugar
1 tsp active dry yeast
¾ tsp salt

1 tsp dried oregano
2 cups mozzarella cheese
1 cup sliced pepperoni

Sift flour and salt in a bowl and stir in yeast. Mix lukewarm water, olive oil, and sugar in another bowl. Add the wet mixture to the dry mixture and whisk until you obtain a soft dough. Place the dough on a lightly floured work surface and knead it thoroughly for 4-5 minutes until elastic. Transfer the dough to a greased bowl. Cover with cling film and leave to rise for 50-60 minutes in a warm place until doubled in size. Roll out the dough to a thickness of around 12 inches. Preheat oven to 400 F. Line a round pizza pan with parchment paper. Spread the dough on the pizza pan and top with the mozzarella cheese, oregano, and pepperoni slices. Bake in the oven for 15 minutes or until the cheese melts. Remove the pizza from the oven and let it cool slightly. Slice and serve.

193. Olive & Arugula Pizza with Balsamic Glaze

Serves: 4 | Ready in about: 90 minutes

2 tbsp olive oil
2 cups flour
1 cup lukewarm water
1 pinch sugar

1 tsp active dry yeast
2 tbsp honey
½ cup balsamic vinegar
4 cups arugula

Salt to taste
1 cup mozzarella, grated
¾ tsp dried oregano
6 black olives, drained

Sift flour and ¾ tsp salt in a bowl and stir in yeast. Mix lukewarm water, olive oil, and sugar in another bowl. Add the wet mixture to the dry mixture and whisk until you obtain a soft dough. Place the dough on a lightly floured work surface and knead it thoroughly for 4-5 minutes until elastic. Transfer the dough to a greased bowl. Cover with cling film and leave to rise for 50-60 minutes in a warm place. Roll out the dough to a thickness of around 12 inches. Place the balsamic vinegar and honey in a saucepan over medium heat and simmer for 5 minutes until syrupy. Preheat oven to 390 F. Transfer the pizza crust to a baking sheet and sprinkle with oregano and mozzarella cheese; bake for 10-15 minutes. Remove the pizza from the oven and top with arugula. Sprinkle with balsamic glaze and olives, and serve.

194. Italian Sausage Pizza Wraps

Serves: 2 | Ready in about: 20 minutes

1 tbsp basil, chopped
1 tsp olive oil
6 oz spicy Italian sausage
1 shallot, chopped

1 tsp Italian seasoning
4 oz marinara sauce
2 flour tortillas
½ cup mozzarella, shredded

1/3 cup Parmesan, grated
1 tsp red pepper flakes

Warm olive oil in a skillet over medium heat. Add and cook the sausage for 5-6 minutes, stirring and breaking up larger pieces, until cooked through. Remove to a bowl. Sauté the shallot for 3 minutes until soft, stirring frequently. Stir in Italian seasoning, marinara sauce, and reserved sausage. Bring to a simmer and cook for about 2 minutes. Divide the mixture between the tortillas, top with the cheeses, add red pepper flakes and basil, and fold over. Serve.

195.   Easy Salami Pizza

Serves: 4 | Ready in about: 45 minutes

For the crust

2 tbsp olive oil	1 cup lukewarm water	1 tsp active dry yeast
2 cups flour	1 pinch of sugar	¾ tsp salt

For the topping

1 cup sliced smoked mozzarella cheese

1 tbsp olive oil	¼ cup marinara sauce	¼ red onion, thinly sliced
1 cup sliced salami	¼ bell pepper, sliced	

Sift flour and salt in a bowl and stir in yeast. Mix lukewarm water, olive oil, and sugar in another bowl. Add the wet mixture to the dry mixture and whisk until you obtain a soft dough. Place the dough on a lightly floured work surface and knead it thoroughly for 4-5 minutes until elastic. Transfer the dough to a greased bowl. Cover with cling film and leave to rise for 50-60 minutes in a warm place until doubled in size. Roll out the dough to a thickness of around 12 inches. Preheat the oven to 400 F. Line a pizza pan with parchment paper. Heat the olive oil and cook the salami until brown, 5 minutes. Spread the marinara sauce on the crust, and top with the mozzarella cheese, salami, bell pepper, and onion. Bake in the oven until the cheese melts, 15 minutes. Remove it from the oven, slice, and serve warm.

196.   Submarine-Style Sandwiches

Serves: 4 | Ready in about: 35 minutes

½ lb sliced deli ham	1 Italian bread loaf, unsliced	½ lb sliced mozzarella cheese
½ lb sliced deli turkey	⅓ cup honey mustard	

Preheat oven to 410 F. Cut the bread horizontally in half. Spread the honey mustard over the bottom half. Layer ham, turkey, and mozzarella cheese over, then top with the remaining bread half. Wrap the sandwich in foil and bake for 20 minutes or until the bread is toasted. Open the foil and bake for 5 minutes or until the top is crisp. Serve sliced.

197.   Pepper-Broccoli Pizza

Serves: 4 | Ready in about: 25 minutes

For the crust

1 tbsp olive oil	¼ tsp salt	1 cup lukewarm water
½ cup almond flour	2 tbsp ground psyllium husk	

For the topping

1 tbsp olive oil	3 cups broccoli florets	4 tomatoes, sliced
1 cup sliced fresh mushrooms	4 garlic cloves, minced	1 ½ cups grated mozzarella
1 white onion, thinly sliced	½ cup pizza sauce	½ cup grated Parmesan cheese

Preheat oven to 400 F. Line a baking sheet with parchment paper. In a bowl, mix the almond flour, salt, psyllium powder, olive oil, and lukewarm water until the dough forms. Spread the mixture on the pizza pan and bake in the oven until crusty, 10 minutes. Remove and allow cooling. Heat olive oil in a skillet and sauté the mushrooms, onion, garlic, and broccoli until softened, 5 minutes. Spread the pizza sauce on the crust and top with the broccoli mixture, tomato, mozzarella and Parmesan. Bake for 5 minutes.

198.   Artichoke & Bean Dip

Serves: 4 | Ready in about: 10 minutes

2 tbsp olive oil	6 oz canned artichoke hearts,	½ lemon, juiced and zested
15 oz canned Cannellini beans	4 garlic cloves, minced	Salt and black pepper to taste
1 red onion, chopped	1 tbsp thyme, chopped	

Warm the olive oil in a skillet over medium heat and sauté onion and garlic for 4-5 minutes until translucent. Add in the artichoke hearts and cook for 2-3 more minutes. Set aside to cool slightly. Transfer the cooled mixture to a blender along with cannellini beans, thyme, lemon juice, lemon zest, salt, and pepper and blitz until it becomes smooth.

199.   One-Skillet Pesto Pizza

Serves: 2 | Ready in about: 10 minutes

1 tbsp butter	2 tbsp pesto	2 large eggs
2 pieces of focaccia bread	1 medium tomato, sliced	

Place a skillet over medium heat. Place the focaccia in the skillet and let it warm for about 4 minutes on both sides until softened and just starting to turn golden. Remove to a platter. Spread 1 tablespoon of the pesto on one side of each slice. Cover with tomato slices. Melt the butter in the skillet over medium heat. Crack in the eggs, keeping them separated, and cook until the whites are no longer translucent and the yolk is cooked to the desired doneness. Spoon one egg onto each pizza. Serve and enjoy!

200.   Spinach Pizza Bagels

Serves: 6 | Ready in about: 20 minutes

2 tbsp olive oil	1 cup pizza sauce	1 ¼ cups mozzarella, grated
6 bagels, halved and toasted	¼ tsp dried oregano	¼ cup Parmesan cheese, grated
2 green onions, chopped	1 cup spinach, torn	

Arrange the bagels on a baking sheet. Warm the olive oil in a saucepan over medium heat and sauté the green onions for 3-4 minutes until tender. Pour in the pizza sauce and oregano and bring to a simmer. Preheat your broiler. Spread the bagel halves with the sauce mixture and top with spinach. Sprinkle with mozzarella and Parmesan cheeses. Place under the preheated broiler for 5-6 minutes or until the cheeses melt.

201.   Rich Sicilian Sandwich Muffuletta

Serves: 6 | Ready in about: 10 minutes

1 focaccia bread	2 tbsp black olive tapenade	¼ lb smoked turkey, sliced
2 tbsp drained capers	½ lb fontina cheese, sliced	¼ lb salami, thinly sliced

Slice the focaccia in half horizontally. Spread each piece with olive tapenade. Layer half of the fontina cheese, a layer of capers, smoked turkey, olive tapenade, salami, and capers, and finish with fontina cheese. Top with the remaining focaccia half and press the sandwich together gently. Serve sliced into wedges.

202.   Spinach-Olive Pizza

Serves: 4 | Ready in about: 40 minutes

For the crust

1 tbsp olive oil	¼ tsp salt	1 cup lukewarm water
½ cup almond flour	2 tbsp ground psyllium husk	

For the topping

½ cup tomato sauce	1 cup grated mozzarella	3 tbsp sliced black olives
½ cup baby spinach	1 tsp dried oregano	

Preheat oven to 400 F. Line a baking sheet with parchment paper. In a medium bowl, mix the almond flour, salt, psyllium powder, olive oil, and water until dough forms. Spread the mixture on the pizza pan and bake in the oven until crusty, 10 minutes. When ready, remove the crust and spread the tomato sauce on top. Add the spinach, mozzarella cheese, oregano, and olives. Bake until the cheese melts, 15 minutes. Take out of the oven, slice and serve.

203.   Cauliflower Steaks

Serves: 4 | Ready in about: 35 minutes

1 head cauliflower, cut into steaks	2 tbsp olive oil	Salt and paprika to taste

Preheat oven to 370 F. Line a baking sheet with aluminum foil. Rub each cauliflower steak with olive oil, salt, and paprika. Arrange on the baking sheet and bake for 10-15 minutes; flip, and bake for another 15 minutes until crispy.

204. Sweet & Spice Roasted Almonds

Serves: 4 | Ready in about: 15 minutes

2 tbsp olive oil
3 cups almonds

1 tbsp curry powder
¼ cup honey

1 tsp salt

Preheat oven to 270 F. Coat almonds with olive oil, curry powder, and salt in a bowl; mix well. Arrange on a lined with aluminum foil sheet and bake for 15 minutes. Remove from the oven and let cool for 10 minutes. Drizzle with honey and let cool at room temperature. Enjoy!

205. Lentil & Roasted Garlic Dip

Serves: 6 | Ready in about: 40 minutes

1 roasted red bell pepper, chopped
4 tbsp olive oil
1 cup split red lentils
½ red onion

1 garlic bulb, top removed
½ tsp cumin seeds
1 tsp coriander seeds
¼ cup walnuts

2 tbsp tomato paste
½ tsp Cayenne powder
Salt and black pepper to taste

Preheat oven to 360 F. Drizzle the garlic with some olive oil and wrap it in a piece of aluminum foil. Roast for 35-40 minutes. Remove and allow to cool for a few minutes. Cover the lentils with salted water in a pot over medium heat and bring to a boil. Simmer for 15 minutes. Drain and set aside. Squeeze out the garlic cloves and place them in a food processor. Add in the cooled lentils, cumin seeds, coriander seeds, roasted red bell pepper, onion, walnuts, tomato paste, Cayenne powder, remaining olive oil, salt, and black pepper. Pulse until smooth. Serve with crostini if desired.

206. Curly Kale Flatbread with Artichokes

Serves: 4 | Ready in about: 25 minutes

3 tbsp olive oil
1 cup curly kale, chopped
1 tbsp garlic powder
2 tbsp parsley, chopped

2 flatbread wraps
4 tbsp Parmesan cheese, grated
½ cup mozzarella, grated
14 oz canned artichokes

12 cherry tomatoes, halved
Salt and black pepper to taste

Preheat oven to 390 F. Line a baking sheet with parchment paper. Brush the flatbread wrap with some olive oil and sprinkle with garlic, salt, and pepper. Top with half of the Parmesan and mozzarella cheeses. Combine artichokes, tomatoes, salt, pepper, and remaining olive oil in a bowl. Spread the mixture on top of the wraps and top with the remaining Parmesan cheese. Transfer to the baking sheet and bake for 15 minutes. Top with curly kale and parsley.

207. Bell Pepper & Eggplant Spread

Serves: 4 | Ready in about: 55 minutes

¼ cup olive oil
1 cup light mayonnaise

2 eggplants, sliced
Salt and black pepper to taste

4 garlic cloves, minced
1 tbsp chives, chopped

Preheat oven to 360 F. Arrange bell peppers and eggplants on a baking pan. Sprinkle with salt, pepper, and garlic and drizzle with some olive oil. Bake for 45 minutes. Transfer to a food processor and pulse until smooth a few times while gradually adding the remaining olive oil. Remove to a bowl and mix in mayonnaise. Top with chives and serve.

208. Tomato & BasilBruschetta

Serves: 4 | Ready in about: 20 minutes

1 ciabatta loaf, halved lengthwise
2 tbsp olive oil
3 tbsp basil, chopped

4 tomatoes, cubed
1 shallot, sliced
2 garlic cloves, minced

Salt and black pepper to taste
1 tbsp balsamic vinegar
½ tsp garlic powder

Preheat oven to 380 F. Line a baking sheet with parchment paper. Cut in half each half of the ciabatta loaf. Place them on the sheet and sprinkle with some olive oil. Bake for 10 minutes. Mix tomatoes, shallot, basil, garlic, salt, pepper, olive oil, vinegar, and garlic powder in a bowl and let sit for 10 minutes. Apportion the mixture among bread pieces.

209. Spring Cucumber Sticks with Dill-Cheese Dip

Serves: 4 | Ready in about: 10 minutes

3 cucumbers, julienned and deseeded
¼ cup olive oil
¼ tsp salt

1 garlic clove, minced
2 tbsp dill, chopped
¼ cup grated Parmesan cheese

¼ cup almonds, chopped
½ tsp paprika

Season the cucumbers and arrange them on a platter. Mix dill, almonds, garlic, Parmesan cheese, and olive oil in a food processor until smooth. Spoon the dip over the cucumbers and season with paprika to serve.

210. Parmesan Crispy Potato Chips

Serves: 4 | Ready in about: 40 minutes

2 tbsp olive oil
4 potatoes, cut into wedges

2 tbsp grated Parmesan cheese
Salt and black pepper to taste

Preheat oven to 340 F. In a bowl, combine the potatoes, olive oil, salt, and black pepper. Spread on a lined baking sheet and bake for 40 minutes until the edges are browned. Serve sprinkled with Parmesan cheese.

211. Orange Cantaloupe & Watermelon Balls

Serves: 4 | Ready in about: 5 minutes + chilling time

2 cups watermelon balls
2 cups cantaloupe balls

½ cup orange juice
¼ cup lemon juice

1 tbsp orange zest

Place the watermelon and cantaloupe in a bowl. In another bowl, mix the lemon juice, orange juice, and zest. Pour over the fruit. Transfer to the fridge covered for 5 hours. Serve.

212. Baked Veggies with Marsala Sauce

Serves: 4 | Ready in about: 30 minutes

Vegetables:
¼ cup olive oil
1 lb green beans, trimmed
½ lb carrots, trimmed
1 fennel bulb, sliced
¼ cup dry white wine
Sauce:
2 tbsp olive oil
2 tbsp Marsala wine
2 tbsp plain yogurt

¼ tsp oregano
½ tsp thyme
½ tsp rosemary
¼ tsp coriander seeds
¼ tsp celery seeds

1 tbsp yellow mustard
1 tsp honey
1 tbsp lemon juice

¼ tsp dried dill weed
1 head garlic, halved
1 red onion, sliced
Salt and black pepper to taste

1 yolk from 1 hard-boiled egg
Salt to taste
1 tbsp paprika

Preheat oven to 380 F. In a bowl, combine the olive oil, white wine, oregano, thyme, rosemary, coriander seeds, celery seeds, dill weed, salt, and black pepper and mix well. Add in carrots, green beans, fennel, garlic, and onion and toss to coat. Spread the mixture on a baking dish and roast in the oven for 15-20 minutes until tender. In a food processor, place the honey, yogurt, mustard, lemon juice, Marsala wine, yolk, olive oil, salt, and paprika, and blitz until smooth and uniform. Transfer to a bowl and place in the fridge until ready to use. When the veggies are ready, remove and serve with the prepared sauce on the side.

213. Grana Padano Charred Asparagus

Serves: 4 | Ready in about: 25 minutes

2 tbsp olive oil
1 lb asparagus, trimmed

4 tbsp Grana Padano, grated
½ tsp garlic powder

Salt to taste
2 tbsp parsley, chopped

Preheat your grill to high. Season the asparagus with salt and garlic powder and coat with olive oil. Grill the asparagus for 10 minutes, turning often until lightly charred and tender. Sprinkle with cheese and parsley and serve.

214. Artichoke Hearts with Aioli

Serves: 4 | Ready in about: 25 minutes

1 tbsp olive oil
1 red onion, chopped
2 garlic cloves, minced

Salt and black pepper to taste
10 oz canned artichoke hearts
1 tsp lemon juice

1 cup light mayonnaise
2 tbsp thyme, chopped

Warm olive oil in a skillet over medium heat and cook the onion for 3 minutes. Stir in artichokes, salt, and pepper and stir-fry for 4-5 minutes; reserve. In a bowl, mix mayonnaise, lemon juice, and garlic. Sprinkle the artichokes with thyme and serve with aioli. Enjoy!

215. Ground Lamb Ragu Tagliatelle

Serves: 4 | Ready in about: 25 minutes

2 tbsp olive oil
16 oz tagliatelle
1 tsp paprika

1 tsp cumin
Salt and black pepper to taste
1 lb ground lamb

1 cup onions, chopped
¼ cup parsley, chopped
2 garlic cloves, minced

Boil the tagliatelle pasta in a pot over medium heat for 9-11 minutes or until "al dente". Drain and set aside. Warm the olive oil in a skillet over medium heat and sauté lamb, onions, and garlic until the meat is browned, about 10-15 minutes. Stir in cumin, paprika, salt, and pepper for 1-2 minutes. Spoon tagliatelle on a platter and scatter lamb over. Top with parsley and serve.

216. Anchovy Tapenade

Serves: 4 | Ready in about: 10 minutes

1 cup roasted red peppers, chopped
3 tbsp olive oil
2 anchovy fillets, chopped

2 tbsp parsley, chopped
14 oz canned artichokes
¼ cup capers, drained

1 tbsp lemon juice
2 garlic cloves, minced

Blend roasted peppers, anchovies, parsley, artichokes, oil, capers, lemon juice, and garlic until a paste is formed, in a food processor. Serve at room temperature.

217. Cumin Vegetarian Patties

Serves: 4 | Ready in about: 20 minutes

3 tbsp olive oil
2 carrots, grated
2 zucchini, grated and drained
2 garlic cloves, minced
2 spring onions, chopped

1 tsp cumin
½ tsp turmeric powder
Salt and black pepper to taste
¼ tsp ground coriander
2 tbsp parsley, chopped

¼ tsp lemon juice
½ cup flour
1 egg, whisked
¼ cup breadcrumbs

Mix garlic, spring onions, carrot, cumin, turmeric, salt, pepper, coriander, parsley, lemon juice, flour, zucchini, egg, and breadcrumbs in a bowl and mix well. Form balls out of the mixture and flatten them to form patties. Warm olive oil in a skillet over medium heat. Fry the cakes for 10 minutes on both sides. Remove to a paper-lined plate to drain the excessive grease. Serve warm.

218. Tuna Stuffed Zucchini Rolls

Serves: 4 | Ready in about: 5 minutes

5 oz canned tuna, drained and mashed
2 tbsp olive oil
½ cup mayonnaise

2 tbsp capers
2 zucchini, sliced lengthwise
Salt and black pepper to taste

1 tsp lime juice

Drizzle the zucchini slices with olive oil and season with salt and pepper. Heat a grill pan over medium heat and grill zucchini for 5-6 minutes on both sides. In a bowl, mix tuna, capers, lime juice, mayonnaise, salt, and pepper until well combined. Spread the tuna mixture onto zucchini slices and roll them up. Transfer the rolls to a plate and serve.

219.   Squash Wedges with Walnuts

Serves: 4 | Ready in about: 50 minutes

1 lb butternut squash, peeled and cut into wedges
3 tbsp olive oil
1 cup walnuts, chopped

1 tbsp chili paste
1 tbsp balsamic vinegar

1 tbsp chives, chopped

Preheat oven to 370 F. Line a baking sheet with parchment paper. Combine squash wedges, chili paste, olive oil, vinegar, and chives in a bowl and arrange on the sheet. Bake for 40 minutes, turning often. Sprinkle with walnuts.

220.   Kale & Shallot Spread

Serves: 4 | Ready in about: 10 minutes

2 shallots, chopped
1 lb kale, roughly chopped

2 tbsp mint, chopped
¾ cup cream cheese, soft

Salt and black pepper to taste

In a food processor or a blender, blend kale, shallots, mint, cream cheese, salt, and pepper until smooth. Serve.

221.   Lighter Roasted Carrot Ribbons with Mayo Sauce

Serves: 4 | Ready in about: 50 minutes

2 tbsp olive oil
1 lb carrots, shaved into ribbons
Salt and black pepper to taste

½ lemon, zested
1/3 cup light mayonnaise
1 garlic clove, minced

1 tsp cumin, ground
1 tbsp dill, chopped

Preheat oven to 380 F. Spread carrot ribbons on a paper-lined roasting tray. Drizzle with some olive oil and sprinkle with cumin, salt, and pepper. Roast for 20-25 minutes until crisp and golden. In a bowl, mix mayonnaise, lemon zest, garlic, dill, and remaining olive oil. Serve the roasted carrots with mayo sauce.

222.   Savory Salmon-Cucumber Rolls

Serves: 4 | Ready in about: 5 minutes

8 black olives, chopped
4 oz smoked salmon strips
1 cucumber, sliced lengthwise

2 tsp lime juice
4 oz cream cheese, soft
1 tsp lemon zest, grated

Salt and black pepper to taste
2 tsp dill, chopped

Place the cucumber slices on a flat surface and top each with a salmon strip. Combine olives, lime juice, cream cheese, lemon zest, salt, pepper, and dill in a bowl. Smear the cream mixture over the salmon and roll them up. Serve.

223.   Grilled Eggplant Rounds

Serves: 4 | Ready in about: 25 minutes

1 cup roasted peppers, chopped
4 tbsp olive oil
2 eggplants, cut into rounds

12 olives, chopped
1 tsp red chili flakes, crushed
Salt and black pepper to taste

2 tbsp basil, chopped
2 tbsp Parmesan cheese, grated

Combine the roasted peppers, half of the olive oil, olives, red chili flakes, salt, and pepper in a bowl. Rub each eggplant slice with the remaining olive oil and salt. Grill them on the preheated grill for 14 minutes on both sides. Remove to a platter. To serve, distribute the pepper mixture across the eggplant rounds and top with basil and Parmesan cheese.

224.   Quick Avocado Spread

Serves: 4 | Ready in about: 5 minutes

2 avocados, chopped
½ cup heavy cream

1 serrano pepper, chopped
Salt and black pepper to taste

2 tbsp cilantro, chopped
¼ cup lime juice

In a food processor or a blender, blitz heavy cream, serrano pepper, salt, pepper, avocados, cilantro, and lime juice until smooth. Refrigerate before serving.

225.　Easy Red Dip

Serves: 4 | Ready in about: 10 minutes

1 cup roasted red peppers, chopped
3 tbsp olive oil
1 lb tomatoes, chopped

Salt and black pepper to taste
1 ½ tsp balsamic vinegar
½ tsp oregano, chopped

2 garlic cloves, minced
2 tbsp parsley, chopped

In a food processor or a blender, blend tomatoes, red peppers, salt, pepper, vinegar, oregano, olive oil, garlic, and parsley until smooth. Store this in the fridge for a few days, up to a week.

226.　Crispy Eggplant Fries

Serves: 4 | Ready in about: 35 minutes

2 tbsp olive oil
2 eggplants, sliced
½ tbsp smoked paprika

Salt and black pepper to taste
½ tsp onion powder
2 tsp dried sage

1 cup fine breadcrumbs
1 large egg white, beaten

Preheat oven to 350 F. Line a baking sheet with parchment paper. In a bowl, mix olive oil, paprika, salt, pepper, onion powder, and sage. Dip the eggplant slices in the egg white, then coat in the breadcrumb mixture. Arrange them on the sheet and roast in the oven for 25 minutes, flipping once.

227.　Spinach Salad with Almonds & Chickpeas

Serves: 4 | Ready in about: 5 minutes

2 tbsp olive oil
3 spring onions, chopped
1 cup baby spinach

15 oz canned chickpeas
Salt and black pepper to taste
2 tbsp lemon juice

1 tbsp cilantro, chopped
2 tbsp almonds flakes, toasted

Toss the chickpeas, spring onions, spinach, salt, pepper, olive oil, lemon juice, and cilantro in a salad bowl. Top with almond flakes. Serve and enjoy!

228.　Ricotta Spread

Serves: 4 | Ready in about: 5 minutes

2 tbsp extra virgin olive oil
8 oz ricotta cheese, crumbled

2 tbsp fresh parsley, chopped
¼ cup chives, chopped

Salt and black pepper to taste

In a blender, blend the ricotta, parsley, chives, salt, pepper, and olive oil until smooth. Serve.

229.　Prosciutto Wrapped Pears

Serves: 4 | Ready in about: 5 minutes

4 oz prosciutto slices, halved lengthwise
2 pears, cored and cut into wedges

1 tbsp chives, chopped

1 tsp red pepper flakes

Wrap the wedges with prosciutto slices. Transfer them to a platter. Garnish with chives and pepper flakes. Serve.

230.　Eggplant Balls

Serves: 4 | Ready in about: 55 minutes

3 tbsp olive oil
2 cups eggplants, chopped
3 garlic cloves, minced

2 eggs, whisked
Salt and black pepper to taste
2 tbsp parsley, chopped

½ cup Pecorino cheese, grated
¾ cups panko breadcrumbs

Preheat oven to 360 F. Warm olive oil in a skillet over medium heat and sauté garlic and eggplants for 15 minutes. Mix cooked eggplants, eggs, salt, pepper, parsley, Pecorino cheese, and breadcrumbs in a bowl and form medium balls out of the mixture. Bake the balls for 30 minutes. Serve.

231. Pepper & Eggplant Spread on Toasts

Serves: 4 | Ready in about: 10 minutes

1 red bell pepper, roasted and chopped
1 lb eggplants, baked, peeled and chopped
¾ cup olive oil

1 lemon, zested
1 red chili pepper, chopped
1 ½ tsp capers
1 garlic clove, minced

Salt and black pepper to taste
1 baguette, sliced and toasted

In a food processor, add the eggplants, lemon zest, red chili pepper, bell pepper, garlic, salt, and pepper. Blend while gradually adding the olive oil until smooth. Spread each baguette slice with the spread and top with capers to serve.

232. Lentil Spread

Serves: 6 | Ready in about: 10 minutes

3 tbsp olive oil
1 garlic clove, minced

1 cup split red lentils, rinsed
½ tsp dried thyme

1 tbsp balsamic vinegar
Salt and black pepper to taste

In a pot, bring to a boil salted water over medium heat. Add in the lentils and cook for 15 minutes until cooked through. Drain and set aside to cool. In a food processor, place the lentils, garlic, thyme, vinegar, salt, and pepper. Gradually add olive oil while blending until smooth. Serve.

233. Arugula Dip with Pesto

Serves: 4 | Ready in about: 5 minutes

1 cup arugula, chopped
3 tbsp basil pesto

1 cup cream cheese, soft
Salt and black pepper to taste

1 cup heavy cream
1 tbsp chives, chopped

Combine the arugula, basil pesto, salt, pepper, and heavy cream in a blender and pulse until smooth. Transfer to a bowl and mix in cream cheese. Serve topped with chives.

234. Cucumber & Prawn Bites

Serves: 4 | Ready in about: 5 minutes

1 lb prawns, cooked and chopped
1 cucumber, cubed

2 tbsp cream cheese
Salt and black pepper to taste

12 whole-grain crackers

Combine the cucumber, prawns, cream cheese, salt, and pepper in a bowl. Place crackers on a plate and top them with the prawn mixture. Serve right away.

235. Egg Avocado Boats

Serves: 2 | Ready in about: 15 minutes

1 halved avocado, pitted
2 large eggs

Salt and black pepper to taste
2 tbsp jarred pesto

2 sundried tomatoes, chopped

Preheat the oven to 420 F. Scoop out the middle of each avocado half. Arrange them on a baking sheet, cutside up. Crack an egg into each avocado half and season to taste. Bake until the eggs are set and cooked to your desired level of doneness, 10-12 minutes. Remove from the oven and top with pesto and sundried tomatoes. Serve and enjoy!

236. Apple Chips with Choco-Tahini Glaze

Serves: 2 | Ready in about: 10 minutes

1 tbsp roasted, salted sunflower seeds
2 tbsp tahini

1 tbsp honey
1 tbsp cocoa powder

2 apples, thinly sliced

Mix tahini, honey, and cocoa powder in a small bowl. Add 1-2 tbsp of warm water and stir until thin enough to drizzle. Lay the apple chips out on a plate and drizzle them with the chocolate tahini sauce. Sprinkle sunflower seeds.

237.   Stuffed Potato Skins with Cheese

Serves: 4 | Ready in about: 40 minutes

2 tbsp olive oil
1 lb red baby potatoes
1 cup ricotta cheese, crumbled

2 garlic cloves, minced
1 tbsp chives, chopped
½ tsp hot chili sauce

Salt and black pepper to taste

Place the potatoes and enough water in a pot over medium heat and bring to a boil. Simmer for 15 minutes and drain. Let them cool. Cut them in halves and scoop out the pulp. Place the pulp in a bowl and mash it a bit with a fork. Add in the ricotta cheese, olive oil, garlic, chives, chili sauce, salt, and pepper. Mix to combine. Fill potato skins with the mixture. Preheat oven to 360 F. Line a baking sheet with parchment paper. Place filled skins on the sheet and bake for 10 minutes.

238.   Seedy Crackers

Serves: 6 | Ready in about: 20 minutes

1 cup almond flour
1 tbsp sesame seeds
1 tbsp sunflower seeds

1 tbsp flaxseed
1 tbsp chia seeds
¼ tsp baking soda

Salt and black pepper to taste
1 egg, beaten

Preheat your oven to 350 F. In a bowl, mix the almond flour, sesame seeds, flaxseed, chia seeds, sunflower seeds, baking soda, salt, and pepper and stir well. Add the egg and stir well to combine and form the dough into a ball. Place one layer of parchment paper on your counter-top and place the dough on top. Cover with a second layer of parchment and, using a rolling pin, roll the dough to ¼-inch thickness, aiming for a rectangular shape. Cut the dough into crackers and bake on parchment until crispy and slightly golden, 10-15 minutes, depending on thickness. Alternatively, you can bake the large rolled dough before cutting and break into free-form crackers once baked and crispy. Store in an airtight container for up to 1 week.

239.   Crunchy Kale Chips

Serves: 4 | Ready in about: 15 minutes

2 tbsp olive oil

2 heads curly leaf kale

Sea salt to taste

Tear the kale into bite-sized pieces. Toss with the olive oil, and lay on a baking sheet in a single layer. Sprinkle with a pinch of sea salt. Bake for 10 to 15 minutes until crispy. Serve or store in an airtight container.

240.   Strawberry Caprese Skewers

Serves: 6 | Ready in about: 15 minutes + cooling time

1 tbsp olive oil
1 cup balsamic vinegar

24 whole, hulled strawberries
24 basil leaves, halved

12 fresh mozzarella balls

Pour the vinegar into a small saucepan and simmer for 10 minutes or until it's reduced by half and is thick enough to coat the back of a spoon. Set aside to cool completely. Thread the strawberries onto wooden skewers, followed by basil leaves folded in half and mozzarella balls. Drizzle with balsamic glaze and olive oil and serve.

241.   Lemon Shrimp

Serves: 6 | Ready in about: 10 minutes

24 large shrimp, peeled and deveined
½ cup olive oil
5 garlic cloves, minced

1 tsp red pepper flakes
1 lemon, juiced and zested
1 tsp dried dill

1 tsp dried thyme
Salt and black pepper to taste

Warm olive oil in a large skillet over medium heat. Add the garlic and red pepper flakes and cook for 1 minute. Add the shrimp and cook an additional 3 minutes, stirring frequently. Remove from the pan, and sprinkle with lemon juice, lemon zest, thyme, dill, salt, and pepper. Serve.

242. Mascarpone & Almonds Stuffed Dates

Serves: 6 | Ready in about: 15 minutes

20 blanched almonds
8 oz mascarpone cheese

20 Medjool dates
2 tbsp honey

With a knife, cut one side of the date lengthwise from the stem to the bottom. Gently remove the stone and replace it with a blanched almond. Spoon the cheese into a piping bag. Squeeze a generous amount of cheese into each date. Set the dates on a serving plate and drizzle with honey. Serve immediately or chill in the fridge.

243. Toasted Balsamic Beet Rounds

Serves: 6 | Ready in about: 45 minutes

4 tbsp olive oil
4 beets, peeled, cut into wedges

Salt and black pepper to taste
3 tsp fresh thyme

⅓ cup balsamic vinegar
1 tbsp fresh dill, chopped

Preheat your oven to 400 F. Place the beets into a large bowl. Add 2 tbsp of olive oil, salt, and thyme and toss to combine. Spread the beets onto a baking sheet. Bake for 35-40 minutes, turning once or twice until the beets are tender. Remove and let them cool for 10 minutes. In a small bowl, whisk together the remaining olive oil, vinegar, dill, and black pepper. Transfer the beets into a serving bowl, spoon the vinegar mixture over the beets, and serve.

244. Speedy Spicy Popcorn

Serves: 6 | Ready in about: 10 minutes

3 tbsp olive oil
¼ tsp garlic powder
Salt and black pepper to taste

½ tsp dried thyme
½ tsp chili powder
½ tsp dried oregano

12 cups plain popped popcorn

Warm olive oil in a large pan over medium heat. Add the garlic powder, black pepper, salt, chili powder, and thyme, and stir oregano until fragrant, 1 minute. Place the popcorn in a large bowl and drizzle the infused oil over. Toss to coat.

245. Power Granola Bites

Serves: 5 | Ready in about: 10 minutes

¾ cup diced dried figs
½ cup chopped walnuts

¼ cup old-fashioned oats
2 tbsp ground flaxseed

2 tbsp peanut butter
2 tbsp honey

In a bowl, mix together the figs, walnuts, oats, flaxseed, and peanut butter. Drizzle with the honey, and mix everything with a wooden spoon. Freeze the dough for 5 minutes. Divide the dough evenly into four sections in the bowl. Dampen your hands with water—but don't get them too wet, or the dough will stick to them. With hands, roll three bites out of each of the four sections of dough, making 10 energy bites. Store in the fridge for up to a week.

246. Trail Mix

Serves: 4 | Ready in about: 20 minutes

1 tbsp olive oil
1 tbsp maple syrup
1 tsp vanilla
½ tsp paprika

½ tsp cardamom
½ tsp allspice
2 cups mixed, unsalted nuts
¼ cup sunflower seeds

½ cup dried apricots, diced
½ cup dried figs, diced
Salt to taste

Mix olive oil, maple syrup, vanilla, cardamom, paprika, and allspice in a pan over medium heat. Stir to combine. Add the nuts and seeds and stir well to coat. Let the nuts and seeds toast for about 10 minutes, stirring often. Remove from the heat, and add the dried apricots and figs. Stir everything well and season with salt. Store in an airtight container.

BEANS, RICE & GRAINS

247.   White Wine Barley Risotto

Serves: 6 | Ready in about: 1 hour 20 minutes

2 tbsp olive oil
4 cups vegetable broth
4 cups water
1 onion, chopped fine

1 carrot, chopped
1 ½ cups pearl barley
1 cup dry white wine
¼ tsp dried oregano

2 oz Parmesan cheese, grated
Salt and black pepper to taste

In a saucepan, bring broth and water to a simmer. Reduce heat to low and cover to keep warm. Heat 1 tbsp of oil in a pot over medium heat until sizzling. Stir-fry onion and carrot until softened, 6-7 minutes. Add barley and cook, stirring often, until lightly toasted and aromatic, 4 minutes. Add wine and cook, stirring frequently for 2 minutes. Stir in 3 cups of water and oregano, bring to a simmer, and cook, stirring occasionally until liquid is absorbed, 25 minutes. Stir in 2 cups of broth, bring to a simmer, and cook until the liquid is absorbed, 15 minutes. Continue stirring often, and adding warm broth as needed to prevent the pot bottom from becoming dry until barley is cooked through but still somewhat firm in the center, 15-20 minutes. Off heat, adjust consistency with the remaining warm broth as needed. Stir in Parmesan and the remaining oil and season with salt and pepper to taste.

248.   Beanballs in Marinara Sauce

Serves: 4 | Ready in about: 45 minutes

Beanballs
2 tbsp olive oil
½ yellow onion, minced
1 tsp coriander seeds
½ tsp dried oregano
Marinara
1 (28-oz) can diced tomatoes with juice
1 tbsp olive oil
3 garlic cloves, minced

½ tsp dried thyme
½ tsp red pepper flakes
1 tsp garlic powder
1 (15-oz) can white beans

2 tbsp basil leaves
Salt to taste

½ cup bread crumbs
Salt and black pepper to taste

Preheat your oven to 350 F. Warm 2 tbsp of olive oil in a skillet over medium heat. Sauté the onion for 3 minutes. Sprinkle with coriander seeds, oregano, thyme, pepper flakes, and garlic powder, then cook for 1 minute or until aromatic. Pour the sautéed mixture into a food processor and add the beans and bread crumbs. Sprinkle with salt and black pepper and pulse to combine well, and the mixture holds together. Shape the mixture into balls. Arrange them on a greased baking sheet. Bake for 30 minutes or until lightly browned. Flip the balls halfway through the cooking time. Meanwhile, heat 1 tbsp of olive oil in a saucepan over medium heat. Add the garlic and basil and sauté for 2 minutes or until fragrant. Fold in the tomatoes and juice. Bring to a boil. Reduce the heat to low. Put the lid on and simmer for 15 minutes. Sprinkle with salt. Transfer the beanballs to a large plate and drizzle with marinara sauce. Serve.

249.   Classic Ribollita (Tuscan Bean Soup)

Serves: 6 | Ready in about: 1 hour 45 minutes

3 tbsp olive oil
Salt and black pepper to taste
2 cups canned cannellini beans
6 oz pancetta, chopped
¼ tsp red pepper flakes

1 onion, chopped
2 carrots, chopped
1 celery rib, chopped
3 garlic cloves, minced
4 cups chicken broth

1 lb lacinato kale, chopped
1 (14-oz) can diced tomatoes
1 rosemary sprig, chopped
Crusty bread for serving

Warm olive oil in a skillet over medium heat and add the pancetta. Cook, stirring occasionally, until pancetta is lightly browned and fat has rendered, 5-6 minutes. Add onion, carrots, and celery and cook, stirring occasionally, until softened and lightly browned, 4-6 minutes. Stir in garlic and red pepper flakes and cook until fragrant, 1 minute. Stir in broth, 2 cups of water, and beans and bring to a boil. Cover and simmer for 15 minutes. Stir in lacinato kale and tomatoes and cook for another 5 minutes. Sprinkle with rosemary and adjust the taste. Serve with crusty bread.

250.   Bean & Vegetable Gratin

Serves: 4 | Ready in about: 50 minutes

½ cup Parmigiano Reggiano, grated
4 pancetta slices
2 tbsp olive oil
4 garlic cloves, minced
1 onion, chopped
½ fennel bulb, chopped

1 tbsp brown rice flour
2 (15-oz) cans white beans
1 (16-oz) can tomatoes, diced
1 medium zucchini, chopped
1 tsp porcini powder
1 tbsp fresh basil, chopped

½ tsp dried oregano
1 tsp red pepper flakes
Salt to taste
2 tbsp butter, cubed

Heat olive oil in a skillet over medium heat. Fry the pancetta for 5 minutes until crispy. Drain on paper towels, chop, and reserve. Add garlic, onion, and fennel to the skillet and sauté for 5 minutes until softened. Stir in rice flour for 3 minutes. Preheat oven to 350 F. Add the beans, tomatoes, and zucchini to a casserole dish and pour in the sautéed vegetable and chopped pancetta; mix well. Sprinkle with porcini powder, oregano, red pepper flakes, and salt. Top with Parmigiano Reggiano cheese and butter and bake for 25 minutes or until the cheese is lightly browned. Garnish with basil and serve.

251.   Bean Stuffed Sweet Potatoes

Serves: 4 | Ready in about: 50 minutes

4 sweet potatoes, pierced with a fork
2 tbsp olive oil
1 cup canned cannellini beans
1 small red pepper, chopped

1 tbsp lemon zest
2 tbsp lemon juice
1 garlic clove, minced
1 tbsp oregano, chopped

1 tbsp parsley, chopped
Salt and black pepper to taste
1 avocado, mashed
1 tbsp tahini paste

Preheat your oven to 360 F. Line a baking sheet with parchment paper and place in the sweet potatoes. Bake for 40 minutes. Let cool and cut in half. Using a spoon, remove some flesh of the potatoes and place it in a bowl. Mix in beans, red pepper, lemon zest, half of the lemon juice, half of the oil, half of the garlic, oregano, half of the parsley, salt, and pepper. Divide the mixture between the potato halves. In another bowl, combine avocado, 2 tbsp of water, tahini, remaining lemon juice, remaining oil, remaining garlic, and remaining parsley and scatter over stuffed potatoes. Serve chilled.

252.   Egg Noodles with Bean & Lemon Sauce

Serves: 4 | Ready in about: 20 minutes

3 tbsp olive oil
12 oz egg noodles
1 (14-oz) can diced tomatoes
1 (13-oz) can cannellini beans
½ cup heavy cream

1 cup vegetable stock
2 garlic cloves, minced
1 onion, chopped
1 cup spinach, chopped
1 tsp dill

1 tsp thyme
½ tsp red pepper, crushed
1 tsp lemon juice
1 tbsp fresh basil, chopped

Warm olive oil in a pot over medium heat. Add in onion and garlic and cook for 3 minutes until softened. Stir in dill, thyme, and red pepper for 1 minute. Add in spinach, vegetable stock, and tomatoes. Bring to a boil, add the egg noodles, cover, and lower the heat. Cook for 5-7 minutes. Put in beans and cook until heated through. Combine the heavy cream, lemon juice, and basil. Serve the dish with creamy lemon sauce on the side.

253.   Borlotti Bean Stew

Serves: 6 | Ready in about: 25 minutes

3 tbsp olive oil
1 onion, chopped
1 (12-oz) can tomato paste

¼ cup red wine vinegar
8 fresh sage leaves, chopped
2 garlic cloves, minced

½ cup water
2 (15-oz) cans borlotti beans

Warm olive oil in a saucepan over medium heat. Sauté the onion and garlic for 5 minutes, stirring frequently. Add the tomato paste, vinegar, and 1 cup of water, and mix well. Turn the heat to low. Drain and rinse one can of the beans in a colander and add to the saucepan. Pour the entire second can of beans (including the liquid) into the saucepan. Simmer for 10 minutes, stirring occasionally. Serve warm sprinkled with sage.

254.   Cumin Spinach Lentils

Serves: 6 | Ready in about: 30 minutes

2 tbsp olive oil
4 garlic cloves, sliced thin
Salt and black pepper to taste

1 onion, chopped
1 tsp ground coriander
1 tsp dried thyme

1 tsp ground cumin
1 cup lentils, rinsed
8 oz spinach, chopped

Warm olive oil in a pot over medium heat. Sauté the garlic for 2-3 minutes, stirring often, until crisp and golden but not brown. Remove the garlic to a paper towel–lined plate and season lightly with salt; set aside. Add the onion to the pot and cook for 3 minutes until softened and lightly browned. Stir in salt, thyme, coriander, and cumin for 1 minute until fragrant. Pour in 2 ½ cups of water and lentils and bring to a simmer. Lower the heat to low, cover, and simmer gently, stirring occasionally for 15 minutes until lentils are mostly tender but still intact. Stir in spinach and cook until spinach is wilted, about 5 minutes. Adjust the taste with salt and pepper. Sprinkle with toasted garlic and serve warm.

255.   Brown Rice & Vegetable Lentils

Serves: 4 | Ready in about: 40 minutes

1 ½ tbsp olive oil
2 ¼ cups vegetable broth
½ cup green lentils
½ cup brown rice

½ cup diced carrots
½ cup diced celery
1 (2 ¼-oz) can olives, sliced
¼ cup diced red onion

¼ cup cilantro, chopped
1 tbsp lemon juice
1 garlic clove, minced
Salt and black pepper to taste

In a large saucepan over high heat, bring the broth and lentils to a boil, cover, and lower the heat to medium-low. Cook for 8 minutes. Raise the heat to medium, and stir in the rice. Cover the pot and cook the mixture for 14 minutes or until the liquid is absorbed. Remove the pot from the heat and let sit covered for 2 minutes, then stir. While the lentils and rice are cooking, combine carrots, celery, olives, onion, and cilantro in a serving bowl. In a small bowl, whisk together the oil, lemon juice, garlic, salt, and black pepper. Set aside. Once the lentils and rice are done, add them to the serving bowl. Pour the dressing on top, and mix well. Serve warm.

256.   Risotto ai Funghi

Serves: 6 | Ready in about: 35 minutes

½ cup Pecorino-Romano, grated
2 tbsp olive oil
2 oz dried porcini mushrooms

4 ½ cups chicken stock
1 onion, minced
2 cups brown rice

Salt and black pepper to taste

In a bowl, cover the mushrooms with hot water. Set aside for 25 minutes. Then drain them, keeping the liquid, and rinse. Strain the liquid through a sieve lined with cheesecloth. Add the liquid to the stock. Warm the stock and mushroom liquid in a saucepan until it simmers. Lower the heat. Warm the olive oil in a saucepan over medium heat. Sauté onion for 5 minutes. Stir in the rice and mushrooms and ¾ cup of stock. Cook the rice, stirring constantly, adding more liquid, so the rice can absorb the liquid until it's tender, 20-30 minutes. Always keep some liquid visible in the pan. Remove from the heat, stir in the cheese, and season to taste.

257.   Paprika Chickpeas

Serves: 4 | Ready in about: 30 minutes

¼ cup extra-virgin olive oil
4 garlic cloves, sliced thin
½ tsp red pepper flakes
1 onion, chopped fine

Salt and black pepper to taste
1 tsp smoked paprika
2 (15-oz) cans chickpeas
1 cup chicken broth

2 tbsp minced fresh parsley
2 tsp lemon juice

Warm 3 tablespoons of olive oil in a skillet over medium heat. Cook garlic and pepper flakes until the garlic turns golden but not brown, about 3 minutes. Stir in onion and salt and cook until softened and lightly browned, 5 minutes. Stir in smoked paprika, chickpeas, and broth and bring to a boil. Simmer covered for 7 minutes until chickpeas are heated through. Uncover, increase the heat to high, and continue to cook until nearly all liquid has evaporated, about 3 minutes. Remove and stir in parsley and lemon juice. Season with salt and pepper and drizzle with remaining olive oil.

258.   Chicken Risotto

Serves: 4 | Ready in about: 45 minutes

4 chicken thighs, bone-in and skin-on
2 tbsp olive oil
1 cup arborio rice
2 lemons, juiced

1 tsp oregano, dried
1 red onion, chopped
Salt and black pepper to taste
2 garlic cloves, minced

2 ½ cups chicken stock
1 cup green olives, sliced
2 tbsp parsley, chopped
½ cup Parmesan, grated

Warm olive oil in a skillet over medium heat and brown chicken thighs skin-side down for 3-4 minutes, turn, and cook for 3 minutes. Remove to a plate. Place garlic and onion in the same skillet and sauté for 3 minutes. Stir in rice, salt, pepper, oregano, and lemon juice. Add 1 cup of chicken stock, reduce the heat and simmer the rice while stirring until it is absorbed. Add another cup of chicken broth and continue simmering until the stock is absorbed. Pour in the remaining chicken stock and return the chicken; cook until the rice is tender. Turn the heat off. Stir in Parmesan cheese and top with olives and parsley. Serve into plates. Enjoy!

259.   Tomato Cannellini Beans

Serves: 4 | Ready in about: 10 minutes

2 tbsp olive oil
15 oz canned cannellini beans
10 cherry tomatoes, halved

2 spring onions, chopped
1 tsp paprika
Salt and black pepper to taste

½ tsp ground cumin
1 tbsp lime juice

Place the beans, cherry tomatoes, spring onions, olive oil, paprika, salt, pepper, cumin, and lime juice in a bowl and toss to combine. Transfer to the fridge for 10 minutes. Serve.

260.   Caper & Carrot Chickpeas

Serves: 4 | Ready in about: 35 minutes

3 tbsp olive oil
3 tbsp capers, drained
1 lemon, juiced and zested

1 red onion, chopped
14 oz canned chickpeas
4 carrots, peeled and cubed

1 tbsp parsley, chopped
Salt and black pepper to taste

Warm olive oil in a skillet over medium heat and cook onion, lemon zest, lemon juice, and capers for 5 minutes. Stir in chickpeas, carrots, parsley, salt, and pepper and cook for another 20 minutes. Serve and enjoy!

261.   Fava Bean Purée

Serves: 4 | Ready in about: 20 minutes

3 tbsp olive oil
4 garlic cloves, minced
1 tsp ground cumin
2 (15-oz) cans fava beans

3 tbsp tahini
2 tbsp lemon juice
4 lemon wedges
Salt and black pepper to taste

1 tomato, chopped
1 small onion, chopped
2 hard-cooked eggs, chopped
1 tbsp rosemary, chopped

Warm 2 tablespoons of olive oil in a saucepan over medium heat. Cook garlic cumin until fragrant, about 2 minutes. Stir in beans and their liquid and tahini. Bring to a simmer and cook until liquid thickens slightly, 8-10 minutes. Heat off. Mash beans to a coarse consistency using a potato masher. Stir in lemon juice. Season with salt and pepper. Top with tomato, onion, rosemary, and eggs, and drizzle with the remaining oil. Serve with lemon wedges.

262.   Brown Rice Pilaf with Capers

Serves: 4 | Ready in about: 30 minutes

2 tbsp olive oil
1 cup brown rice
1 onion, chopped

1 celery stalk, chopped
2 garlic cloves, minced
½ cup capers, rinsed

Salt and black pepper to taste
2 tbsp parsley, chopped

Warm olive oil in a skillet over medium heat. Sauté celery, garlic, and onion for 10 minutes. Stir in rice, capers, 2 cups of water, salt, and pepper and cook for 25 minutes. Serve topped with parsley.

263. Bean & Sausage Casserole

Serves: 4 | Ready in about: 45 minutes

2 tbsp olive oil
1 lb Italian sausages
1 (15-oz) can cannellini beans
1 carrot, chopped

1 onion, chopped
2 garlic cloves, minced
1 tsp paprika
1 (14-oz) can tomatoes, diced

1 celery stalk, chopped
Salt and black pepper to taste

Warm olive oil in a pot over medium heat. Sauté onion, garlic, celery, and carrot for 3-4 minutes, stirring often until softened. Add in sausages and cook for another 3 minutes, turning occasionally. Stir in paprika for 30 seconds. Heat off. Mix in tomatoes, beans, salt, and pepper. Preheat oven to 350 F. Pour into a baking dish and bake for 30 minutes.

264. Spinach & Cannellini Bean Stew

Serves: 4 | Ready in about: 40 minutes

2 tbsp olive oil
1 onion, chopped
1 (15-oz) can diced tomatoes
2 (15-oz) cans cannellini beans

1 cup carrots, chopped
1 celery stalk, chopped
4 cups vegetable broth
½ tsp dried thyme

1 lb baby spinach
Salt and black pepper to taste

Warm olive oil in a saucepan over medium heat. Sauté the onion, celery, and carrots for 5 minutes until tender. Add the tomatoes, beans, carrots, broth, thyme, pepper, and salt. Stir and cook for 20 minutes. Add the spinach and cook for 5 minutes until the spinach wilts. Serve warm.

265. Hot Bean Rolls

Serves: 4 | Ready in about: 25 minutes

1 tbsp olive oil
1 red onion, chopped
2 garlic cloves, minced
1 green bell pepper, sliced

2 cups canned cannellini beans
1 red chili pepper, chopped
1 tbsp cilantro, chopped
1 tsp cumin, ground

Salt and black pepper to taste
4 whole-wheat tortillas
1 cup mozzarella, shredded

Warm olive oil in a skillet over medium heat and sauté onion for 3 minutes. Stir in garlic, bell pepper, cannellini beans, red chili pepper, cilantro, cumin, salt, and pepper and cook for 15 minutes. Spoon bean mixture on each tortilla and top with cheese. Roll up and serve right away.

266. Pork Rice

Serves: 4 | Ready in about: 8 hours 10 minutes

3 tbsp olive oil
2 lb pork loin, sliced
1 cup chicken stock

½ tbsp chili powder
2 tsp thyme, dried
½ tbsp garlic powder

Salt and black pepper to taste
2 cups rice, cooked

Place the pork, chicken stock, oil, chili powder, garlic powder, salt, and pepper in your slow cooker. Cover with the lid and cook for 8 hours on Low. Share pork into plates with a side of rice and garnish with thyme to serve.

267. Asparagus Chickpea Sautée

Serves: 4 | Ready in about: 25 minutes

2 tbsp olive oil
2 garlic cloves, minced
2 potatoes, cubed
1 yellow onion, chopped

1 cup canned chickpeas
Salt and black pepper to taste
1 lb asparagus, chopped
1 tsp sweet paprika

1 tsp ground coriander
2 tomatoes, chopped
2 tbsp parsley, chopped
½ cup ricotta cheese, crumbled

Warm olive oil in a skillet over medium heat and sauté potatoes, onion, garlic, salt, and pepper for 7 minutes, stirring occasionally. Add in chickpeas, salt, pepper, asparagus, paprika, and coriander and sauté another 6-7 minutes. Remove to a bowl. Mix in tomatoes, parsley, and ricotta cheese and serve right away.

268. Chicken Lentils

Serves: 4 | Ready in about: 1 hour 20 minutes

1 lb chicken thighs, skinless, boneless, and cubed
2 tbsp olive oil
1 tbsp coriander seeds
1 bay leaf
1 tbsp tomato paste

2 carrots, chopped
1 onion, chopped
2 garlic cloves, chopped
½ tsp red chili flakes

½ tsp paprika
4 cups chicken stock
1 cup brown lentils
Salt and black pepper to taste

Warm the olive oil in a pot over medium heat and cook chicken, onion, and garlic for 6-8 minutes. Stir in carrots, tomato paste, coriander seeds, bay leaf, red chili pepper, and paprika for 3 minutes. Pour in the chicken stock and bring to a boil. Simmer for 25 minutes. Add in lentils, season with salt and pepper and cook for another 15 minutes. Discard bay leaf and serve right away.

269. Rich Sun-Dried Tomato & Basil Risotto

Serves: 4 | Ready in about: 35 minutes

10 oz sundried tomatoes in olive oil, drained and chopped
2 tbsp olive oil
2 cups chicken stock
1 onion, chopped

1 cup Arborio rice
Salt and black pepper to taste
1 cup Pecorino cheese, grated

¼ cup basil leaves, chopped

Warm olive oil in a skillet over medium heat and cook onion and sundried tomatoes for 5 minutes. Stir in rice, chicken stock, salt, pepper, and basil and bring to a boil. Cook for 20 minutes. Mix in Pecorino cheese and serve.

270. Cheese & Mushroom Wild Rice

Serves: 4 | Ready in about: 30 minutes

2 cups chicken stock
1 cup wild rice
1 onion, chopped

½ lb wild mushrooms, sliced
2 garlic cloves, minced
1 lemon, juiced and zested

1 tbsp chives, chopped
½ cup mozzarella, grated
Salt and black pepper to taste

Warm 2 cups of chicken stock in a pot over medium heat and add in wild rice, onion, mushrooms, garlic, lemon juice, zest, salt, and pepper. Bring to a simmer and cook for 20 minutes. Transfer to a baking tray and top with mozzarella cheese. Place the tray under the broiler for 4 minutes until the cheese is melted. Sprinkle with chives and serve.

271. Cherry Tomato & Pistachio Rice Pilaf

Serves: 4 | Ready in about: 30 minutes

2 tbsp olive oil
1 cup basmati rice
1 carrot, shredded
½ cup scallions, chopped

12 cherry tomatoes, halved
1 oz pistachios, crushed
2 cups vegetable broth
1 garlic clove, minced

1 tsp ground coriander
2 tbsp fresh parsley, chopped

Heat the olive oil in a saucepan over medium heat. Add in the carrot, garlic, and scallions and cook for 3-4 minutes, stirring often. Stir in the rice for 1-2 minutes. Pour in the vegetable broth. Bring to a quick boil and sprinkle with ground coriander. Lower the heat and simmer covered for 10-12 minutes until the liquid has absorbed. Fluff the rice with a fork and transfer to a serving plate. Top with cherry tomatoes and pistachios and sprinkle with parsley. Serve.

272. Brown Rice Bowl

Serves: 4 | Ready in about: 25 minutes

½ lb broccoli rabe, halved lengthways
2 tbsp olive oil
1 onion, sliced
1 red bell pepper, cut into strips
½ cup green peas

1 carrot, chopped
1 celery stalk, chopped
1 garlic clove, minced
½ cup brown rice
2 cups vegetable broth

Salt and black pepper to taste
½ tsp dried thyme
¾ tsp paprika
2 green onions, chopped

Warm olive oil in a skillet over medium heat and sauté onion, garlic, carrot, celery, and bell pepper for 10 minutes. Stir in rice, vegetable broth, salt, pepper, thyme, paprika, and green onions and bring to a simmer. Cook for 15 minutes. Add in broccoli rabe and green peas and cook for 5 minutes.

273.   Bean Stew

Serves: 4 | Ready in about: 70 minutes

2 tbsp olive oil
3 tomatoes, cubed
1 yellow onion, chopped
1 celery stalk, chopped

2 tbsp parsley, chopped
2 garlic cloves, minced
1 cup lima beans, soaked
1 tsp paprika

1 tsp dried oregano
½ tsp dried thyme
Salt and black pepper to taste

In a pot, cover the lima beans with water and place over medium heat. Bring to a boil and cook for 30 minutes. Drain and set aside. Warm olive oil in the pot over medium heat and cook onion and garlic for 3 minutes. Stir in tomatoes, celery, oregano, thyme, and paprika and cook for 5 minutes. Pour in 3 cups of water and return the lima beans; season with salt and pepper. Simmer for 30 minutes. Top with parsley.

274.   Lentil & Rice Salad with Caramelized Onions

Serves: 4 | Ready in about: 1 hour 15 minutes

¼ cup olive oil
2 cups lentils
1 cup brown rice

4 ½ cups water
½ tsp dried thyme
½ tsp dried tarragon

3 onions, peeled and sliced
Salt and black pepper to taste

In a large saucepan, place the lentils and rice. Pour the water. Bring to a boil, cover, and simmer for 23 minutes or until almost tender. Stir in the seasonings and cook for 25-30 minutes or until the rice is tender and the water is absorbed. In a separate saucepan, warm the olive oil over medium heat. Add the onions and cook slowly, stirring frequently, until the onions brown and caramelize, for 17-20 minutes. Top with the caramelized onions. Serve.

275.   Olive Green Rice

Serves: 4 | Ready in about: 35 minutes

2 tbsp butter
4 spring onions, sliced
1 leek, sliced
1 medium zucchini, chopped
5 oz broccoli florets

2 oz curly kale
½ cup frozen green peas
2 cloves garlic, minced
1 thyme sprig, chopped
1 rosemary sprig, chopped

1 cup white rice
2 cups vegetable broth
1 large tomato, chopped
2 oz black olives, sliced

In a saucepan, melt the butter over medium heat. Cook the spring onions, leek, and zucchini for 4-5 minutes or until tender. Add in the garlic, thyme, and rosemary and continue to sauté for about 1 minute or until aromatic. Add in the rice, broth, and tomato. Bring to a boil, turn the heat to a gentle simmer, and cook for about 10-12 minutes. Stir in broccoli, kale, and green peas, and continue cooking for 5 minutes. Fluff the rice with a fork and garnish with olives.

276.   Cavolo Nero Farro Pilaf

Serves: 4 | Ready in about: 50 minutes

2 tbsp olive oil
1 cup green peas
4 cups cavolo nero, torn
½ cup hummus
½ cup scallions, sliced

1 garlic clove, minced
1 cup farro
2 cups water
1 cup chopped tomatoes
1 tbsp tomato paste

1 tsp cumin
½ tsp oregano
2 tbsp fresh cilantro, chopped
Salt and black pepper to taste

Heat olive oil in a skillet over medium heat. Add in scallions, sauté until tender. Add in garlic, cumin, and oregano and cook for another 30 seconds. Stir in farro, water, chopped tomatoes, and tomato paste. Bring to a boil, then lower the heat, and simmer for 30-40 minutes. Stir in peas, cavolo nero, salt, and black pepper. Let sit covered for 8 minutes. Serve topped with hummus and cilantro.

277. Autenthic Milanese-Style Risotto

Serves: 4 | Ready in about: 10 minutes

2 tbsp olive oil
2 tbsp butter, softened
1 cup Arborio rice, cooked

½ cup white wine
1 onion, chopped
Salt and black pepper to taste

2 cups hot chicken stock
1 pinch of saffron, soaked
½ cup Parmesan, grated

Warm olive oil in a skillet over medium heat and sauté onion for 3 minutes. Stir in rice, salt, and pepper for 1 minute. Pour in white wine and saffron and stir to deglaze the bottom of the skillet. Gradually add in the chicken stock while stirring; cook for 15-18 minutes. Turn off the heat and mix in butter and Parmesan cheese. Serve immediately.

278. Rice Stuffed Bell Peppers

Serves: 4 | Ready in about: 35 minutes

1 tbsp olive oil
2 lb mixed bell peppers, halved
1 cup white rice, rinsed

½ cup ricotta cheese, crumbled
2 tomatoes, pureed
1 onion, chopped

1 tsp ground cumin
1 tsp ground fennel seeds
Salt and black pepper to taste

In a pot, blanch the peppers with salted water over medium heat for 1-2 minutes, drain and set aside. Add the rice to the pot, bring to a boil and simmer for 15 minutes. Drain and remove to a bowl. Add in olive oil, cumin, ground fennel seeds, onion, tomatoes, salt, and pepper and stir to combine. Divide the mixture between the pepper halves and top with ricotta cheese. Bake for 8-10 minutes. Serve right away.

279. Green Onion Mushroom Rice Pilaf

Serves: 4 | Ready in about: 30 minutes

2 tbsp olive oil
1 cup rice, rinsed
2 greens onions, chopped

2 cups chicken stock
1 cup mushrooms, sliced
1 garlic clove, minced

Salt and black pepper to taste
½ cup Parmesan cheese, grated
2 tbsp cilantro, chopped

Warm olive oil in a skillet over medium heat and cook onion, garlic, and mushrooms for 5 minutes until tender. Stir in rice, salt, and pepper for 1 minute. Pour in chicken stock and cook for 15-18 minutes. Transfer to a platter, scatter Parmesan cheese all over, and sprinkle with cilantro to serve.

280. Lamb Risotto

Serves: 4 | Ready in about: 90 minutes

2 tbsp olive oil
2 garlic cloves, minced
1 onion, chopped

1 lb lamb, cubed
Salt and black pepper to taste
2 cups vegetable stock

1 cup arborio rice
2 tbsp mint, chopped
1 cup Parmesan, grated

Warm olive oil in a skillet over medium heat and cook the onion for 5 minutes. Put in lamb and cook for another 5 minutes. Stir in garlic, salt, pepper, and stock and bring to a simmer; cook for 1 hour. Stir in rice and cook for 18-20 minutes. Top with Parmesan cheese and mint and serve.

281. Minty Farro

Serves: 6 | Ready in about: 30 minutes

3 tbsp olive oil
1 ½ cups whole farro
Salt and black pepper to taste

1 onion, chopped fine
1 garlic clove, minced
¼ cup chopped fresh cilantro

¼ cup chopped fresh mint
1 tbsp lemon juice

Bring 4 quarts of water to boil in a pot. Add the farro and season with salt and pepper, bring to a boil and cook until grains are tender with a slight chew, 20-25 minutes. Drain farro, return to the empty pot and cover to keep warm. Heat 2 tbsp of oil in a large skillet over medium heat. Stir-fry onion for 5 minutes. Stir in garlic and cook until fragrant, about 30 seconds. Add the remaining oil and farro and stir-fry for 2 minutes. Remove from heat, stir in cilantro, mint, and lemon juice. Season to taste and serve.

282.　Tarragon Buckwheat

Serves: 6 | Ready in about: 55 minutes

3 tbsp olive oil
1 ½ cups buckwheat, soaked
3 cups vegetable broth
½ onion, finely chopped

1 garlic clove, minced
2 tsp fresh tarragon, minced
Salt and black pepper to taste
2 oz Parmesan cheese, grated

2 tbsp parsley, minced
2 tsp lemon juice

In your blender, pulse buckwheat until about half of the grains are broken into smaller pieces. Bring broth and 3 cups of water to a boil in a medium saucepan over high heat. Reduce heat to low, cover, and keep warm. Warm 2 tablespoons oil in a pot over medium heat. Add onion and cook until softened, 5 minutes. Stir in garlic and cook until fragrant, about 30 seconds. Add farro and cook, stirring frequently, until grains are lightly toasted, 3 minutes. Stir 5 cups warm broth mixture into farro mixture, reduce heat to low, cover, and cook until almost all liquid has been absorbed and farro is just al dente, about 25 minutes, stirring twice during cooking. Add tarragon, salt, and pepper and keep stirring for 5 minutes. Remove from heat and stir in Parmesan cheese, parsley, lemon juice, and the remaining olive oil. Adjust the seasoning and serve.

283.　Vegetable Millet

Serves: 6 | Ready in about: 35 minutes

6 oz okra, cut into 1-inch lengths
3 tbsp olive oil
6 oz asparagus, chopped
Salt and black pepper to taste

1 ½ cups whole millet
2 tbsp lemon juice
2 tbsp minced shallot
1 tsp Dijon mustard

6 oz cherry tomatoes, halved
3 tbsp chopped fresh dill
2 oz goat cheese, crumbled

In a large pot, bring 4 quarts of water to a boil. Add asparagus, snap peas, and salt and cook until crisp-tender, about 3 minutes. Using a slotted spoon, transfer vegetables to a large plate and let cool completely, about 15 minutes. Add millet to water, return to a boil, and cook until grains are tender, 15-20 minutes. Drain the millet, spread in rimmed baking sheet; let cool completely for 15 minutes. Whisk oil, lemon juice, shallot, mustard, salt, and pepper in a large bowl. Add vegetables, millet, tomatoes, dill, and half of the goat cheese and toss gently to combine. Season with salt and pepper. Sprinkle with remaining goat cheese to serve.

284.　Brown Rice with Roasted Peppers

Serves: 6 | Ready in about: 1 hour 50 minutes

2 tbsp Pecorino-Romano, grated
¾ cup roasted red peppers, chopped
4 tsp olive oil

2 onions, finely chopped
Salt and black pepper to taste
1 ½ cups vegetable broth

1 ½ cups brown rice, rinsed
1 lemon, cut into wedges

Preheat your oven to 370 F. Heat oil in a pot over medium heat until sizzling. Stir-fry the onions for 10-12 minutes until soft. Season with salt. Stir in 2 cups of water and broth and bring to a boil. Add in rice, cover, and transfer the pot to the oven. Cook until the rice is tender and liquid absorbed, 50-65 minutes. Remove from the oven. Sprinkle with red peppers and let sit for 5 minutes. Season to taste and stir in Pecorino-Romano cheese. Serve with lemon wedges.

285.　Cheesy Polenta

Serves: 6 | Ready in about: 50 minutes

1 ½ cups coarse-ground cornmeal
2 tbsp olive oil

6 ½ cups water
Salt and black pepper to taste

½ tsp baking soda
2 oz Pecorino cheese, grated

In a saucepan, bring water to a boil over medium heat. Stir in 1 teaspoon of salt and baking soda. Slowly pour cornmeal into water in a steady stream while stirring back and forth with a wooden spoon or rubber spatula. Bring mixture to boil, stirring constantly, about 1 minute. Reduce heat to the lowest setting and cover. After 4 minutes, whisk polenta to smooth out any lumps that may have formed, about 20 seconds. Cover and continue to cook, without stirring, until polenta grains are tender but slightly al dente, about 23 minutes longer. Off heat, stir in Pecorino and oil and season with pepper to taste. Cover and let sit for 5 minutes. Serve along with extra Pecorino cheese on the side.

286.   Tuna Barley with Capers

Serves: 4 | Ready in about: 50 minutes

2 tbsp olive oil
3 cups chicken stock
10 oz canned tuna, flaked

1 cup barley
Salt and black pepper to taste
12 cherry tomatoes, halved

½ cup pepperoncini, sliced
¼ cup capers, drained
½ lemon, juiced

Boil 3 cups of chicken stock in a saucepan over medium heat and add in barley. Cook covered for 40 minutes. Fluff the barley and remove to a bowl. Stir in tuna, salt, pepper, tomatoes, pepperoncini, olive oil, capers, and lemon juice.

287.   Barley with Walnuts

Serves: 4 | Ready in about: 45 minutes

2 tbsp olive oil
½ cup diced onion
½ cup diced celery
1 carrot, peeled and diced

3 cups water
1 cup barley
½ tsp thyme
½ tsp rosemary

¼ cup pine nuts
Salt and black pepper to taste

Warm olive oil in a medium saucepan over medium heat. Sauté the onion, celery, and carrot over medium heat until tender. Add the water, barley, and seasonings, and bring to a boil. Reduce the heat and simmer for 23 minutes or until tender. Stir in the pine nuts and season to taste. Serve warm.

288.   Parmesan Pearl Barley with Artichoke Hearts

Serves: 4 | Ready in about: 50 minutes

½ cup artichoke hearts, chopped
2 tbsp olive oil
1 cup pearl barley
2 tbsp grated Parmesan cheese
1 bay leaf

1 fresh cilantro sprig
1 fresh thyme sprig
1 onion, chopped
1 tbsp Italian seasoning
3 garlic cloves, minced

1 cup chicken broth
1 lemon, zested
Salt and black pepper to taste

Place the barley, cilantro, bay leaf, and thyme in a pot over medium heat and cover with water. Bring to a boil, then lower the heat and simmer for 25 minutes. Drain, discard the bay leaf, rosemary, and thyme and reserve. Warm the olive oil in a pan over medium heat. Sauté onion, artichoke, and Italian seasoning for 5 minutes. Add garlic and stir-fry for 40 seconds. Pour in some broth and cook until the liquid absorbs, add more, and keep stirring until absorbed. Mix in zest, salt, pepper, and cheese and stir for 2 minutes until the cheese has melted. Pour over the barley and serve.

289.   Green Quinoa

Serves: 4 | Ready in about: 30 minutes

2 tbsp olive oil
1 onion, chopped
2 garlic cloves, minced
1 cup quinoa, rinsed

1 lb asparagus, chopped
2 tbsp fresh parsley, chopped
2 tbsp lemon juice
1 tsp lemon zest, grated

½ lb green beans, trimmed and halved
Salt and black pepper to taste
½ lb cherry tomatoes, halved

Heat the olive oil in a pot over medium heat and sauté onion and garlic for 3 minutes until soft. Stir in quinoa for 1-2 minutes. Pour in 2 cups of water and season with salt and pepper. Bring to a bowl and reduce the heat. Simmer for 5 minutes. Stir in green beans and asparagus and cook for another 10 minutes. Remove from the heat and mix in cherry tomatoes, lemon juice and lemon zest. Top with parsley and serve.

290.   Zucchini Millet

Serves: 4 | Ready in about: 30 minutes

3 tbsp olive oil
2 tomatoes, chopped
2 zucchinis, chopped

1 cup millet
2 spring onions, chopped
½ cup cilantro, chopped

1 tsp chili paste
½ cup lemon juice
Salt and black pepper to taste

Warm olive oil in a skillet over medium heat and sauté millet for 1-2 minutes. Pour in 2 cups of water, salt, and pepper and bring to a simmer. Cook for 15 minutes. Mix in spring onions, tomatoes, zucchini, chili paste, and lemon juice. Serve topped with cilantro.

291. Egg Quinoa with Pancetta

Serves: 4 | Ready in about: 35 minutes

4 pancetta slices, cooked and crumbled

2 tbsp olive oil

1 small red onion, chopped

1 red bell pepper, chopped

1 sweet potato, grated

1 green bell pepper, chopped

2 garlic cloves, minced

1 cup mushrooms, sliced

½ cup quinoa

1 cup chicken stock

4 eggs, fried

¼ tsp red pepper flakes

Salt and black pepper to taste

Warm olive oil in a skillet over medium heat and cook onion, garlic, bell peppers, sweet potato, and mushrooms for 5 minutes, stirring often. Stir in quinoa for another minute. Mix in stock, salt, and pepper for 15 minutes. Share into plates and serve topped with fried eggs, salt, pepper, red pepper flakes, and crumbled pancetta.

292. Green Oats with Parmesan

Serves: 4 | Ready in about: 15 minutes

2 tbsp olive oil

2 cups collard greens, torn

½ cup black olives, sliced

1 cup rolled oats

2 tomatoes, diced

2 spring onions, chopped

1 tsp garlic powder

½ tsp hot paprika

A pinch of salt

2 tbsp fresh parsley, chopped

1 tbsp lemon juice

½ cup Parmesan cheese, grated

In a pot, pour 2 cups of water over medium heat. Bring to a boil, then lower the heat, and add the rolled oats. Cook for 4-5 minutes. Mix in tomatoes, spring onions, hot paprika, garlic powder, salt, collard greens, black olives, parsley, lemon juice, and olive oil. Cook for another 5 minutes. Ladle into bowls and top with Parmesan cheese. Serve warm.

293. Nut & Quinoa Watercress Salad with Nuts

Serves: 4 | Ready in about: 5 minutes

2 boiled eggs, cut into wedges

2 cups watercress

2 cups cherry tomatoes, halved

1 cucumber, sliced

1 cup quinoa, cooked

1 cup almonds, chopped

2 tbsp olive oil

1 avocado, peeled and sliced

2 tbsp fresh cilantro, chopped

Salt to taste

1 lemon, juiced

Place the watercress, cherry tomatoes, cucumber, quinoa, almonds, olive oil, cilantro, salt, and lemon juice in a bowl and toss to combine. Top with egg wedges and avocado slices and serve immediately.

294. Walnut Raspberry Quinoa

Serves: 4 | Ready in about: 5 minutes

1 tbsp honey

2 cups almond milk

2 cups quinoa, cooked

½ tsp cinnamon powder

1 cup raspberries

¼ cup walnuts, chopped

Combine the quinoa, milk, cinnamon powder, honey, raspberries, and walnuts in a bowl. Serve in individual bowls.

295. Sage & Cheese Farro

Serves: 4 | Ready in about: 50 minutes

2 tbsp olive oil

1 cup farro

1 red onion, chopped

5 sage leaves

1 garlic clove, minced

1 tbsp Parmesan cheese, grated

6 cups veggie stock

Salt and black pepper to taste

Warm olive oil in a skillet over medium heat and cook onion and garlic for 5 minutes. Stir in sage leaves, faro, veggie stock, salt, and pepper and bring to a simmer. Cook for 40 minutes. Mix in Parmesan cheese and serve.

FISH & SEAFOOD

296.   Lemon Salmon Packets

Serves: 4 | Ready in about: 25 minutes

2 tbsp olive oil
½ cup apple juice

4 salmon fillets
4 tsp lemon zest

4 tbsp chopped parsley
Salt and black pepper to taste

Preheat your oven to 380 F. Brush salmon with olive oil and season with salt and pepper. Cut four pieces of nonstick baking paper and divide the salmon between them. Top each one with apple juice, lemon zest, and parsley. Wrap the paper to make packets and arrange them on a baking sheet. Cook for 15 minutes until the salmon is cooked through. Remove the packets to a serving plate, open them, and drizzle with cooking juices to serve.

297.   Asparagus & Salmon Roast

Serves: 4 | Ready in about: 20 minutes

2 tbsp olive oil
4 salmon fillets, skinless

2 tbsp balsamic vinegar
1 lb asparagus, trimmed

Salt and black pepper to taste

Preheat your oven to 380 F. In a roasting pan, arrange the salmon fillets and asparagus spears. Season with salt and pepper and drizzle with olive oil and balsamic vinegar; roast for 12-15 minutes. Serve warm.

298.   Salmon & Shrimp in Tomato Sauce

Serves: 4 | Ready in about: 30 minutes

1 lb shrimp, peeled and deveined
2 tbsp olive oil
1 lb salmon fillets
Salt and black pepper to taste

1 cups tomatoes, chopped
1 onion, chopped
2 garlic cloves, minced
¼ tsp red pepper flakes

1 cup fish stock
1 tbsp cilantro, chopped

Preheat your oven to 360 F. Line a baking sheet with parchment paper. Season the salmon with salt and pepper, drizzle with some olive oil, and arrange them on the sheet. Bake for 15 minutes. Remove to a serving plate. Warm the remaining olive oil in a skillet over medium heat and sauté onion and garlic for 3 minutes until tender. Pour in tomatoes, fish stock, salt, pepper, and red pepper flakes and bring to a boil. Simmer for 10 minutes. Stir in shrimp and cook for another 8 minutes. Pour the sauce over the salmon and serve sprinkled with cilantro.

299.   Salmon Bake

Serves: 4 | Ready in about: 20 minutes

2 tbsp olive oil
1 lb salmon fillets
¼ fresh parsley, chopped

1 garlic clove, minced
¼ tsp dried dill
¼ tsp chili powder

¼ tsp garlic powder
1 lemon, grated
Salt and black pepper to taste

Preheat your oven to 350 F. Sprinkle the salmon with dill, chili powder, garlic powder, salt, and pepper. Warm olive oil in a pan over medium heat and sear salmon skin-side down for 5 minutes. Transfer to the oven and bake for another 4-5 minutes. Combine parsley, lemon zest, garlic, and salt in a bowl. Serve salmon topped with the mixture.

300.   Avocado & Salmon Tartare

Serves: 4 | Ready in about: 10 minutes + chilling time

1 lb salmon, skinless, boneless and cubed
1 tbsp olive oil
4 tbsp scallions, chopped

2 tsp lemon juice
1 avocado, chopped
Salt and black pepper to taste

1 tbsp parsley, chopped

Mix the scallions, lemon juice, olive oil, salmon, salt, pepper, and parsley in a bowl. Place in the fridge for 1 hour. Place a baking ring on a serving plate and pour in the salmon mixture. Top with avocado and gently press down.

301. Rosemary Trout with Roasted Beets

Serves: 4 | Ready in about: 45 minutes

1 lb medium beets, peeled and sliced
3 tbsp olive oil
4 trout fillets, boneless

Salt and black pepper to taste
1 tbsp rosemary, chopped
2 spring onions, chopped

2 tbsp lemon juice
½ cup vegetable stock

Preheat oven to 390 F. Line a baking sheet with parchment paper. Arrange the beets on the sheet, season with salt and pepper, and drizzle with some olive oil. Roast for 20 minutes. Warm the remaining oil in a skillet over medium heat. Cook trout fillets for 8 minutes on all sides; reserve. Add spring onions to the skillet and sauté for 2 minutes. Stir in lemon juice and stock and cook for 5-6 minutes until the sauce thickens. Remove the beets to a plate and top with trout fillets. Pour the sauce all over and sprinkle with rosemary.

302. Baked Salmon with Celery & Eggs

Serves: 4 | Ready in about: 40 minutes

2 tbsp olive oil
2 tbsp butter, melted
4 oz smoked salmon, flaked
1 cup cheddar cheese, grated

4 eggs, whisked
¼ cup plain yogurt
1 cup cream of celery soup
1 shallot, chopped

2 garlic cloves, minced
½ cup celery, chopped
8 slices fresh toast, cubed
1 tbsp mint leaves, chopped

Preheat oven to 360 F. In a bowl, mix eggs, yogurt, and celery soup. Warm olive oil in a skillet over medium heat and cook the shallot, garlic, and celery until tender. Place the toast cubes in a greased baking dish, top with cooked vegetables and salmon, and cover with egg mixture and butter. Bake for 22-25 minutes until it is cooked through. Scatter cheddar cheese on top and bake for another 5 minutes until the cheese melts. Serve garnished with mint leaves.

303. Saucy Salmon

Serves: 4 | Ready in about: 25 minutes

2 tbsp olive oil
4 salmon fillets, boneless

1 tsp thyme, chopped
Salt and black pepper to taste

1 lb cherry tomatoes, halved

Warm olive oil in a skillet over medium heat and sear salmon for 6 minutes, turning once; set aside. In the same skillet, stir in cherry tomatoes for 3-4 minutes and sprinkle with thyme, salt, and pepper. Pour the sauce over the salmon.

304. Salmon with Olives & Escarole in a Skillet

Serves: 4 | Ready in about: 25 minutes

3 tbsp olive oil
1 head escarole, torn
4 salmon fillets, boneless

1 lime, juiced
Salt and black pepper to taste
¼ cup fish stock

¼ cup green olives, pitted and chopped
¼ cup fresh chives, chopped

Warm half of the oil in a skillet over medium heat and sauté escarole, lime juice, salt, pepper, fish stock, and olives for 6 minutes. Share into plates. Warm the remaining oil in the same skillet. Sprinkle salmon with salt and pepper and fry for 8 minutes on both sides until golden brown. Transfer to the escarole plates and serve warm, topped with chives.

305. Tomato & Caper Roasted Salmon

Serves: 4 | Ready in about: 25 minutes

1 tbsp olive oil
4 salmon steaks
Salt and black pepper to taste
¼ mustard powder

½ tsp garlic powder
2 Roma tomatoes, chopped
¼ cup green olives, chopped
1 tsp capers

½ cup breadcrumbs
1 lemon, cut into wedges

Preheat oven to 370 F. Arrange the salmon fillets on a greased baking dish. Season with salt, pepper, garlic powder, and mustard powder and coat with the breadcrumbs. Drizzle with olive oil. Scatter the tomatoes, green olives, garlic, and capers around the fish fillets. Bake for 15 minutes until the salmon steaks flake easily with a fork. Serve with lemon wedges.

306. Almond-Crusted Salmon

Serves: 4 | Ready in about: 20 minutes

1 tbsp olive oil
½ tsp lemon zest
¼ cup breadcrumbs

½ cup toasted almonds, ground
½ tsp dried thyme
Salt and black pepper to taste

4 salmon steaks
1 lemon, cut into wedges

Preheat oven to 350 F. In a shallow dish, combine the lemon zest, breadcrumbs, almonds, thyme, salt, and pepper. Coat the salmon steaks with olive oil and arrange them on a baking sheet. Cover them with the almond mixture, pressing down lightly with your fingers to create a tightly packed crust. Bake for 10-12 minutes or until the almond crust is lightly browned and the fish is cooked through. Serve garnished with lemon wedges.

307. Trout Bowls with Avocado & Farro

Serves: 4 | Ready in about: 50 minutes

4 tbsp olive oil
8 trout fillets, boneless
1 cup farro
Juice of 2 lemons

Salt and black pepper to taste
1 avocado, chopped
¼ cup balsamic vinegar
1 garlic clove, minced

¼ cup parsley, chopped
¼ cup mint, chopped
2 tbsp yellow mustard

Boil salted water in a pot over medium heat and stir in farro. Simmer for 30 minutes and drain. Remove to a bowl and combine with lemon juice, mustard, garlic, salt, pepper, and half olive oil. Set aside. Mash the avocado with a fork in a bowl and mix with vinegar, salt, pepper, parsley, and mint. Warm the remaining oil in a skillet over medium heat and brown trout fillets skin-side down for 10 minutes on both sides. Let cool and cut into pieces. Put over farro and stir in avocado dressing. Serve immediately.

308. Bell Pepper & Fennel Salmon

Serves: 4 | Ready in about: 30 minutes

2 tbsp olive oil
4 salmon fillets, boneless
1 fennel bulb, sliced

Salt and black pepper to taste
½ tsp chili powder
1 yellow bell pepper, diced

1 red bell pepper, chopped
1 green bell pepper, chopped

In a skillet, warm the olive oil over medium heat. Season the salmon with chili powder, salt, and pepper and cook for 6-8 minutes, turning once. Remove to a serving plate. Add fennel and peppers to the skillet and cook for another 10 minutes until tender. Top the salmon with the mixture.

309. Baked Walnut-Crusted Salmon

Serves: 4 | Ready in about: 25 minutes

2 tbsp olive oil
4 salmon fillets, boneless
2 tbsp mustard

5 tsp honey
1 cup walnuts, chopped
1 tbsp lemon juice

2 tsp parsley, chopped
Salt and pepper to the taste

Preheat your oven to 380 F. Line a baking tray with parchment paper. In a bowl, whisk the olive oil, mustard, and honey. In a separate bowl, combine walnuts and parsley. Sprinkle salmon with salt and pepper and place them on the tray. Rub each fillet with mustard mixture and scatter with walnut mixture; bake for 15 minutes. Drizzle with lemon juice.

310. Smoked Salmon Crostini

Serves: 4 | Ready in about: 10 minutes + chilling time

4 oz smoked salmon, sliced
2 oz ricotta cheese, crumbled
4 oz cream cheese, softened

2 tbsp horseradish sauce
2 tsp orange zest
1 red onion, chopped

2 tbsp chives, chopped
1 baguette, sliced and toasted

In a large bowl, mix cream cheese, horseradish sauce, onion, ricotta cheese, and orange zest until smooth. Spread the mixture on the baguette slices. Top with salmon and chives to serve.

311.   Tasty Roman-Style Cod

Serves: 2 | Ready in about: 40 minutes

2 cod fillets, cut into 4 portions
¼ tsp paprika
¼ tsp onion powder
3 tbsp olive oil
4 medium scallions
2 tbsp fresh chopped basil

3 tbsp minced garlic
Salt and black pepper to taste
¼ tsp dry marjoram
6 sun-dried tomato slices
½ cup dry white wine
½ cup ricotta cheese, crumbled

1 (15-oz) can artichoke hearts
1 lemon, sliced
1 cup pitted black olives
1 tsp capers

Preheat oven to 370 F. Warm the olive oil in a skillet over medium heat. Sprinkle the cod with paprika and onion powder. Sear it for about 1 minute per side or until golden; reserve. Add the scallions, basil, garlic, salt, pepper, marjoram, tomatoes, and wine to the same skillet. Bring to a boil. Remove the skillet from the heat. Arrange the fish on top of the sauce and sprinkle with ricotta cheese. Place the artichokes in the pan and top with lemon slices. Sprinkle with black olives and capers. Place the skillet in the oven. Bake for 15-20 minutes until it flakes easily with a fork.

312.   Baked Cod with Cabbage

Serves: 4 | Ready in about: 30 minutes

2 tbsp olive oil
1 white cabbage head, shredded
1 tsp garlic powder

1 tsp smoked paprika
4 cod fillets, boneless
½ cup tomato sauce

1 tsp Italian seasoning
1 tbsp chives, chopped

Preheat oven to 390 F. Mix cabbage, garlic powder, paprika, olive oil, tomato sauce, Italian seasoning, and chives in a roasting pan. Top with cod fillets and bake covered with foil for 20 minutes. Serve immediately.

313.   Poached Cod

Serves: 4 | Ready in about: 20 minutes

4 cod fillets, skins removed
3 cups olive oil

Salt and black pepper to taste
1 lemon, zested and juiced

3 fresh thyme sprigs

Heat the oil with thyme sprigs in a pot over low heat. Gently add the cod fillets and poach them for about 6 minutes or until the fish is completely opaque. Using a slotted spoon, carefully remove the fish to a plate lined with paper towels. Sprinkle with lemon zest, salt, and pepper. Drizzle with lemon juice and serve immediately.

314.   Horseradish Trout fillets

Serves: 4 | Ready in about: 35 minutes

3 tbsp olive oil
2 tbsp horseradish sauce
1 onion, sliced

2 tsp Italian seasoning
4 trout fillets, boneless
¼ cup panko breadcrumbs

½ cup green olives, chopped
Salt and black pepper to taste
1 lemon, juiced

Preheat the oven to 380 F. Line a baking sheet with parchment paper. Sprinkle trout fillets with salt and pepper and dip in breadcrumbs. Arrange them along with the onion on the sheet. Sprinkle with olive oil, Italian seasoning, and lemon juice and bake for 15-18 minutes. Transfer to a serving plate and top with horseradish sauce and olives. Serve.

315.   Salmon with Balsamic Haricots Vert

Serves: 4 | Ready in about: 25 minutes

2 tbsp olive oil
3 tbsp balsamic vinegar
1 garlic clove, minced

½ tsp red pepper flakes
1 ½ lb haricots vert, chopped
Salt and black pepper to taste

1 red onion, sliced
4 salmon fillets, boneless

Warm half of the oil in a skillet over medium heat and sauté vinegar, onion, garlic, red pepper flakes, haricots vert, salt, and pepper for 6 minutes. Share into plates. Warm the remaining oil. Sprinkle salmon with salt and pepper and sear for 8 minutes on all sides. Serve with haricots vert.

316.　　Eggplant Wrapped Smoked Salmon

Serves: 4 | Ready in about: 20 minutes

2 eggplants, lengthwise cut into thin slices
2 tbsp olive oil
1 cup ricotta cheese, soft

4 oz smoked salmon, chopped
2 tsp lemon zest, grated

1 small red onion, sliced
Salt and pepper to the taste

Mix the salmon, cheese, lemon zest, onion, salt, and pepper in a bowl. Grease the eggplant with olive oil and grill them on a preheated grill pan for 3-4 minutes per side. Set aside to cool. Spread the cooled eggplant slices with the salmon mixture. Roll out and secure with toothpicks and serve.

317.　　Stuffed Peppers with Salmon

Serves: 4 | Ready in about: 25 minutes

4 bell peppers
10 oz canned salmon, drained
12 black olives, chopped

1 red onion, finely chopped
½ tsp garlic, minced
1/3 cup mayonnaise

1 cup cream cheese
1 tsp Mediterranean seasoning
Salt and pepper flakes to taste

Preheat your oven to 390 F. Cut the peppers into halves and remove the seeds. In a mixing bowl, combine the salmon, onion, garlic, mayonnaise, olives, salt, red pepper, Mediterranean spice mix, and cream cheese. Divide the mixture between the peppers and bake them in the oven for 10-12 minutes or until cooked through. Serve and enjoy!

318.　　Orange Salmon

Serves: 4 | Ready in about: 25 minutes

2 tbsp butter, melted
4 salmon fillets

Salt and black pepper to taste
1 orange, juiced and zested

4 tbsp fresh dill, chopped

Preheat oven to 370 F. Coat the salmon fillets on both sides with butter. Season with salt and pepper and divide them between 4 pieces of parchment paper. Drizzle the orange juice over each piece of fish and top with orange zest and dill. Wrap the paper around the fish to make packets. Place on a baking sheet and bake for 15-20 minutes until the cod is cooked through. Serve and enjoy!

319.　　Effortless Cod Fettuccine

Serves: 4 | Ready in about: 30 minutes

1 lb cod fillets, cubed
16 oz fettuccine
3 tbsp olive oil

1 onion, finely chopped
Salt and lemon pepper to taste
1 ½ cups heavy cream

1 cup Parmesan cheese, grated

Boil salted water in a pot over medium heat and stir in fettuccine. Cook according to package directions and drain. Heat the olive oil in a large saucepan over medium heat and add the onion. Stir-fry for 3 minutes until tender. Sprinkle cod with salt and lemon pepper and add to saucepan; cook for 4–5 minutes until fish fillets and flakes easily with a fork. Stir in heavy cream for 2 minutes. Add in the pasta, tossing gently to combine. Cook for 3–4 minutes until the sauce is slightly thickened. Sprinkle with Parmesan cheese.

320.　　Dad's Cod with Mozzarella & Tomatoes

Serves: 4 | Ready in about: 30 minutes

2 tbsp olive oil
4 cod fillets, boneless
Salt and black pepper to taste

12 cherry tomatoes, halved
1 red chili pepper, chopped
1 tbsp cilantro, chopped

2 tbsp balsamic vinegar
1 oz fresh mozzarella, torn

Preheat oven to 380 F. Drizzle the cod fillets with some olive oil and season with salt and pepper. Place them on a roasting tray, top with mozzarella cheese, and bake for 15 minutes until golden and crispy. Warm the remaining oil in a skillet over medium heat and cook the cherry tomatoes for 5 minutes. Stir in red chili pepper, cilantro, and balsamic vinegar for 1-2 minutes. Serve the fish with sautéed veggies.

321.   Cod with Potatoes

Serves: 4 | Ready in about: 35 minutes

1 tbsp olive oil
2 cod fillets
1 tbsp basil, chopped

Salt and black pepper to taste
2 potatoes, peeled and sliced
2 tsp turmeric powder

1 garlic clove, minced

Preheat oven to 360 F. Spread the potatoes on a greased baking dish and season with salt and pepper. Bake for 10 minutes. Arrange the cod fillets on top of the potatoes, sprinkle with salt and pepper, and drizzle with some olive oil. Bake for 10-12 more minutes until the fish flakes easily. Warm the remaining olive oil in a skillet over medium heat and sauté garlic for 1 minute. Stir in basil, salt, pepper, turmeric powder, and 3-4 tbsp of water; cook for another 2-3 minutes. Pour the sauce over the cod fillets and serve warm.

322.   Cod Fillets with Cherry Tomatoes

Serves: 4 | Ready in about: 35 minutes

2 tbsp olive oil
1 tsp lime juice
Salt and black pepper to taste
1 tsp sweet paprika

1 tsp chili powder
1 onion, chopped
2 garlic cloves, minced
4 cod fillets, boneless

1 tsp ground coriander
½ cup fish stock
½ lb cherry tomatoes, cubed

Warm olive oil in a skillet over medium heat. Season the cod with salt, pepper, and chili powder and cook in the skillet for 8 minutes on all sides; set aside. In the same skillet, cook onion and garlic for 3 minutes. Stir in lime juice, paprika, coriander, fish stock, and cherry tomatoes and bring to a boil. Simmer for 10 minutes. Serve topped with cod fillets.

323.   Juicy Cod Fillets in Mushroom Sauce

Serves: 4 | Ready in about: 45 minutes

2 cups cremini mushrooms, sliced
¼ cup olive oil
4 cod fillets
½ cup shallots, chopped
2 garlic cloves, minced

2 cups canned diced tomatoes
½ cup clam juice
¼ tsp chili flakes
¼ tsp sweet paprika
1 tbsp capers

¼ cup raisins, soaked
1 lemon, cut into wedges
Salt to taste

Heat olive oil in a skillet over medium heat. Sauté shallots and garlic for 2-3 minutes. Add in mushrooms and cook for another 4 minutes. Stir in tomatoes, clam juice, chili flakes, paprika, capers, and salt. Bring to a boil and simmer for 15 minutes. Preheat oven to 380 F. Arrange the cod fillets on a greased baking pan. Cover with the mushroom mixture and top with the soaked raisins. Bake for 18-20 minutes. Serve garnished with lemon wedges.

324.   Haddock in Tomato Sauce

Serves: 4 | Ready in about: 20 minutes

4 haddock fillets, boneless
1 cup vegetable stock

2 garlic cloves, minced
2 cups cherry tomatoes, halved

Salt and black pepper to taste
2 tbsp dill, chopped

In a skillet over medium heat, cook the cherry tomatoes, garlic, salt, and pepper for 5 minutes. Stir in haddock fillets and vegetable stock and bring to a simmer. Cook covered for 10-12 minutes. Serve topped with dill.

325.   Haddock with Capers

Serves: 4 | Ready in about: 25 minutes

2 tbsp olive oil
4 haddock fillets, boneless
¼ cup capers, drained

1 tbsp tarragon, chopped
Salt and black pepper to taste
2 tbsp parsley, chopped

1 tbsp lemon juice

Warm the olive oil in a skillet over medium heat and sear haddock for 6 minutes on both sides. Stir in capers, tarragon, salt, pepper, parsley, and lemon juice and cook for another 6-8 minutes. Serve right away.

326.   Spicy Cod Stew

Serves: 4 | Ready in about: 35 minutes

4 cod fillets, boneless, skinless, cubed
2 tbsp olive oil
2 tbsp parsley, chopped
2 tomatoes, chopped
2 tbsp cilantro, chopped

2 garlic cloves, minced
½ tsp paprika
2 cups chicken stock
Salt and black pepper to taste
1 carrot, sliced

1 red bell pepper, chopped
½ cup black olives, pitted and halved
1 red onion, sliced

Warm olive oil in a saucepan over medium heat and cook garlic, carrot, bell pepper, and onion for 5 minutes. Stir in cod fillets, parsley, tomatoes, and paprika for 3-4 minutes. Pour in chicken stock and olives and bring to a boil. Cook for 15 minutes. Adjust the seasoning and sprinkle with cilantro.

327.   Mustardy Cod Skewers

Serves: 4 | Ready in about: 30 minutes

1 lb cod fillets, cut into chunks
2 sweet peppers, cut into chunks
2 tbsp olive oil

2 oranges, juiced
1 tbsp yellow mustard
1 tsp dried dill

1 tsp dried parsley
Salt and black pepper to taste

Mix the olive oil, orange juice, dill, parsley, mustard, salt, and pepper in a bowl. Stir in cod to coat. Allow sitting for 10 minutes. Heat the grill over medium heat. Thread the cod and peppers onto skewers. Grill for 7-8 minutes, turning regularly until the fish is cooked through.

328.   Cod with Calamari Rings

Serves: 4 | Ready in about: 20 minutes

1 lb cod, skinless and cubed
2 tbsp olive oil
1 mango, peeled and cubed
½ lb calamari rings

1 tbsp garlic chili sauce
¼ cup lime juice
½ tsp smoked paprika
½ tsp cumin, ground

2 garlic cloves, minced
Salt and black pepper to taste

Warm olive oil in a skillet over medium heat and cook chili sauce, lime juice, paprika, cumin, garlic, salt, pepper, and mango for 3 minutes. Stir in cod and calamari and cook for another 7 minutes. Serve warm.

329.   Olive & Leek Cod Casserole

Serves: 4 | Ready in about: 30 minutes

½ cup olive oil
1 lb fresh cod fillets
1 cup black olives, chopped

4 leeks, trimmed and sliced
1 cup breadcrumbs
¾ cup chicken stock

Salt and black pepper to taste

Preheat oven to 350 F. Brush the cod with some olive oil, season with salt and pepper, and bake for 5-7 minutes. Let it cool, then cut it into 1-inch pieces. Warm the remaining olive oil in a skillet over medium heat. Stir-fry the olives and leeks for 4 minutes until the leeks are tender. Add the breadcrumbs and chicken stock, stirring to mix. Fold in the pieces of cod. Pour the mixture into a greased baking dish and bake for 15 minutes or until cooked through.

330.   Oven-Baked Haddock with Rosemary Gremolata

Serves: 6 | Ready in about: 35 minutes +marinating time

1 cup milk
Salt and black pepper to taste

2 tbsp rosemary, chopped
1 garlic clove, minced

1 lemon, zested
1 ½ lb haddock fillets

In a bowl, coat the fish with milk, salt, pepper, and 1 tablespoon of rosemary. Refrigerate for 2 hours. Preheat oven to 380 F. Carefully remove the haddock from the marinade, drain thoroughly, and place in a greased baking dish. Cover and bake 15–20 minutes until the fish is flaky. Remove the fish from the oven and let it rest for 5 minutes. To make the gremolata, mix the remaining rosemary, lemon zest, and garlic. Sprinkle the fish with gremolata and serve.

331. Wine Cod Fillets

Serves: 4 | Ready in about: 40 minutes

4 cod fillets
Salt and black pepper to taste
½ fennel seeds, ground

1 tbsp olive oil
½ cup dry white wine
½ cup vegetable stock

2 garlic cloves, minced
1 tsp chopped fresh sage
4 rosemary sprigs

Preheat oven to 370 F. Season the cod fillets with salt, pepper, and ground fennel seeds and place them in a greased baking dish. Add the wine, stock, garlic, and sage and drizzle with olive oil. Cover with foil and bake for 20 minutes until the fish flakes easily with a fork. Remove the fillets from the dish. Place the liquid in a saucepan over high heat and cook, stirring frequently, until reduced by half, about 10 minutes. Serve the fish topped with sauce and rosemary.

332. White Wine Poached Haddock

Serves: 4 | Ready in about: 40 minutes

4 haddock fillets
Salt and black pepper to taste

2 garlic cloves, minced
½ cup dry white wine

½ cup seafood stock
4 rosemary sprigs for garnish

Preheat oven to 380 F. Sprinkle haddock fillets with salt and black pepper and arrange them on a baking dish. Pour in the wine, garlic, and stock. Bake covered for 20 minutes until the fish is tender; remove to a serving plate. Pour the cooking liquid into a pot over high heat. Cook for 10 minutes until reduced by half. Place on serving dishes and top with the reduced poaching liquid. Serve garnished with rosemary.

333. Tilapia Pilaf

Serves: 4 | Ready in about: 45 minutes

3 tbsp olive oil
2 tilapia fillets, boneless
½ tsp Italian seasoning

½ cup brown rice
½ cup green bell pepper, diced
½ cup white onions, chopped

½ tsp garlic powder
Salt and black pepper to taste

Warm one tbsp of olive oil in a saucepan over medium heat. Cook onions, bell pepper, garlic powder, Italian seasoning, salt, and pepper for 3 minutes. Stir in brown rice and 2 cups of water and bring to a simmer. Cook for 18 minutes. Warm the remaining oil in a skillet over medium heat. Season the tilapia with salt and pepper. Fry for 10 minutes on both sides. Share the rice among plates and top with the tilapia fillets.

334. Onion-Avocado Tilapia

Serves: 4 | Ready in about: 10 minutes

1 tbsp olive oil
1 tbsp orange juice
¼ tsp kosher salt

½ tsp ground coriander seeds
4 tilapia fillets, skin-on
¼ cup chopped red onions

1 avocado, skinned and sliced

In a large bowl, mix together the olive oil, orange juice, ground coriander seeds, and salt. Add the fish and turn to coat on all sides. Arrange the fillets on a greased microwave-safe dish. Top with onion and cover the dish with plastic wrap, leaving a small part open at the edge to vent the steam. Microwave on high for about 3 minutes. The fish is done when it just begins to separate into chunks when pressed gently with a fork. Top the fillets with the avocado to serve.

335. Hazelnut & Date Crusted Barramundi

Serves: 2 | Ready in about: 25 minutes

2 tbsp olive oil
2 barramundi fillets, boneless
1 shallot, sliced

4 lemon slices
½ lemon, zested and juiced
1 cup baby spinach

¼ cup hazelnuts, chopped
4 dates, pitted and chopped
Salt and black pepper to taste

Preheat oven to 380 F. Sprinkle barramundi with salt and pepper and place on 2 parchment paper pieces. Top each fillet with lemon slices, lemon juice, shallot, lemon zest, spinach, hazelnuts, dates, and parsley. Sprinkle each fillet with 1 tbsp of oil and fold the paper around it. Place them on a baking sheet and bake for 12 minutes. Serve and enjoy!

336.   Easy Tuna Burgers

Serves: 4 | Ready in about: 20 minutes

2 tbsp olive oil
2 (5-oz) cans tuna, flaked
4 hamburger buns
3 green onions, chopped
¼ cup breadcrumbs

1 egg, beaten
2 tbsp chopped fresh parsley
1 tbsp Italian seasoning
1 lemon, zested
½ cup mayonnaise

1 tbsp chopped fresh dill
1 tbsp green olives, chopped
Sea salt to taste

Combine the tuna, breadcrumbs, green onions, eggs, Italian seasoning, parsley, and lemon zest in a bowl. Shape the mixture into 6 patties. Warm olive oil in a skillet over medium heat and brown patties for 8 minutes on both sides. Mix mayonnaise, green olives, dill, and salt in a bowl. Spoon the mixture on the buns and top with the patties.

337.   Tomato Tilapia

Serves: 4 | Ready in about: 20 minutes

2 tbsp olive oil
4 tilapia fillets, boneless

½ cup tomato sauce
2 tbsp parsley, chopped

Salt and black pepper to taste

Warm olive oil in a skillet over medium heat. Sprinkle tilapia with salt and pepper and cook until golden brown, flipping once, about 6 minutes. Pour in the tomato sauce and parsley and cook for an additional 4 minutes. Serve.

338.   Garlic-Lemon Sea Bass

Serves: 2 | Ready in about: 25 minutes

2 tbsp olive oil
2 sea bass fillets

1 lemon, juiced
4 garlic cloves, minced

Salt and black pepper to taste

Preheat oven to 380 F. Line a baking sheet with parchment paper. Brush sea bass fillets with lemon juice, olive oil, garlic, salt, and pepper and arrange them on the sheet. Bake for 15 minutes. Serve with salad.

339.   Onion Sea Bass

Serves: 4 | Ready in about: 25 minutes

1 tbsp butter, melted
4 skinless sea bass fillets

Salt and black pepper to taste
½ tsp onion powder

Preheat oven to 420 F. Rub the fish with salt, pepper, and onion powder and place on a greased baking dish. Drizzle the butter all over and bake for 20 minutes or until opaque.

340.   Tuna Gratin

Serves: 4 | Ready in about: 20 minutes

10 oz canned tuna, flaked
4 eggs, whisked

½ cup mozzarella, shredded
1 tbsp chives, chopped

1 tbsp parsley, chopped
Salt and black pepper to taste

Preheat oven to 360 F. Mix tuna, eggs, chives, parsley, salt, and pepper in a bowl. Transfer to a greased baking dish and bake for 15 minutes. Scatter cheese on top and let sit for 5 minutes. Cut before serving.

341.   Flounder with Pasta Salad

Serves: 4 | Ready in about: 25 minutes

2 tbsp olive oil
4 flounder fillets, boneless
1 tsp rosemary, dried
2 tsp cumin, ground
1 tbsp coriander, ground

2 tsp cinnamon powder
2 tsp oregano, dried
Salt and black pepper to taste
2 cups macaroni, cooked
1 cup cherry tomatoes, halved

1 avocado, peeled and sliced
1 cucumber, cubed
½ cup black olives, sliced
1 lemon, juiced

Preheat oven to 390 F. Combine rosemary, cumin, coriander, cinnamon, oregano, salt, and pepper in a bowl. Add in the flounder and toss to coat. Warm olive oil in a skillet over medium heat. Brown the fish fillets for 4 minutes on both sides. Transfer to a baking tray and bake in the oven for 7-10 minutes. Combine macaroni, tomatoes, avocado, cucumber, olives, and lemon juice in a bowl; toss to coat. Serve the fish with pasta salad on the side.

342. One-Pan Tuna with Vegetables

Serves: 4 | Ready in about: 25 minutes

2 tbsp olive oil
4 tuna fillets, boneless
1 red bell pepper, chopped
1 onion, chopped

4 garlic cloves, minced
½ cup fish stock
1 tsp basil, dried
½ cup cherry tomatoes, halved

½ cup black olives, halved
Salt and black pepper to taste

Warm olive oil in a skillet over medium heat and fry tuna for 10 minutes on both sides. Divide the fish among plates. In the same skillet, cook onion, bell pepper, garlic, and cherry tomatoes for 3 minutes. Stir in salt, pepper, fish stock, basil, and olives and cook for another 3 minutes. Top the tuna with the mixture and serve immediately.

343. Canned Tuna & Bean Bowl

Serves: 6 | Ready in about: 30 minutes

3 tbsp olive oil
1 lb kale, chopped
1 onion, chopped
3 garlic cloves, minced

18 black olives, sliced
¼ cup capers
¼ tsp red pepper flakes
2 (6-oz) cans tuna in olive oil

1 (15-oz) can cannellini beans
½ cup chicken broth
Salt and black pepper to taste

Steam the kale for 4 minutes or until crisp-tender and set aside. Warm the olive oil in a saucepan over medium heat. Sauté the onion and garlic for 4 minutes, stirring often. Add the chicken broth, olives, capers, and crushed red pepper flakes and cook for 4-5 minutes, stirring often. Add the kale and stir. Remove to a bowl and mix in the tuna, beans, pepper, and salt. Serve and enjoy!

344. Flounder Parcels

Serves: 4 | Ready in about: 20 minutes

2 tbsp olive oil
4 flounder fillets
¼ tsp red pepper flakes
4 fresh rosemary sprigs

2 garlic cloves, thinly sliced
1 cup cherry tomatoes, halved
½ chopped onion
2 tbsp capers

8 black olives, sliced
2 tbsp dry white wine
Salt and black pepper to taste

Preheat oven to 420 F. Drizzle the flounder with olive oil and season with salt, pepper, and red pepper flakes. Divide fillets between 4 pieces of aluminium foil. Top each one with garlic, cherry tomatoes, capers, onion, and olives. Fold the edges to form packets with opened tops. Add in a rosemary sprig in each one and drizzle with the white wine. Seal the packets and arrange them on a baking sheet. Bake for 10 minutes or until the fish is cooked. Serve warm.

345. Halibut with Roasted Peppers

Serves: 4 | Ready in about: 45 minutes

3 tbsp olive oil
1 tsp butter
2 red peppers, cut into wedges

4 halibut fillets
2 shallots, cut into rings
2 garlic cloves, minced

¾ cup breadcrumbs
2 tbsp chopped fresh parsley
Salt and black pepper to taste

Preheat oven to 440 F. Combine red peppers, garlic, shallots, 1 tbsp of olive oil, salt, and pepper in a bowl. Spread on a baking sheet and bake for 40 minutes. Warm the remaining olive oil in a pan over medium heat and brown the breadcrumbs for 4-5 minutes, stirring constantly. Set aside. Clean the pan and add in the butter to melt. Sprinkle the fish with salt and pepper. Add to the butter and cook for 8-10 minutes on both sides. Divide the pepper mixture between 4 plates and top with halibut fillets. Spread the crunchy breadcrumbs all over and top with parsley. Serve.

346. Mackerel Fillets in Red Sauce

Serves: 2 | Ready in about: 15 minutes

1 tbsp butter
2 mackerel fillets
¼ cup white wine
½ cup spring onions, sliced

2 garlic cloves, minced
½ tsp dried thyme
1 tsp dried parsley
Salt and black pepper to taste

½ cup vegetable broth
½ cup tomato sauce
½ tsp hot sauce
1 tbsp fresh mint, chopped

In a pot, melt the butter over medium heat. Add in fish and cook for 6 minutes in total; set aside. Pour in the wine and scrape off any bits from the bottom. Add in spring onions and garlic; cook for 3 minutes until fragrant. Sprinkle with thyme, parsley, salt, and pepper. Stir in vegetable broth, and tomato sauce, and add back the fillets. Cook for 3-4 minutes. Stir in hot sauce and top with mint. Serve and enjoy!

347. Zesty Halibut Confit with Sautéed Leeks

Serves: 4 | Ready in about: 45 minutes

1 tsp fresh lemon zest
¼ cup olive oil
4 skinless halibut fillets

Salt and black pepper to taste
1 lb leeks, sliced
1 tsp Dijon mustard

¾ cup dry white wine
1 tbsp fresh cilantro, chopped
4 lemon wedges

Warm olive oil in a skillet over medium heat. Season the halibut with salt and pepper. Sear in the skillet for 6-7 minutes until cooked through. Carefully transfer the halibut to a large plate. Add leeks, mustard, salt, and pepper to the skillet and sauté for 10-12 minutes, stirring frequently, until softened. Pour in the wine and lemon zest and bring to a simmer. Top with halibut. Reduce the heat to low, cover, and simmer for 6-10 minutes. Carefully transfer halibut to a serving platter, tent loosely with aluminum foil, and let rest while finishing leeks. Increase the heat and cook the leeks for 2-4 minutes until the sauce is slightly thickened. Adjust the seasoning with salt and pepper. Pour the leek mixture around the halibut, sprinkle with cilantro, and serve with lemon wedges.

348. Red Snapper with Citrus Topping Roast

Serves: 2 | Ready in about: 35 minutes

2 tbsp olive oil
1 tsp fresh cilantro, chopped
½ tsp grated lemon zest
½ tbsp lemon juice

½ tsp grated grapefruit zest
½ tbsp grapefruit juice
½ tsp grated orange zest
½ tbsp orange juice

½ shallot, minced
¼ tsp red pepper flakes
Salt and black pepper to taste
1 whole red snapper, cleaned

Preheat oven to 380 F. Whisk the olive oil, cilantro, lemon juice, orange juice, grapefruit juice, shallot, and pepper flakes together in a bowl. Season with salt and pepper. Set aside the citrus topping until ready to serve. In a separate bowl, combine lemon zest, orange zest, grapefruit zest, salt, and pepper. With a sharp knife, make 3-4 shallow slashes, about 2 inches apart, on both sides of the snapper. Spoon the citrus mixture into the fish cavity and transfer to a greased baking sheet. Roast for 25 minutes until the fish flakes. Serve drizzled with citrus topping, and enjoy!

349. Quick Grilled Sardines with Herby Sauce

Serves: 4 | Ready in about: 15 minutes + marinating time

12 sardines, gutted and cleaned
1 lemon, cut into wedges
2 garlic cloves, minced
2 tbsp capers, finely chopped

1 tbsp whole capers
1 shallot, diced
1 tsp anchovy paste
1 lemon, zested and juiced

2 tbsp olive oil
1 tbsp parsley, finely chopped
1 tbsp basil, finely chopped

In a large bowl, blend garlic, chopped capers, shallot, anchovy paste, lemon zest, and olive oil. Add the sardines and toss to coat; let them sit to marinate for about 30 minutes. Preheat your grill to high. Place the sardines on the grill. Cook for 3-4 minutes per side until the skin is browned and beginning to blister. Pour the marinade into a saucepan over medium heat and add the whole capers, parsley, basil, and lemon juice. Cook for 2-3 minutes until thickens. Pour the sauce over grilled sardines. Serve with lemon wedges.

350. Eggplant & Halibut Bake

Serves: 4 | Ready in about: 35 minutes

2 tbsp olive oil
¼ cup tomato sauce
4 halibut fillets, boneless

2 eggplants, sliced
Salt and black pepper to taste
2 tbsp balsamic vinegar

2 tbsp chives, chopped

Preheat oven to 380 F. Warm the olive oil in a skillet over medium heat and fry the eggplant slices for 5-6 minutes, turning once; reserve. Add the tomato sauce, salt, pepper, and vinegar to the skillet and cook for 5 minutes. Return the eggplants to the skillet and cook for 2 minutes. Remove to a plate. Place the halibut fillets on a greased baking tray and bake for 12-15 minutes. Serve the halibut over the eggplants sprinkled with chives.

351. Golden Sole Fillets

Serves: 4 | Ready in about: 10 minutes

¼ cup olive oil
½ cup flour

½ tsp paprika
8 skinless sole fillets

Salt and black pepper to taste
4 lemon wedges

Warm olive oil in a skillet over medium heat. Mix the flour with paprika in a shallow dish. Coat the fish with the flour, shaking off any excess. Sear the sole fillets for 2-3 minutes per side until lightly browned. Serve with lemon wedges.

352. Hake with Potatoes

Serves: 4 | Ready in about: 40 minutes

1 ½ lb russet potatoes, unpeeled
¼ cup olive oil
½ tsp garlic powder

½ tsp paprika
Salt and black pepper to taste
4 skinless hake fillets

4 fresh thyme sprigs
1 lemon, sliced

Preheat oven to 420 F. Slice the potatoes and toss them with some olive oil, salt, pepper, paprika, and garlic powder in a bowl. Microwave for 12-14 minutes until potatoes are just tender, stirring halfway through microwaving. Transfer the potatoes to a baking dish and press gently into an even layer. Season the hake with salt and pepper, and arrange it skinned side down over the potatoes. Drizzle with the remaining olive oil, then place thyme sprigs and lemon slices on top. Bake for 15-18 minutes until the hake flakes apart when gently prodded with a paring knife. Serve and enjoy!

353. Rich Hake Fillet in Herby Tomato Sauce

Serves: 4 | Ready in about: 30 minutes

2 tbsp olive oil
1 onion, sliced thin
1 fennel bulb, sliced
Salt and black pepper to taste

4 garlic cloves, minced
1 tsp fresh thyme, chopped
1 (14-oz) can diced tomatoes,
½ cup dry white wine

4 skinless hake fillets
2 tbsp fresh basil, chopped

Warm olive oil in a skillet over medium heat. Sauté the onion and fennel for about 5 minutes until softened. Stir in garlic and thyme and cook for about 30 seconds until fragrant. Pour in tomatoes and wine and bring to simmer. Season the hake with salt and pepper. Nestle hake a skinned side down into the tomato sauce and spoon some sauce over the top. Bring to a simmer. Cook for 10-12 minutes until the hake easily flakes with a fork. Sprinkle with basil and serve.

354. Chili-Garlic Topped Baked Anchovies

Serves: 2 | Ready in about: 10 minutes

½ tsp red pepper flakes
16 canned anchovies

4 garlic cloves, minced
Salt and black pepper to taste

Preheat your broiler. Arrange the anchovies on a foil-lined baking dish. In a bowl, mix anchovy olive oil, garlic, salt, red flakes, and pepper and pour over anchovies. Broil for 3-4 minutes. Divide between 4 plates and drizzle with the remaining mixture from the dish. Serve and enjoy!

355.　Shrimp with White Beans

Serves: 4 | Ready in about: 25 minutes

1 lb large shrimp, peeled and deveined
3 tbsp olive oil
Salt and black pepper to taste

1 red bell pepper, chopped
1 small red onion, chopped
2 garlic cloves, minced

¼ tsp red pepper flakes
2 (15-oz) cans cannellini beans
2 tbsp lemon zest

Warm olive oil in a skillet over medium heat. Add the shrimp and cook, without stirring, until spotty brown and edges turn pink, about 2 minutes. Remove the skillet from the heat, turn over the shrimp, and let sit until opaque throughout, about 30 seconds. Transfer shrimp to a bowl and cover with foil to keep warm. Return the skillet to heat and reheat the olive oil. Sauté the bell pepper, garlic, and onion until softened, about 5 minutes. Stir in pepper flakes and salt for about 30 seconds. Pour in the beans and cook until heated through, 5 minutes. Add the shrimp with any accumulated juices back to the skillet and cook for about 1 minute. Stir in lemon zest and serve.

356.　Easy Shrimp & Mushroom Rice

Serves: 4 | Ready in about: 40 minutes

2 tbsp olive oil
1 lb shrimp, peeled, deveined
1 cup white rice
4 garlic cloves, sliced

¼ tsp hot paprika
1 cup mushrooms, sliced
¼ cup green peas
Juice of 1 lime

Sea salt to taste
¼ cup chopped fresh chives

Bring a large pot of salted water to a boil. Cook the rice for 15-18 minutes, stirring occasionally. Drain and place in a bowl. Add in the green peas and mix to combine well. Taste and adjust the seasoning. Remove to a serving plate. Heat the olive oil in a saucepan over medium heat and sauté garlic and hot paprika for 30-40 seconds until garlic is light golden brown. Remove the garlic with a slotted spoon. Add the mushrooms to the saucepan and sauté them for 5 minutes until tender. Put in the shrimp, lime juice, and salt and stir for 4 minutes. Turn the heat off. Add the chives and reserved garlic to the shrimp and pour over the rice. Serve and enjoy!

357.　Avocado & Anchovy Spread

Serves: 2 | Ready in about: 5 minutes

1 avocado, peeled and pitted
1 tsp lemon juice

¼ celery stalk, chopped
¼ cup chopped shallots

2 anchovy fillets in olive oil
Salt and black pepper to taste

Combine the lemon juice, avocado, celery, shallots, and anchovy fillets (along with their olive oil) in a food processor. Blitz until smooth. Season with salt and black pepper. Serve.

358.　Sardine Cakes

Serves: 4 | Ready in about: 20 minutes

3 tbsp olive oil
1 tsp mustard powder
1 tsp chili powder
20 oz canned sardines, mashed

2 garlic cloves, minced
2 tbsp dill, chopped
1 onion, chopped
1 cup panko breadcrumbs

1 egg, whisked
Salt and black pepper to taste
2 tbsp lemon juice

Combine the sardines, garlic, dill, onion, breadcrumbs, egg, mustard powder, chili powder, salt, pepper, and lemon juice in a bowl and form medium patties out of the mixture. Warm the olive oil in a skillet over medium heat and fry the cakes for 10 minutes on both sides. Serve with aioli.

359.　Crispy Pollock Fillets

Serves: 4 | Ready in about: 25 minutes

4 pollock fillets, boneless

2 cups potato chips, crushed

2 tbsp mayonnaise

Preheat oven to 380F. Line a baking sheet with parchment paper. Rub each fillet with mayonnaise and dip them in the potato chips. Place fillets on the sheet and bake for 12 minutes. Serve with salad.

360.   Tomato & Squid Stew

Serves: 4 | Ready in about: 50 minutes

1 (28-oz) cans whole peeled tomatoes, diced

¼ cup olive oil	¼ tsp red pepper flakes	Salt and black pepper to taste
1 onion, chopped	1 red chili, minced	⅓ cup green olives, chopped
1 celery rib, sliced	½ cup dry white wine	1 tbsp capers
3 garlic cloves, minced	2 lb squid, sliced into rings	2 tbsp fresh parsley, chopped

Warm olive oil in a pot over medium heat. Sauté the onion, garlic, red chili, and celery until softened, about 5 minutes. Stir in pepper flakes and cook for about 30 seconds. Stir in wine, scraping up any browned bits, and cook until nearly evaporated, about 1 minute. Add 1 cup of water and season with salt and pepper. Stir the squid in the pot. Reduce heat to low, cover, and simmer until squid has released its liquid, about 15 minutes. Pour in tomatoes, olives, and capers, and continue to cook until squid is very tender, 30-35 minutes. Top with parsley. Serve and enjoy!

361.   Balsamic Prawns with Mushrooms

Serves: 4 | Ready in about: 25 minutes

1 lb tiger prawns, peeled and deveined	2 green onions, sliced	2 tbsp balsamic vinegar
3 tbsp olive oil	½ lb white mushrooms, sliced	2 tsp garlic, minced

Warm olive oil in a skillet over medium heat and cook green onions and garlic for 2 minutes. Stir in mushrooms and balsamic vinegar and cook for an additional 6 minutes. Put in prawns and cook for 4 minutes. Serve right away.

362.   Herring Stuffed Eggs with Capers

Serves: 6 | Ready in about: 20 minutes

1/3 cup aioli	1 tbsp tarragon, chopped	1 (6.7-oz) can smoke herring
1 tbsp capers, drained	2 pickled jalapenos, minced	1 tsp paprika
12 eggs	Salt and black pepper to taste	

Fill a large pot over medium heat with water by 1 inch. Bring to a boil. Carefully add the eggs, one at a time to the pot, cover, and boil them for 10 minutes. Cool the eggs in cold water. Peel the eggs and slice them in half lengthwise; mix the yolks with the aioli, herring, paprika, capers, tarragon, jalapenos, salt, and pepper. Divide the mixture between the egg whites. Arrange the deviled eggs on a serving platter.

363.   Shrimp & Vegetable Roast

Serves: 4 | Ready in about: 30 minutes

2 lb shrimp, peeled and deveined	2 red onions, cut into wedges	2 tsp oregano, dried
4 tbsp olive oil	4 garlic cloves, unpeeled	2 tbsp parsley, chopped
2 bell peppers, cut into chunks	8 Kalamata olives, halved	Salt and black pepper to taste
2 fennel bulbs, cut into wedges	1 tsp lemon zest, grated	

Preheat oven to 390 F. Place bell peppers, garlic, fennel, red onions, and olives in a roasting tray. Add in the lemon zest, oregano, half of the olive oil, salt, and pepper and toss to coat; roast for 15 minutes. Coat the shrimp with the remaining olive oil and pour over the veggies; roast for another 7 minutes. Serve topped with parsley.

364.   Sicilian-Style Squid with Zucchini

Serves: 4 | Ready in about: 25 minutes

2 tbsp olive oil	2 tbsp cilantro, chopped	Salt and black pepper to taste
10 oz squid, cut into pieces	1 jalapeno pepper, chopped	1 tbsp dill, chopped
2 zucchinis, chopped	3 tbsp balsamic vinegar	

Warm olive oil in a skillet over medium heat and sauté squid for 5 minutes. Stir in zucchini, cilantro, jalapeño pepper, vinegar, salt, pepper, and dill and cook for another 10 minutes. Serve right away.

365.   Shrimp with Lemon & Black Olives

Serves: 4 | Ready in about: 25 minutes

1 lb shrimp, peeled and deveined
3 tbsp olive oil
1 lemon, juiced

1 tbsp flour
1 cup fish stock
Salt and black pepper to taste

1 cup black olives, halved
1 tbsp rosemary, chopped

Warm olive oil in a skillet over medium heat and sear the shrimp for 4 minutes on both sides; set aside. In the same skillet over low heat, stir in the flour for 2-3 minutes. Gradually pour in the fish stock and lemon juice while stirring and simmer for 3-4 minutes until the sauce thickens. Adjust the seasoning with salt and pepper and mix in shrimp, olives, and rosemary. Serve immediately.

366.   One-Pot Lime-Orange Squid Meal

Serves: 4 | Ready in about: 30 minutes

1 lb baby squid, cleaned, body and tentacles chopped
3 tbsp olive oil
½ cup green olives, chopped
½ tsp lime zest, grated

1 tbsp lime juice
½ tsp orange zest, grated
1 tsp red pepper flakes
1 tbsp parsley, chopped
4 garlic cloves, minced

1 shallot, chopped
1 cup vegetable stock
2 tbsp red wine vinegar
Salt and black pepper to taste

Warm olive oil in a skillet over medium heat and stir in lime zest, lime juice, orange zest, red pepper flakes, garlic, shallot, olives, stock, vinegar, salt, and pepper. Bring to a boil and simmer for 10 minutes. Mix in squid and parsley and cook for another 10 minutes. Serve hot.

367.   Seafood Medley

Serves: 4 | Ready in about: 25 minutes

2 tbsp butter
½ lb squid rings
1 lb shrimp, peeled, deveined
Salt and black pepper to taste

2 garlic cloves, minced
1 tsp rosemary, dried
1 red onion, chopped
1 cup vegetable stock

1 lemon, juiced
1 tbsp parsley, chopped

Melt the butter in a skillet over medium heat and cook onion and garlic for 4 minutes. Stir in shrimp, salt, pepper, squid rings, rosemary, vegetable stock, and lemon juice and bring to a boil. Simmer for 8 minutes. Put in parsley and serve.

Serves: 4 | Ready in about: 25 minutes

368.   Favorite Prawn Scampi

Serves: 4 | Ready in about: 25 minutes

1 lb prawns, peeled and deveined
2 tbsp olive oil
1 onion, chopped

6 garlic cloves, minced
1 lemon, juiced and zested
½ cup dry white wine

Salt and black pepper to taste
2 cups fusilli, cooked
½ tsp red pepper flakes

Warm olive oil in a pan over medium heat and sauté onion and garlic for 3 minutes, stirring often, until fragrant. Stir in prawns and cook for 3-4 minutes. Mix in lemon juice, lemon zest, salt, pepper, wine, and red flakes. Bring to a boil, then decrease the heat, and simmer for 2 minutes until the liquid is reduced by half. Turn the heat off. Stir in pasta and serve.

369.   Celery Sticks Stuffed with Crab

Serves: 4 | Ready in about: 10 minutes

1 cup cream cheese
6 oz crab meat

1 tsp Mediterranean seasoning
2 tbsp apple cider vinegar

8 celery sticks, halved
Salt and black pepper to taste

In a large mixing bowl, combine the cream cheese, crab meat, apple cider vinegar, salt, pepper, and Mediterranean seasoning. Divide the crab mixture between the celery sticks. Serve.

370. Authentic Tuscan Scallops

Serves: 4 | Ready in about: 25 minutes

2 tbsp olive oil
1 lb sea scallops, rinsed

4 cups Tuscan kale
1 orange, juiced

Salt and black pepper to taste
¼ tsp red pepper flakes

Season the scallops with salt and pepper. Warm olive oil in a skillet over medium heat and brown scallops for 6-8 minutes on all sides. Remove to a plate and keep warm, covering with foil. In the same skillet, add the kale, red pepper flakes, orange juice, salt, and pepper and cook until the kale wilts, about 4-5 minutes. Share the kale mixture into 4 plates and top with the scallops. Serve warm.

371. Speedy Jumbo Shrimp

Serves: 4 | Ready in about: 20 minutes

2 lb shell-on jumbo shrimp, deveined
¼ cup olive oil
Salt and black pepper to taste

6 garlic cloves, minced
1 tsp anise seeds
½ tsp red pepper flakes

2 tbsp minced fresh cilantro
1 lemon, cut into wedges

Combine olive oil, garlic, anise seeds, pepper flakes, and black pepper in a large bowl. Add the shrimp and cilantro and toss well, making sure the oil mixture gets into the interior of the shrimp. Arrange shrimp in a single layer on a baking tray. Set under the preheated broiler for approximately 4 minutes. Flip the shrimp and continue to broil until it is opaque and the shells are beginning to brown, about 2 minutes, rotating the sheet halfway through broiling. Serve with lemon wedges.

372. Black Olive & Shrimp Quinoa Bowl

Serves: 4 | Ready in about: 20 minutes

10 black olives, pitted and halved
¼ cup olive oil
1 cup quinoa
1 lemon, cut into wedges

1 lb shrimp, peeled and cooked
2 tomatoes, sliced
2 bell peppers, thinly sliced
1 red onion, chopped

1 tsp dried dill
1 tbsp fresh parsley, chopped
Salt and black pepper to taste

Place the quinoa in a pot and cover with 2 cups of water over medium heat. Bring to a boil, reduce the heat, and simmer for 12-15 minutes or until tender. Remove from heat and fluff it with a fork. Mix in the quinoa with olive oil, dill, parsley, salt, and black pepper. Stir in tomatoes, bell peppers, olives, and onion. Serve decorated with shrimp and lemon wedges.

373. Stewed Squid with Capers

Serves: 4 | Ready in about: 25 minutes

2 tbsp olive oil
1 onion, chopped
1 celery stalk, chopped
1 lb calamari rings

2 red chili peppers, chopped
2 garlic cloves, minced
14 oz canned tomatoes, diced
2 tbsp tomato paste

Salt and black pepper to taste
2 tbsp capers, drained
12 black olives, pitted and halved

Warm olive oil in a skillet over medium heat and cook onion, celery, garlic, and chili peppers for 2 minutes. Stir in calamari rings, tomatoes, tomato paste, salt, and pepper and bring to a simmer. Cook for 20 minutes. Put in olives and capers and cook for another 5 minutes. Serve right away.

374. One-Skillet Scallops

Serves: 4 | Ready in about: 25 minutes

3 tbsp olive oil
2 celery stalks, sliced
2 lb sea scallops, halved
3 garlic cloves, minced

Juice of 1 lime
1 red bell pepper, chopped
1 tbsp capers, chopped
1 tbsp mayonnaise

1 tbsp rosemary, chopped
1 cup chicken stock

Warm the oil in a skillet over medium heat and cook celery and garlic for 2 minutes. Stir in bell pepper, lime juice, capers, rosemary, and stock and bring to a boil. Simmer for 8 minutes. Mix in scallops and mayonnaise and cook for 5 minutes.

375.   Fried Chili Sea Scallops

Serves: 4 | Ready in about: 25 minutes

1 ½ lb sea scallops, tendons removed
3 tbsp olive oil
1 garlic clove, finely chopped

½ red pepper flakes
2 tbsp chili sauce
¼ cup tomato sauce

1 small shallot, minced
1 tbsp minced fresh cilantro
Salt and black pepper to taste

Warm olive oil in a skillet over medium heat. Add the scallops and cook for 2 minutes without moving them. Flip them and continue to cook for 2 more minutes, without moving them, until golden browned. Set aside. Add the shallot and garlic to the skillet and sauté for 3-5 minutes until softened. Pour in the chili sauce, tomato sauce, and red pepper flakes and stir for 3-4 minutes. Add the scallops back and warm through. Adjust the taste and top with cilantro.

376.   Typical Clams with Snow Peas

Serves: 4 | Ready in about: 30 minutes

2 tbsp olive oil
1 tbsp basil, chopped
2 lb clams
1 onion, chopped

4 garlic cloves, minced
Salt and black pepper to taste
½ cup vegetable stock
1 cup snow peas, sliced

½ tbsp balsamic vinegar
1 cup scallions, sliced

Warm the olive oil in a skillet over medium heat. Sauté onion and garlic for 2 to 3 minutes until tender and fragrant, stirring often. Add in the clams, salt, pepper, vegetable stock, snow peas, balsamic vinegar, and basil and bring to a boil. Lower the heat and simmer for 10 minutes. Remove from the heat. Discard any unopened clams. Scatter with scallions.

377.   Crispy Scallops with Bean Mash

Serves: 4 | Ready in about: 20 minutes

4 tbsp olive oil
2 garlic cloves
2 tsp fresh thyme, minced

1 (15-oz) can cannellini beans
½ cup chicken stock
Salt and black pepper to taste

10 oz sea scallops

Warm 2 tbsp of olive oil in a saucepan over medium heat. Sauté the garlic for 30 seconds or just until it's fragrant. Stir in the beans and stock, and bring to a boil. Simmer for 5 minutes. Remove the beans to a bowl and mash them with a potato mash. Season with thyme, salt, and pepper. Warm the remaining oil in a large sauté pan. Add the scallops, flat-side down, and cook for 2 minutes or until they're golden on the bottom. Flip over and cook for another 1-2 minutes or until opaque and slightly firm. Divide the bean mash between plates and top with scallops.

378.   Lemon Pancetta-Wrapped Scallops

Serves: 6 | Ready in about: 25 minutes

2 tsp olive oil
12 thin pancetta slices

12 medium scallops
2 tsp lemon juice

1 tsp chili powder

Wrap the pancetta around scallops and secure them with toothpicks. Warm the olive oil in a skillet over medium heat and cook scallops for 6 minutes on all sides. Serve sprinkled with chili powder and lemon juice.

379.   Perfect Wine-Steamed Clams

Serves: 4 | Ready in about: 30 minutes

4 lb clams, scrubbed and debearded
3 tbsp butter
3 garlic cloves, minced

¼ tsp red pepper flakes
1 cup dry white wine
3 fresh thyme sprigs

2 tbsp fresh dill, minced

Melt butter in a large saucepan over medium heat and cook garlic and pepper flakes, stirring constantly, until fragrant, about 30 seconds. Stir in wine and thyme sprigs and cook until wine is slightly reduced, about 1 minute. Stir in clams. Cover the saucepan and simmer for 15-18 minutes. Remove and discard thyme sprigs and any clams that refuse to open. Sprinkle with dill and serve.

380.   Decadent Seafood Cakes with Radicchio Salad

Serves: 4 | Ready in about: 30 minutes

2 tbsp butter
2 tbsp extra-virgin olive oil
1 lb lump crabmeat
4 scallions, sliced

1 garlic clove, minced
¼ cup cooked shrimp
2 tbsp heavy cream
¼ head radicchio, thinly sliced

1 green apple, shredded
2 tbsp lemon juice
Salt and black pepper to taste

In a food processor or a blender, place the shrimp, heavy cream, salt, and pepper. Blend until smooth. Mix crab meat and scallions in a bowl. Add in shrimp mixture and toss to combine. Make 4 patties out of the mixture. Transfer to the fridge for 10 minutes. Warm butter in a skillet over medium heat and brown patties for 8 minutes on all sides. Remove to a serving plate. Mix radicchio and apple in a bowl. Combine olive oil, lemon juice, garlic, and salt in a small bowl and stir well. Pour over the salad and toss to combine. Serve and enjoy!

381.   Clam Stew with Chickpeas

Serves: 4 | Ready in about: 40 minutes

2 tbsp olive oil
1 yellow onion, chopped
1 fennel bulb, chopped
1 carrot, chopped

1 red bell pepper, chopped
2 garlic cloves, minced
3 tbsp tomato paste
16 oz canned chickpeas, drained

1 tsp dried thyme
¼ tsp smoked paprika
Salt and black pepper to taste
1 lb clams, scrubbed

Warm the olive oil in a pot over medium heat and sauté fennel, onion, bell pepper, and carrot for 5 minutes until they're tender. Stir in garlic and tomato paste and cook for another minute. Mix in the chickpeas, thyme, paprika, salt, pepper, and 2 cups of water and bring to a boil; cook for 20 minutes. Rinse the clams under cold, running water. Discard any clams that remain open when tapped with your fingers. Put the unopened clams into the pot and cook everything for 4-5 minutes until the shells have opened. When finished, discard any clams that haven't opened fully during the cooking process. Adjust the seasoning with salt and pepper. Serve.

382.   Homemade Lemon Cioppino

Serves: 6 | Ready in about: 10 minutes

1 lb mussels, scrubbed, debearded
1 lb large shrimp, peeled and deveined
1 ½ lb haddock fillets, cut into chunks
3 tbsp olive oil
1 fennel bulb, thinly sliced
1 onion, chopped

3 large shallots, chopped
Salt to taste
4 garlic cloves, minced
¼ tsp red pepper flakes
¼ cup tomato paste
1 (28-oz) can diced tomatoes

1 ½ cups dry white wine
5 cups vegetable stock
1 bay leaf
1 lb clams, scrubbed
2 tbsp basil, chopped

Warm olive oil in a large pot over medium heat. Sauté the fennel, onion, garlic, and shallots for 8-10 minutes until tender. Add the red pepper flakes and sauté for 2 minutes. Stir in the tomato paste, tomatoes with their juices, wine, stock, salt, and bay leaf. Cover and bring to a simmer. Lower the heat to low and simmer for 30 minutes until the flavors blend. Pour in the clams and mussels and cook for about 5 minutes. Add the shrimp and fish. Simmer gently until the fish and shrimp are just cooked through, 5 minutes. Discard any clams and mussels that refuse to open and bay leaf. Top with basil.

383.   Delectable Littleneck Clams in Sherry Sauce

Serves: 4 | Ready in about: 20 minutes

2 tbsp olive oil
1 cup dry sherry
3 shallots, minced

4 garlic cloves, minced
4 lb littleneck clams, scrubbed
2 tbsp minced fresh parsley

½ tsp cayenne pepper
1 Lemon, cut into wedges

Bring sherry wine, shallots, and garlic to a simmer in a large saucepan and cook for 3 minutes. Add clams, cover, and cook, stirring twice, until clams open, about 7 minutes. With a slotted spoon, transfer clams to a serving bowl, discarding any that refuse to open. Stir in olive oil, parsley, and cayenne pepper. Pour sauce over clams and serve with lemon wedges.

384.   Pasta with Steamed Mussels

Serves: 4 | Ready in about: 30 minutes

2 lb mussels, cleaned and beards removed

1 lb cooked spaghetti

3 tbsp butter

2 garlic cloves, minced

1 carrot, diced

1 onion, chopped

2 celery sticks, chopped

1 cup white wine

2 tbsp parsley, chopped

½ tsp red pepper flakes

1 lemon, juiced

Melt the butter in a saucepan over medium heat and sauté the garlic, carrot, onion, and celery for 4-5 minutes, stirring occasionally until softened. Add the mussels, white wine, and lemon juice, cover, and bring to a boil. Reduce the heat and steam for 4-6 minutes. Discard any unopened mussels. Stir in spaghetti to coat. Sprinkle with parsley and red pepper flakes to serve.

385.   Mussels in Butter Sauce with Lemon

Serves: 4 | Ready in about: 15 minutes

4 lb mussels, cleaned

4 tbsp butter

½ cup chopped parsley

1 white onion, chopped

2 cups dry white wine

½ tsp sea salt

6 garlic cloves, minced

Juice of ½ lemon

Add the wine, garlic, salt, onion, and ¼ cup of parsley in a pot over medium heat and let simmer. Put in mussels and simmer covered for 7-8 minutes. Divide mussels between four bowls. Stir butter and lemon juice into the pot and drizzle over the mussels. Top with parsley and serve.

386.   Saucy Basil-Tomato Scallops

Serves: 4 | Ready in about: 20 minutes

2 tbsp olive oil

1 tbsp basil, chopped

1 lb scallops, scrubbed

1 tbsp garlic, minced

1 onion, chopped

6 tomatoes, cubed

1 cup heavy cream

1 tbsp parsley, chopped

Warm olive oil in a skillet over medium heat and cook garlic and onion for 2 minutes. Stir in scallops, basil, tomatoes, heavy cream, and parsley and cook for an additional 7 minutes. Serve immediately.

387.   Weeknight Calamari with Garlic Sauce

Serves: 4 | Ready in about: 25 minutes

2 tbsp olive oil

2 lb calamari, sliced into rings

4 garlic cloves, minced

1 lime, juiced

2 tbsp balsamic vinegar

3 tbsp cilantro, chopped

Warm olive oil in a skillet over medium heat and sauté garlic, lime juice, balsamic vinegar, and cilantro for 5 minutes. Stir in calamari rings and cook for 10 minutes.

388.   Sunday Seafood Stew

Serves: 4 | Ready in about: 25 minutes

½ lb skinless trout, cubed

2 tbsp olive oil

½ lb clams

½ lb cod, cubed

1 onion, chopped

½ fennel bulb, chopped

2 garlic cloves, minced

¼ cup dry white wine

2 tbsp chopped fresh parsley

1 (32-oz) can tomato sauce

1 cup fish broth

1 tbsp Italian seasoning

⅛ tsp red pepper flakes

Salt and black pepper to taste

Warm the olive oil in a pot over medium heat and sauté onion and fennel for 5 minutes. Add in garlic and cook for 30 seconds. Pour in the wine and cook for 1 minute. Stir in tomato sauce, clams, broth, cod, trout, salt, Italian seasoning, red pepper flakes, and pepper. Bring just a boil and simmer for 5 minutes. Discard any unopened clams. Top with parsley.

389.   Delicious Seafood Soup

Serves: 4 | Ready in about: 30 minutes

½ lb cod, skinless and cubed
2 tbsp olive oil
½ lb shrimp, deveined
1 yellow onion, chopped

1 carrot, finely chopped
1 celery stalk, finely chopped
1 small pepper, chopped
1 garlic clove, minced

½ cup tomatoes, crushed
4 cups fish stock
¼ tsp rosemary, dried
Salt and black pepper to taste

Warm olive oil in a pot over medium heat. Cook onion, garlic, carrot, celery, and pepper for 5 minutes until soft, stirring occasionally. Stir in the tomatoes, stock, cod, shrimp, rosemary, salt, and pepper and simmer for 15 minutes.

390.   Stuffed Cucumbers with Avocado & Salmon

Serves: 4 | Ready in about: 10 minutes

1 tbsp extra-virgin olive oil
2 large cucumbers, peeled

1 (4-oz) can red salmon
1 ripe avocado, mashed

2 tbsp chopped fresh dill
Salt and black pepper to taste

Cut the cucumber into 1-inch-thick pieces, and using a spoon, scrape seeds out of the center of each piece and stand up on a plate. In a bowl, mix the salmon, avocado, olive oil, lime zest and juice, dill, salt, and pepper, and blend until creamy. Spoon the salmon mixture into the center of each cucumber segment and serve chilled.

391.   Shrimp Salad with Beans

Serves: 4 | Ready in about: 15 minutes

1 lb shrimp, peeled and deveined
30 oz canned cannellini beans, drained
4 tbsp olive oil
10 cherry tomatoes, halved

1 tsp lemon zest
½ cup red onion, chopped
5 oz spring mix salad
Salt and black pepper to taste

2 tbsp red wine vinegar
2 garlic cloves, minced

In a skillet, warm half of the olive oil over medium heat and cook the shrimp, turning once until just pink and opaque, about 4 minutes. Set aside to cool. Place the salad mix on a serving plate. In a bowl, mix cooled shrimp, cannellini beans, cherry tomatoes, and onion. Pour the mixture over the salad. In another bowl, whisk the remaining olive oil, red wine vinegar, garlic, lemon zest, salt, and pepper. Drizzle the dressing over the salad. Serve immediately.

392.   Restaurant-Style Marinara Mussels

Serves: 4 | Ready in about: 25 minutes

2 lb mussels, cleaned and de-bearded
2 tbsp olive oil
2 leeks, chopped

1 red onion, chopped
Salt and black pepper to taste
1 tbsp parsley, chopped

1 tbsp chives, chopped
½ cup tomato sauce

Warm the oil in a skillet over medium heat and cook leeks and onion for 5 minutes. Stir in mussels, salt, pepper, parsley, chives, and tomato sauce and cook for 10 minutes. Discard any unopened mussels. Serve right away.

POULTRY

393.   Cacciatore Chicken Stir-Fry

Serves: 4 | Ready in about: 20 minutes

3 tbsp olive oil
1 lb chicken thigh strips
¼ cup Marsala white wine
1 tsp dried oregano
Salt and black pepper to taste

2 tsp cornstarch
3 tbsp chicken broth
1 tomato, chopped
1 shallot, chopped
1 garlic clove, minced

¼ lb mushrooms, sliced
1 red bell pepper, sliced
2 fresh rosemary sprigs

Combine 2 tbsp of the wine, oregano, salt, pepper, and cornstarch in a large bowl. Add the chicken and toss to coat; set aside. Warm the olive oil in a skillet over medium heat and stir-fry the shallot and garlic for 1 minute until softened. Add the mushrooms and red bell pepper and sauté for 2-3 minutes until lightly tender. Remove to a plate. Brown the chicken in the same skillet for about 5 minutes until it turns white and is nearly cooked through. Pour in the white wine, broth, and tomato mixture while stir-frying. Bring to a boil. Add the vegetables back to the skillet. Cook, stirring, for another 2 minutes to mix everything. Garnish with rosemary sprigs before serving.

394.   Tuscan Chicken with Chianti Sauce

Serves: 4 | Ready in about: 80 minutes + chilling time

4 tbsp olive oil
2 tbsp butter
3 garlic cloves, minced
1 tbsp lemon zest

2 tbsp fresh thyme, chopped
2 tbsp fresh parsley, chopped
Salt and black pepper to taste
4 bone-in chicken legs

2 cups red grapes (in clusters)
1 red onion, sliced
1 cup Chianti red wine
1 cup chicken stock

Toss the chicken in a bowl with 2 tablespoons of olive oil, garlic, thyme, parsley, lemon zest, salt, and pepper. Refrigerate for 1 hour. Preheat oven to 400 F. Heat the remaining olive oil in a saucepan over medium heat. Sear the chicken for 3–4 minutes per side. Top chicken with grapes. Transfer to the oven and bake for 20–30 minutes or until internal temperature registers 180 F on an instant-read thermometer. Melt the butter in another saucepan and sauté the onion for 3–4 minutes. Add the wine and stock, stir, and simmer the sauce for about 30 minutes until it is thickened. Plate the chicken and grapes and pour the sauce over to serve.

395.   Chicken Breasts with Wine and Capers

Serves: 4 | Ready in about: 25 minutes

2 tbsp butter
1 lb chicken breasts
½ cup flour
½ tsp ground nutmeg

½ cup chicken broth
½ cup dry white wine
1 lemon, juiced and zested
1 tbsp capers

2 tbsp chopped fresh cilantro
Salt and black pepper to taste

Cut the chicken breasts into 4 pieces and pound them to ¼-inch thickness using a meat mallet. Combine flour, nutmeg, salt, and pepper in a bowl. Roll the chicken in the mixture and shake off the excess flour. Warm butter in a skillet over medium heat and brown the chicken for 6-8 minutes on both sides; set aside. Scrape the bottom of the pot with white wine. Add in broth, lemon juice, lemon zest, and capers. Simmer for 3-4 minutes until thickens. Pour the sauce over the chicken and sprinkle with cilantro to serve.

396.   Skewers of Chicken & Vegetables

Serves: 6 | Ready in about: 20 minutes

2 tbsp olive oil
1 ½ lb chicken breasts, cubed
1 tbsp fresh chives, chopped

1 zucchini, sliced thick
1 tbsp Italian seasoning
1 cup bell peppers, sliced

1 red onion, cut into wedges
1 ½ cups cherry tomatoes

Preheat your grill to high. Toss the chicken cubes with olive oil and Italian seasoning. Thread them onto skewers, alternating with the vegetables. Grill the skewers for 10 minutes, turning them occasionally. Top with chives.

397. Green Bean & Chicken Bake

Serves: 4 | Ready in about: 35 minutes

1 lb chicken thighs, boneless and skinless
1 lb green beans, trimmed and halved   ½ cup sour cream
2 tsp turmeric powder   Salt and black pepper to taste

1 tbsp lime juice
1 tbsp thyme, chopped

Preheat oven to 380 F. Place chicken, turmeric, green beans, sour cream, salt, pepper, lime juice, and thyme in a roasting pan and mix well. Bake for 25 minutes. Serve.

398. Simple Chicken Wings

Serves: 4 | Ready in about: 55 minutes

2 tbsp canola oils
12 chicken wings, halved
2 garlic cloves, minced

1 lime, juiced and zested
1 cup raisins, soaked
1 tsp cumin, ground

Salt and black pepper to taste
½ cup chicken stock
1 tbsp chives, chopped

Preheat oven to 340 F. Combine chicken wings, garlic, lime juice, lime zest, canola oil, raisins, cumin, salt, pepper, stock, and chives in a baking pan. Bake for 40 minutes.

399. Sicilian-Inspired Chicken

Serves: 4 | Ready in about: 25 minutes

1 lb chicken breasts, halved
Salt and black pepper to taste
2 tbsp olive oil
1 red onion, thinly sliced

½ cup mixed bell pepper strips
2 garlic cloves, minced
1 tbsp capers, rinsed
3 tbsp fresh basil, chopped

2 tbsp balsamic vinegar
½ tsp red pepper flakes

Warm olive oil in a skillet over medium heat. Season the chicken with salt and pepper. Sear chicken for 4-5 minutes on each side until golden brown; remove to a plate. Sauté the onion, garlic, and peppers in the same skillet for 3-4 minutes until soft, stirring often. Stir in vinegar and red pepper flakes. Return the chicken and add the capers. Cover and reduce the heat. Simmer for about 6 minutes until the chicken is cooked through. Serve hot topped with basil.

400. Chicken Rolls with Spinach & Ricotta

Serves: 4 | Ready in about: 55 minutes

2 tbsp olive oil
4 chicken breast halves
1 lb baby spinach

2 garlic cloves, minced
1 lemon, zested
½ cup crumbled ricotta cheese

1 tbsp pine nuts, toasted
Salt and black pepper to taste

Preheat your oven to 350 F. Pound the chicken breasts to ½-inch thickness with a meat mallet and season with salt and pepper. Warm olive oil in a pan over medium heat and sauté spinach for 4-5 minutes until it wilts. Stir in garlic, salt, lemon zest, and pepper for 20-30 seconds. Let cool slightly and add in ricotta cheese and pine nuts; mix well. Spoon the mixture over the chicken breasts, wrap around the filling, and secure the ends with toothpicks. Arrange the breasts on a greased baking dish and bake for 35-40 minutes. Let sit for a few minutes and slice. Serve immediately.

401. One-Pan Eggplant & Chicken

Serves: 4 | Ready in about: 40 minutes

2 tbsp olive oil
1 lb eggplants, cubed
Salt and black pepper to taste
1 onion, chopped

2 garlic cloves, minced
1 tsp hot paprika
1 tbsp oregano, chopped
1 cup chicken stock

1 lb chicken breasts, cubed
1 cup half and half
3 tsp toasted chopped almonds

Warm olive oil in a skillet over medium heat and sauté chicken for 8 minutes, stirring often. Mix in eggplants, onion, and garlic and cook for another 5 minutes. Season with salt, pepper, hot paprika, and oregano and pour in the stock. Bring to a boil and simmer for 16 minutes. Stir in half and half for 2 minutes. Serve topped with almonds.

402.   Luscious Tomato Chicken

Serves: 4 | Ready in about: 90 minutes

3 tbsp olive oil
1 (32-oz) can diced tomatoes
4 chicken breast halves
2 whole cloves

¼ cup chicken broth
2 tbsp tomato paste
¼ tsp chili flakes
1 tsp ground allspice

½ tsp dried mint
1 cinnamon stick
Salt and black pepper to taste

Place the tomatoes, chicken broth, olive oil, tomato paste, chili flakes, mint, allspice, cloves, cinnamon stick, salt, and pepper in a pot over medium heat and bring just to a boil. Then, lower the heat and simmer for 30 minutes. Strain the sauce through a fine-mesh sieve and discard the cloves and cinnamon stick. Let it cool completely. Preheat oven to 350 F. Lay the chicken on a baking dish and pour the sauce over. Bake covered with aluminum foil for 40-45 minutes. Uncover and continue baking for 5 more minutes. Serve and enjoy!

403.   Peppery Chicken Sausages

Serves: 4 | Ready in about: 30 minutes

2 tbsp olive oil
4 chicken sausage links
2 garlic cloves, minced

1 onion, thinly sliced
1 red bell pepper, sliced
1 green bell pepper, sliced

½ cup dry white wine
Salt and black pepper to taste
½ dried chili pepper, minced

Warm olive oil in a pan over medium heat and brown the sausages for 6 minutes, turning periodically. Set aside. In the same pan, sauté onion and bell peppers and garlic for 5 minutes until tender. Deglaze with the wine and stir in salt, pepper, and chili. Simmer for 4 minutes until the sauce reduces by half. Serve sausages topped with bell peppers.

404.   Piquant Chicken Pot

Serves: 4 | Ready in about: 30 minutes

1 lb chicken thighs, skinless and boneless
2 tbsp olive oil
1 onion, chopped
2 garlic cloves, minced

1 tsp smoked paprika
1 tsp chili powder
½ tsp fennel seeds, ground

2 tsp oregano, dried
14 oz canned tomatoes, diced
½ cup capers

Warm olive oil in a skillet over medium heat and sauté the onion, garlic, paprika, chili powder, fennel seeds, and oregano for 3 minutes. Put in chicken, tomatoes, 1 cup of water, and capers. Bring to a boil and simmer for 20-25 minutes.

405.   Chicken Breasts with Spinach Pesto Topping

Serves: 4 | Ready in about: 25 minutes

¼ cup + 1 tbsp olive oil
4 chicken breasts
1 cup spinach

¼ cup grated Pecorino cheese
Salt and black pepper to taste
¼ cup pine nuts

1 garlic clove, minced

Rub the chicken with salt and black pepper. Grease a grill pan with 1 tbsp of olive oil and place over medium heat. Grill the chicken for 8-10 minutes, flipping once. Mix spinach, garlic, Pecorino cheese, and pine nuts in a food processor. Slowly pour in the remaining oil; pulse until smooth. Spoon 1 tbsp of pesto on each breast and cook for 5 minutes.

406.   Herby Chicken Roast

Serves: 4 | Ready in about: 80 minutes

2 tbsp butter, melted
1 (3 ½-lb) chicken
2 lemons, halved

4 rosemary sprigs
1 bay leaf
6 thyme sprigs

1 tsp lemon juice
Salt and black pepper to taste

Preheat oven to 430 F and fit a rack into a roasting tray. Brush the chicken with butter on all sides. Put the lemons, herbs, and bay leaf inside the cavity. Drizzle with lemon juice and sprinkle with salt and pepper. Roast for 60-65 minutes. Let rest for 10 minutes before carving.

407. Pappardelle with Chicken & Mushrooms

Serves: 4 | Ready in about: 30 minutes

4 oz cremini mushrooms, sliced
2 tbsp olive oil
½ onion, minced
2 garlic cloves, minced

8 oz chicken breasts, cubed
2 tsp tomato paste
2 tsp dried tarragon
2 cups chicken stock

6 oz pappardelle pasta
¼ cup Greek yogurt
Salt and black pepper to taste
¼ tsp red pepper flakes

Warm 1 tbsp of olive oil in a pan over medium heat. Suté the onion, garlic, and mushrooms for 5 minutes. Move the vegetables to the edges of the pan and add the remaining 1 tablespoon of olive oil to the center of the pan. Place the chicken cubes in the center and let them cook for about 6 minutes, stirring often until golden brown. Mix in the tomato paste and tarragon. Add the chicken stock and stir well to combine everything. Bring the mixture to a boil. Add the pappardelle. Simmer covered for 9-11 minutes, stirring occasionally, until the pasta is cooked and the liquid is mostly absorbed. Remove the pan from the heat. Stir 2 tbsp of the hot liquid from the pan into the yogurt. Pour the tempered yogurt into the pan and stir well to mix it into the sauce. Season with salt and pepper. Top with pepper flakes.

408. Roasted Artichokes & Chicken Thighs

Serves: 4 | Ready in about: 25 minutes

2 artichoke hearts, halved lengthwise
2 tbsp butter, melted

3 tbsp olive oil
2 lemons, zested and juiced

½ tsp salt
4 chicken thighs

Preheat your oven to 450 F. Place a large, rimmed baking sheet in the oven. Whisk the olive oil, lemon zest, and lemon juice in a bowl. Add the artichoke hearts and turn them to coat on all sides. Lay the artichoke halves flat-side down in the center of 4 aluminum foil sheets and close up loosely to create packets. Put the chicken in the remaining lemon mixture and toss to coat. Carefully remove the hot baking sheet from the oven and pour on the butter; tilt the pan to coat. Arrange the chicken thighs, skin-side down, on the sheet, add the artichoke packets. Roast for about 20 minutes or until the chicken is cooked through and the skin is slightly charred. Check the artichokes for doneness and bake for another 5 minutes if needed. Serve and enjoy!

409. Caprese-Style Stuffed Chicken Breasts

Serves: 4 | Ready in about: 40 minutes

4 oz fresh mozzarella cheese, shredded
5 tbsp olive oil
2 chicken breasts
1 cup spinach, torn

¼ cup fresh basil, chopped
6 sundried tomatoes, diced
Salt and black pepper to taste
1 tbsp rosemary, chopped

½ tsp garlic powder
1 tbsp balsamic vinegar

Preheat oven to 370 F. In a bowl, mix the spinach, cheese, basil, sun-dried tomatoes, salt, pepper, rosemary, and garlic powder. Cut a pocket in each chicken breast and stuff it with the filling. Press the opening together with your fingers. Warm 2 tablespoons olive oil in a medium skillet over medium heat. Carefully sear the chicken breasts for 3-4 minutes on each side until lightly golden. Transfer to a greased baking dish, incision-side up. Cover with foil and bake for 30-40 minutes until the chicken is cooked through. Remove from the oven and let it sit covered for 10 minutes. In a small bowl, whisk together the remaining 3 tablespoons of olive oil, balsamic vinegar, salt, and pepper. Cut the chicken breasts in half. Serve drizzled with balsamic vinaigrette.

410. Herbed Tomato Chicken

Serves: 4 | Ready in about: 50 minutes

2 tbsp olive oil
1 lb chicken breasts, sliced
1 onion, chopped
1 carrot, chopped

2 garlic cloves, minced
½ cup chicken stock
1 tsp oregano, dried
1 tsp tarragon, dried

1 tsp rosemary, dried
1 cup canned tomatoes, diced
Salt and black pepper to taste

Warm olive oil in a pot over medium heat and cook the chicken for 8 minutes on both sides. Put in carrot, garlic, and onion and cook for an additional 3 minutes. Season with salt and pepper. Pour in the stock, oregano, tarragon, rosemary, and tomatoes and bring to a boil; simmer for 25 minutes. Serve.

411. Juicy Chicken Breasts

Serves: 4 | Ready in about: 30 minutes

1 cup canned cream of onion soup
2 tbsp olive oil
1 lb chicken breasts, cubed
½ tsp dried basil

½ cup flour
½ cup white wine
1 cup heavy cream
4 garlic cloves, minced

¼ tsp chili flakes, crushed
Salt and black pepper to taste
2 tbsp parsley, chopped

In a large bowl, combine salt, black pepper, chili flakes, basil, and flour. Add in chicken and toss to coat. Warm the olive oil in a skillet over medium heat. Add in the chicken and cook for 5 minutes, stirring occasionally. Pour in the white wine to scrape any bits from the bottom. Stir in garlic, onion soup, and ½ cup of water. Bring to a boil, then lower the heat, and simmer covered for 15-18 minutes. Stir in heavy cream, top with parsley and chili flakes; serve.

412. Chicken Breasts with Mushrooms

Serves: 4 | Ready in about: 40 minutes

2 tbsp olive oil
4 chicken breasts, cubed
1 onion, chopped
2 garlic cloves, minced

1 celery stalk chopped
Salt and black pepper to taste
1 tbsp thyme, chopped
3 cups chicken stock

1 cup Bella mushrooms, sliced
1 cup heavy cream
2 tbsp chives, chopped
1 tbsp parsley, chopped

Warm olive oil in a pot over medium heat and cook onion and garlic for 3 minutes. Put in chicken and mushrooms and cook for another 10 minutes, stirring occasionally. Stir in celery, salt, pepper, thyme, and stock and bring to a boil; cook for 15 minutes. Stir in heavy cream for 3-4 minutes. Sprinkle with chives and parsley. Serve and enjoy!

413. Super Easy Chicken & Spinach Dish

Serves: 4 | Ready in about: 60 minutes

2 tbsp olive oil
2 cups baby spinach
1 lb chicken sausage, sliced

1 red bell pepper, chopped
1 onion, sliced
2 tbsp garlic, minced

Salt and black pepper to taste
½ cup chicken stock
1 tbsp balsamic vinegar

Preheat your oven to 380 F. Warm olive oil in a skillet over medium heat. Cook sausages for 6 minutes on all sides. Remove to a bowl. Add the bell pepper, onion, garlic, salt, and pepper to the skillet and sauté for 5 minutes. Pour in stock and vinegar and return the sausages. Bring to a boil and cook for 10 minutes. Add in the spinach and cook until it wilts, about 4 minutes. Serve and enjoy!

414. Buttery Chicken Roast

Serves: 4 | Ready in about: 65 minutes

1 tbsp butter, softened
1 lb chicken drumsticks
2 garlic cloves, minced

1 tsp paprika
1 lemon, zested
1 tbsp chopped fresh thyme

Salt and black pepper to taste

Preheat oven to 360 F. Mix butter, thyme, paprika, salt, garlic, pepper, and lemon zest in a bowl. Rub the mixture over the chicken drumsticks and arrange them on a baking dish. Add ½ cup of water and roast in the oven for 50-60 minutes. Remove the chicken from the oven and let it sit covered with foil for 10 minutes. Serve and enjoy!

415. Chicken & Veggie Casserole

Serves: 4 | Ready in about: 50 minutes

4 fresh prunes, cored and quartered
2 tbsp olive oil
4 chicken legs

1 lb baby potatoes, halved
1 carrot, julienned
2 tbsp chopped fresh parsley

Salt and black pepper to taste

Preheat oven to 430 F. Combine potatoes, carrot, prunes, olive oil, salt, and pepper in a bowl. Transfer to a baking dish. Top with chicken. Season with salt and pepper. Roast for about 40-45 minutes. Serve topped with parsley.

416. Fantastic Turkey Breast

Serves: 4 | Ready in about:1 hour 40 minutes +chilling time

2 tbsp olive oil
1 lb turkey breast
2 garlic cloves, minced
½ cup chicken broth

1 lemon, zested
¼ tsp dried thyme
¼ tsp dried tarragon
½ tsp red pepper flakes

2 tbsp chopped fresh parsley
1 tsp ground mustard
Salt and black pepper to taste

Preheat oven to 320 F. Mix the olive oil, garlic, lemon zest, thyme, tarragon, red pepper flakes, mustard, salt, and pepper in a bowl. Rub the breast with the mixture until well coated and transfer onto a roasting pan skin-side up. Pour in the chicken broth. Roast in the oven for 60-90 minutes. Allow to sit for 10 minutes covered with foil, then remove from the roasting tin and carve. Serve topped with parsley.

417. Chicken & Asparagus Skillet

Serves: 4 | Ready in about: 30 minutes

2 tbsp olive oil
1 lb chicken breasts, sliced
Salt and black pepper to taste

1 lb asparagus, chopped
6 sundried tomatoes, diced
3 tbsp capers, drained

2 tbsp lemon juice

Warm olive oil in a skillet over medium heat. Cook asparagus, tomatoes, salt, pepper, capers, and lemon juice for 10 minutes. Remove to a bowl. Brown chicken in the same skillet for 8 minutes on both sides. Put veggies back into the skillet and cook for another 2-3 minutes. Serve and enjoy!

418. Baked Peppery Chicken

Serves: 4 | Ready in about: 70 minutes

3 tbsp olive oil
1 lb chicken breasts, sliced
2 lb cherry tomatoes, halved

1 onion, chopped
3 garlic cloves, minced
3 red chili peppers, chopped

½ lemon, zested
Salt and black pepper to taste

Warm olive oil in a skillet over medium heat and brown chicken for 8 minutes on both sides. Remove to a roasting pan. In the same skillet, add onion, garlic, and chili peppers and cook for 2 minutes. Pour the mixture over the chicken and toss to coat. Add in tomatoes, lemon zest, 1 cup of water, salt, and pepper. Bake for 45 minutes. Serve.

419. Glazed Chicken Drumsticks

Serves: 4 | Ready in about: 35 minutes

2 tbsp olive oil
8 chicken drumsticks, skinless
3 peaches, peeled and chopped

¼ cup honey
¼ cup cider vinegar
1 sweet onion, chopped

1 tsp minced fresh rosemary
Salt to taste

Warm olive oil in a large skillet over medium heat. Sprinkle chicken with salt and pepper and brown it for about 7 minutes per side. Remove to a plate. Add onion and rosemary to the skillet and sauté for 1 minute or until lightly golden. Add honey, vinegar, salt, and peaches and cook for 10-12 minutes or until peaches are softened. Add the chicken back to the skillet and heat just until warm, brushing with the sauce. Serve chicken thighs with peach sauce.

420. Zucchini & Chicken Stir-Fry

Serves: 4 | Ready in about: 40 minutes

2 tbsp olive oil
2 cups tomatoes, crushed
1 lb chicken breasts, cubed

Salt and black pepper to taste
2 shallots, sliced
3 garlic cloves, minced

2 zucchini, sliced
2 tbsp thyme, chopped
1 cup chicken stock

Warm olive oil in a skillet over medium heat. Sear chicken for 6 minutes, stirring occasionally. Add in shallots and garlic and cook for another 4 minutes. Stir in tomatoes, salt, pepper, zucchini, and stock and bring to a boil; simmer for 20 minutes. Garnish with thyme and serve.

421.   Cheesy Chicken Caprese

Serves: 4 | Ready in about: 50 minutes

1 tsp garlic powder
½ cup basil pesto

4 chicken breast halves
3 tomatoes, sliced

1 cup mozzarella, shredded
Salt and black pepper to taste

Preheat the oven to 400 F. Line a baking dish with parchment paper and grease with cooking spray. Combine chicken, garlic powder, salt, pepper, and pesto in a bowl and arrange them on the sheet. Top with tomatoes and mozzarella and bake for 40 minutes. Serve hot.

422.   Juicy Chicken Breasts

Serves: 4 | Ready in about: 30 minutes

2 tbsp olive oil
2 cups peaches, cubed
1 tbsp smoked paprika

1 lb chicken breasts, cubed
2 cups chicken broth
Salt and black pepper to taste

1 tbsp chives, chopped

Warm olive oil in a skillet over medium heat and sauté chicken, salt, and pepper for 8 minutes, stirring occasionally. Stir in peaches, paprika, and chicken broth and cook for another 15 minutes. Serve topped with chives.

423.   Walnut Chicken with Tomatoes

Serves: 4 | Ready in about: 35 minutes

2 tbsp olive oil
1 lb chicken breast halves
Salt and black pepper to taste

2 tbsp walnuts, chopped
1 tbsp chives, chopped
½ cup tomato sauce

½ cup chicken stock

Warm olive oil in a skillet over medium heat and cook chicken for 8 minutes, flipping once. Season with salt and pepper. Stir in walnuts, tomato sauce, and stock and bring to a boil. Cook for 16 minutes. Serve sprinkled with chives.

424.   Cheesy Chicken Breasts

Serves: 4 | Ready in about: 35 minutes

1 tbsp olive oil
1 ½ lb chicken breasts, cubed
1 tsp ground coriander

1 tsp parsley flakes
2 garlic cloves, minced
1 cup heavy cream

Salt and black pepper to taste
¼ cup Parmesan cheese, grated
1 tbsp basil, chopped

Warm olive oil in a skillet over medium heat and brown chicken, salt, and pepper for 6 minutes on all sides. Add in garlic and cook for another minute. Stir in coriander, parsley, and cream and cook for an additional 20 minutes. Serve scattered with basil and Parmesan cheese.

425.   Tasty Chicken with Bell Peppers

Serves: 4 | Ready in about: 65 minutes

2 tbsp olive oil
2 lb chicken breasts, cubed
2 garlic cloves, minced

1 red onion, chopped
2 red bell peppers, chopped
¼ tsp cumin, ground

2 cups corn
½ cup chicken stock
1 tsp chili powder

Warm olive oil in a skillet over medium heat and sear chicken for 8 minutes on both sides. Put in onion and garlic and cook for another 5 minutes. Stir in bell peppers, cumin, corn, stock, and chili powder. Cook for 45 minutes. Serve.

426.   Tangy Green Pea & Chicken

Serves: 4 | Ready in about: 35 minutes

2 tbsp olive oil
1 lb chicken breasts, halved
1 tsp chili powder
Salt and black pepper to taste

1 tsp garlic powder
1 tbsp smoked paprika
½ cup chicken stock
2 tsp sherry vinegar

3 tsp hot sauce
2 tsp cumin, ground
1 cup green peas
1 carrot, chopped

Warm olive oil in a skillet over medium heat and cook chicken for 6 minutes on both sides. Sprinkle with chili powder, salt, pepper, garlic powder, and paprika. Pour in the chicken stock, vinegar, hot sauce, cumin, carrot, and green peas and bring to a boil; cook for an additional 15 minutes.

427.   Chicken-Mushroom Piccata

Serves: 4 | Ready in about: 25 minutes

3 tbsp olive oil
2 tbsp butter
1 lb chicken breasts, sliced
Salt and black pepper to taste

¼ cup ground flaxseed
2 tbsp almond flour
2 cups mushrooms, sliced
½ cup white wine

¼ cup lemon juice
¼ cup capers, chopped
¼ cup parsley, chopped
16 oz cooked spaghetti

Combine ground flaxseed, almond flour, salt, and pepper in a bowl. Coat the chicken with the mixture. Warm the olive oil in a large skillet over medium heat. Sear the chicken for 3-4 minutes per side until golden; reserve. Add the butter to the skillet and sauté the mushrooms and for 5-7 minutes. Pour in the white wine, lemon juice, capers, and salt and bring to a boil, whisking to incorporate any little browned bits that have stuck to the bottom of the skillet. Lower the heat to low and return the browned chicken. Cover and simmer for 5 more minutes until the sauce thickens. Place the spaghetti on a serving platter and spoon the chicken and mushrooms on top. Garnish with parsley.

428.   Chicken & Bean Bake

Serves: 4 | Ready in about: 40 minutes

1 ½ lb skinless, boneless chicken thighs, cubed
½ cup canned artichokes, drained and chopped
2 tbsp olive oil
2 garlic cloves, minced
1 tbsp oregano, chopped

2 shallots, sliced
1 tsp paprika
1 cup canned white beans

½ cup parsley, chopped
1 cup mozzarella, shredded
Salt and black pepper to taste

Preheat oven to 390 F. Warm the olive oil in a skillet over medium heat and sauté the chicken for 5 minutes. Transfer to a baking pan and garlic, oregano, artichokes, paprika, shallots, beans, parsley, salt, and pepper. Top with mozzarella cheese and bake for 25 minutes.

429.   Chicken Sausage Stew with Farro

Serves: 2 | Ready in about: 55 minutes

8 oz hot Italian chicken sausage, removed from the casing
1 tbsp olive oil
½ onion, diced
1 garlic clove, minced

8 sundried tomatoes, diced
½ cup farro
1 cup chicken stock

2 cups arugula
5 fresh basil, sliced thin

Warm olive oil in a pan over medium heat. Sauté the onion and garlic for 5 minutes. Add the sun-dried tomatoes and chicken sausage, stirring to break up the sausage. Cook for 7 minutes or until the sausage is no longer pink. Stir in the farro for about 2 minutes. Add the chicken stock and bring the mixture to a boil. Cover the pan and reduce the heat to low. Simmer for 30 minutes or until the farro is tender. Stir in arugula and let it wilt slightly, 2 minutes. Sprinkle with basil and serve.

430.   Hazelnut Chicken Breasts with Parmesan

Serves: 4 | Ready in about: 65 minutes

2 tbsp canola oil
1 lb chicken breasts, halved
½ tsp hot paprika
1 cup chicken stock

2 tbsp hazelnuts, chopped
2 spring onions, chopped
2 garlic cloves, minced
¼ cup Parmesan cheese, grated

2 tbsp cilantro, chopped
2 tbsp parsley, chopped
Salt and black pepper to taste

Preheat your oven to 370 F. Combine chicken, canola oil, hot paprika, stock, hazelnuts, spring onions, garlic, salt, and pepper in a greased baking pan and bake for 40 minutes. Sprinkle with Parmesan cheese and bake for an additional 5 minutes until the cheese melts. Top with cilantro and parsley.

431. Potato & Carrot Chicken Bake

Serves: 4 | Ready in about: 60 minutes

2 tbsp olive oil
1 lb chicken breasts, cubed
1 carrot, chopped
2 garlic cloves, minced

Salt and black pepper to taste
2 tsp thyme, dried
1 lb baby potatoes, halved
1 onion, sliced

¾ cup chicken stock
2 tbsp basil, chopped

Preheat oven to 380 F. Grease a baking dish with oil. Put carrot, potatoes, chicken, garlic, salt, pepper, thyme, onion, stock, and basil in the dish and bake for 50 minutes. Serve and enjoy!

432. Prune & Shallot Chicken Stew

Serves: 4 | Ready in about: 50 minutes

2 tbsp olive oil
3 garlic cloves, minced
3 tbsp cilantro, chopped

Salt and black pepper to taste
2 cups chicken stock
2 shallots, thinly sliced

1 lb chicken breasts, cubed
5 oz dried pitted prunes, halved

Warm olive oil in a pot over medium heat and cook shallots and garlic for 3 minutes. Add in chicken breasts and cook for another 5 minutes, stirring occasionally. Pour in chicken stock and prunes and season with salt and pepper. Cook for 30 minutes. Garnish with cilantro and serve.

433. Artichoke Chicken with Lentils

Serves: 4 | Ready in about: 50 minutes

2 tbsp olive oil
4 chicken breasts, halved
1 lemon, juiced and zested
2 garlic cloves, crushed

1 tbsp thyme, chopped
6 oz canned artichokes hearts
1 cup canned lentils, drained
1 cup chicken stock

1 tsp cayenne pepper
Salt and black pepper to taste

Warm olive oil in a skillet over medium heat and cook chicken for 5-6 minutes until browned, flipping once. Mix in lemon zest, garlic, lemon juice, salt, pepper, thyme, artichokes, lentils, stock, and cayenne pepper and bring to a boil. Cook for 35 minutes. Serve immediately.

434. Farro & Carrot Chicken

Serves: 4 | Ready in about: 50 minutes

2 tbsp olive oil
3 carrots, chopped
1 cup farro, soaked
1 lb chicken breasts, cubed

1 red onion, chopped
4 garlic cloves, minced
2 tbsp dill, chopped
2 tbsp tomato paste

2 cups vegetable stock
Salt and black pepper to taste

Warm olive oil in a pressure cooker on Sauté mode and sear the chicken for 10 minutes on all sides, stirring occasionally. Remove to a plate. Add onion, garlic, and carrots to the cooker and sauté for 3 minutes. Stir in tomato paste, farro, and vegetable stock and return the chicken. Seal the lid, select Pressure Cook, and cook for 30 minutes on High. Do a natural pressure release for 10 minutes. Adjust the taste with salt and pepper. Sprinkle with dill and serve.

435. Almond Chicken Balls

Serves: 4 | Ready in about: 30 minutes

2 tbsp olive oil
1 lb ground chicken
2 tsp toasted chopped almonds
1 egg, whisked

2 tsp turmeric powder
2 garlic cloves, minced
Salt and black pepper to taste
1 ¼ cups heavy cream

¼ cup parsley, chopped
1 tbsp chives, chopped

Place the ground chicken, almonds, egg, turmeric powder, garlic, salt, pepper, parsley, and chives in a bowl and toss to combine. Form meatballs out of the mixture. Warm olive oil in a skillet over medium heat. Brown meatballs for 8 minutes on all sides. Stir in cream and cook for another 10 minutes.

436.   Juicy Almond Turkey

Serves: 4 | Ready in about: 40 minutes

2 tbsp canola oil
¼ cup almonds, chopped
1 lb turkey breast, sliced

Salt and black pepper to taste
1 lemon, juiced and zested
1 grapefruit, juiced

1 tbsp rosemary, chopped
3 garlic cloves, minced
1 cup chicken stock

Warm olive oil in a skillet over medium heat and cook garlic and turkey for 8 minutes on both sides. Stir in salt, pepper, lemon juice, lemon zest, grapefruit juice, rosemary, almonds, and stock and bring to a boil. Cook for 20 minutes.

437.   Succulent Grilled Chicken Breasts

Serves: 4 | Ready in about: 25 minutes + marinating time

½ cup olive oil
2 tbsp rosemary, chopped
2 tbsp parsley, chopped

1 tsp minced garlic
1 lemon, zested and juiced
Salt and black pepper to taste

4 chicken breasts
2 tsp basil, chopped

Combine olive oil, rosemary, garlic, lemon juice, lemon zest, parsley, salt, and pepper in a plastic bag. Add the chicken and shake to coat. Refrigerate for 2 hours. Heat your grill to medium heat. Remove the chicken breasts from the marinade and grill them for 6-8 minutes per side. Pour the marinade into a saucepan, add 2 tbsp of water and simmer for 2-3 minutes until the sauce thickens. Sprinkle with basil and serve the grilled chicken. Enjoy!

438.   Chicken Mushroom-Barley Soup

Serves: 6 | Ready in about: 10 minutes

3 tbsp olive oil
1 lb chicken breasts, chopped
1 onion, chopped
1 cup carrots, chopped

½ cup celery, chopped
1 cup mushrooms, chopped
6 cups vegetable broth
1 cup pearl barley

2 tbsp tomato paste
½ tsp dried thyme
½ cup Parmesan cheese

Warm olive oil in a large stockpot over medium heat. Add the chicken, onion, celery, and carrots and cook for 5 minutes, stirring frequently. Add the mushrooms and cook for 3 minutes until tender. Pour in the broth, barley, tomato paste, and thyme. Bring the soup to a boil. Simmer for another 15-18 minutes until the barley is cooked through. Top with cheese and serve.

439.   Penne with Turkey & Asparagus

Serves: 4 | Ready in about: 40 minutes

3 tbsp olive oil
16 oz penne pasta
1 lb turkey breast strips

1 lb asparagus, chopped
1 tsp basil, chopped
Salt and black pepper to taste

½ cup tomato sauce
2 tbsp cilantro, chopped

Bring to a boil salted water in a large pot over medium heat and cook penne until "al dente", 8-9 minutes. Drain and set aside; reserve 1 cup of the cooking water. Warm the olive oil in a skillet over medium heat and sear turkey for 4 minutes, stirring periodically. Add in asparagus and sauté for 3-4 more minutes. Pour in the tomato sauce and reserved pasta liquid and bring to a boil; simmer for 20 minutes. Stir in cooked penne, season with salt and pepper, and top with the basil and cilantro to serve.

440.   Rosemary Turkey Pot

Serves: 4 | Ready in about: 8 hours 10 minutes

2 tbsp capers, drained
1 lb turkey breast, sliced
2 cups canned tomatoes, diced

2 garlic cloves, minced
1 yellow onion, chopped
2 cups chicken stock

¼ cup rosemary, chopped
Salt and black pepper to taste

Place the turkey, tomatoes, garlic, onion, chicken stock, capers, rosemary, salt, and pepper in your slow cooker. Cover with the lid and cook for 8 hours on Low. Serve warm.

441. Asparagus & Artichoke Turkey Dish

Serves: 4 | Ready in about: 40 minutes

3 tbsp olive oil
1 lb asparagus, halved
1 lb turkey breast, sliced
1 cup chicken stock

Salt and black pepper to taste
1 cup canned artichoke hearts
2 tomatoes, chopped
10 Kalamata olives, sliced

1 shallot, chopped
3 garlic cloves, minced
3 tbsp dill, chopped

Warm olive oil in a pot over medium heat and cook turkey and garlic for 8 minutes or until the meat is golden brown. Stir in the asparagus, chopped tomatoes, chicken stock, salt, black pepper, artichoke hearts, Kalamata olives, and shallot and bring to a boil. Lower the heat and simmer for 20 minutes. Garnish with dill and serve.

442. Classic Turkey Stew

Serves: 4 | Ready in about: 60 minutes

1 skinless, boneless turkey breast, cubed
2 tbsp olive oil
Salt and black pepper to taste
1 tbsp sweet paprika
½ cup chicken stock

1 lb pearl onions
2 garlic cloves, minced
1 carrot, sliced
1 tsp cumin, ground

1 tbsp basil, chopped
1 tbsp cilantro, chopped

Warm olive oil in a pot over medium heat and sear turkey for 8 minutes, stirring occasionally. Stir in pearl onions, carrot, and garlic and cook for another 3 minutes. Season with salt, pepper, cumin, and paprika. Pour in the stock and bring to a boil; cook for 40 minutes. Top with basil and cilantro.

443. Pistachio Turkey Breasts

Serves: 4 | Ready in about: 50 minutes

½ cup toasted pistachios, chopped
1 tbsp olive oil
1 lb turkey breast, cubed
1 cup chicken stock

1 tbsp basil, chopped
1 tbsp rosemary, chopped
1 tbsp oregano, chopped
1 tbsp parsley, chopped

1 tbsp tarragon, chopped
3 garlic cloves, minced
3 cups tomatoes, chopped

Warm olive oil in a skillet over medium heat and cook turkey and garlic for 5 minutes. Stir in stock, basil, rosemary, oregano, parsley, tarragon, pistachios, and tomatoes and bring to a simmer. Cook for 35 minutes. Serve immediately.

444. Turkey Vegetable Traybake

Serves: 4 | Ready in about: 80 minutes

2 tbsp olive oil
1 lb turkey breast, cubed
1 head broccoli, cut into florets

2 oz cherry tomatoes, halved
2 tbsp cilantro, chopped
1 lemon, zested

Salt and black pepper to taste
2 spring onions, chopped

Preheat oven to 360 F. Warm the olive oil in a skillet over medium heat and sauté spring onions and lemon zest for 3 minutes. Add in turkey and cook for another 5-6 minutes, stirring occasionally. Transfer to a baking dish, pour in 1 cup of water and bake for 30 minutes. Add in broccoli and tomatoes and bake for another 10 minutes. Top with cilantro.

445. Turkey Bake with Cranberries

Serves: 4 | Ready in about: 40 minutes

2 tbsp canola oil
1 turkey breast, sliced
1 cup chicken stock

½ cup cranberry sauce
½ cup orange juice
1 tsp mustard powder

1 onion, chopped
Salt and black pepper to taste

Warm the canola oil in a saucepan over medium heat. Cook onion for 3 minutes. Put in turkey and cook for another 5 minutes, turning once. Season with mustard powder, salt, and pepper. Pour in the cranberry sauce, chicken stock, and orange juice and bring to a boil; simmer for 20 minutes.

446.   Turkey with Ricotta Cheese

Serves: 4 | Ready in about: 60 minutes

2 tbsp olive oil
1 turkey breast, cubed

1 ½ cups salsa verde
Salt and black pepper to taste

4 oz ricotta cheese, crumbled
2 tbsp cilantro, chopped

Preheat oven to 380 F. Grease a roasting pan with oil. In a bowl, place turkey, salsa verde, salt, and pepper and toss to coat. Transfer to the roasting pan and bake for 50 minutes. Top with ricotta cheese and cilantro and serve.

447.   Olive & Bell Pepper Turkey Breasts

Serves: 4 | Ready in about: 70 minutes

4 mixed bell peppers, chopped
1 lb turkey breast strips
2 leeks, chopped

4 garlic cloves, minced
½ cup black olives, sliced
2 cups chicken stock

1 tbsp oregano, chopped
½ cup cilantro, chopped

Preheat oven to 380 F. Put leeks, bell peppers, garlic, olives, stock, turkey, oregano, and cilantro in a baking pan and roast for 1 hour. Serve right away.

448.   Oven-Baked Turkey with Veggies

Serves: 4 | Ready in about: 70 minutes

2 tbsp olive oil
1 lb turkey breasts, sliced
¼ cup chicken stock

1 carrot, chopped
1 red onion, chopped
2 mixed bell peppers, chopped

Salt and black pepper to taste
1 tbsp cilantro, chopped

Preheat your oven to 380 F. Grease a roasting pan with olive oil. Combine turkey, stock, carrots, bell peppers, onion, salt, and pepper in the pan and bake for 1 hour. Top with cilantro.

449.   Avocado & Chicken Salad

Serves: 4 | Ready in about: 10 minutes

1 cup cooked chicken breasts, chopped
½ cup marinated artichoke hearts
2 tbsp olive oil
6 sundried tomatoes, chopped
1 cucumber, chopped
6 black olives, 6 sliced
2 cups Iceberg lettuce, torn

2 tbsp parsley, chopped
1 avocado, peeled and cubed
½ cup ricotta cheese, crumbled
4 tbsp red wine vinegar
2 tbsp Dijon mustard
1 tsp basil, dried

1 garlic clove, minced
2 tsp honey
Salt and black pepper to taste
3 tbsp lemon juice

Mix the chicken, tomatoes, artichokes, cucumber, olives, lettuce, parsley, and avocado in a bowl. In a separate bowl, whisk vinegar, mustard, basil, garlic, honey, olive oil, salt, pepper, and lemon juice and pour over the salad. Mix well. Top with cheese and serve.

450.   Cannellini Beans with Turkey

Serves: 4 | Ready in about: 50 minutes

1 (28-oz) can Cannellini beans
2 tbsp olive oil, divided
1 lb turkey breast, cubed
Salt and black pepper to taste

2 garlic cloves, minced
1 large onion, diced
1 celery stalk, chopped
1 cup tomatoes, chopped

1 carrot, chopped
⅓ cup tomato paste
1 tsp paprika
1 tsp dried oregano

Warm olive oil in a pot over medium heat. Season the turkey with salt and pepper and sauté for 3-4 minutes until brown, stirring occasionally. Stir in the onion, celery, tomatoes, and carrots and cook for 4-5 minutes. Add the paprika and tomato paste and stir to combine. Pour in the beans and 2 cups water. Bring the mixture to a boil and simmer for 20-25 minutes until the turkey is cooked. Season with salt, pepper, and oregano and serve.

PORK, BEEF & LAMB

451.   Glazed Pork Skewers

Serves: 6 | Ready in about: 50 minutes

2 lb pork tenderloin, cubed
1 cup apricot jam

½ cup apricot nectar
1 cup dried whole apricots

2 onions, cut into wedges
½ tsp dried rosemary

Coat the cubes with apricot jam, cover, and set aside for 10-15 minutes. Bring the apricot nectar, rosemary, and dried apricots to a boil over medium heat. Lower the heat and simmer for 2-3 minutes. Remove the apricots with a perforated spoon and pour the hot liquid over the pork. Stir and drain the pork, reserving the marinade. Preheat your grill to medium-high. Alternate pork cubes, onion wedges, and apricots onto 6 metal skewers. Brush them with some marinade and grill for 10-12 minutes, turning and brushing with some more marinade until the pork is slightly pink, and the onions are crisp-tender. Simmer the remaining marinade for 3-5 minutes. Serve the skewers with marinade on the side.

452.   Tender Pork Chops

Serves: 6 | Ready in about: 20 minutes

2 tbsp butter
3 tbsp olive oil
6 pork chops, boneless

2 fresh eggs
2 tbsp chicken stock
½ cup grated Parmesan cheese

1 cup panko bread crumbs
1 tsp Italian seasoning
½ tsp dried basil

Flatten the pork chops with a meat tenderizer. In a bowl, beat the eggs with chicken stock. Mix the Parmesan cheese, crumbs, Italian seasoning, and basil on a shallow plate. Dip each pork chop into the egg mixture, then coat with the cheese mixture. Warm the butter and olive oil in a large skillet over medium heat. Sear the pork chops for 6-8 minutes on both sides until brown and crisp. Serve immediately.

453.   Pork Chops with Red Sauce

Serves: 4 | Ready in about: 20 minutes

2 tbsp olive oil
½ tsp garlic, minced
For the Sauce:
1 cup cherry tomatoes
2 tbsp fresh basil, chopped
1 tsp rosemary

Salt and black pepper to taste
¼ cup vegetable broth

½ cup red onion, chopped
1 tsp oregano
2 tbsp olive oil

1 fennel, thinly sliced

1 garlic clove, minced
1 cayenne pepper, minced
Salt and black pepper to taste

Warm olive oil in a pan over medium heat. Sauté the garlic until aromatic. Add in the fennel, broth, salt, and pepper and cook until the fennel is just tender; remove to a plate. Puree the sauce ingredients in your food processor until smooth and creamy. Pour the sauce into a pan over medium heat and cook for 5-6 minutes. Pour the sauce over the fennel and serve.

454.   Charred Pork Chops with Apricot Chutney

Serves: 4 | Ready in about: 40 minutes

1 tbsp olive oil
½ tsp garlic powder
4 pork loin chops, boneless
For the chutney
3 cups apricots, peeled and chopped
½ cup red sweet pepper, chopped
1 tsp olive oil

Salt and black pepper to taste
¼ tsp ground cumin
½ tsp sage, dried

¼ cup shallot, minced
½ jalapeno pepper, minced
1 tbsp balsamic vinegar

1 tsp chili powder

2 tbsp cilantro, chopped

Warm olive oil in a skillet over medium heat and cook the shallot for 5 minutes. Stir in sweet pepper, apricots, jalapeño pepper, vinegar, and cilantro and cook for 10 minutes. Remove from heat. In the meantime, sprinkle pork chops with olive oil, salt, pepper, garlic powder, cumin, sage, and chili powder. Preheat the grill to medium heat. Grill pork chops for 12-14 minutes on both sides. Serve topped with apricot chutney.

455.   Green Onion Pork Loin

Serves: 4 | Ready in about: 50 minutes

2 lb pork loin roast, boneless and cubed

2 tbsp olive oil

2 garlic cloves, minced

Salt and black pepper to taste

1 cup tomato sauce

1 tsp rosemary, chopped

4 green onions, chopped

Preheat oven to 360 F. Heat olive oil in a skillet over medium heat and cook pork, garlic, and green onions for 6-7 minutes, stirring often. Add in tomato sauce, rosemary, and 1 cup of water. Season with salt and pepper. Transfer to a baking dish and bake for 40 minutes. Serve warm.

456.   Pork Chops with Pickle Topping

Serves: 4 | Ready in about: 20 minutes

½ cup roasted bell peppers, chopped

6 dill pickles, sliced

1 cup dill pickle juice

6 pork chops, boneless

Salt and black pepper to taste

1 tsp hot pepper sauce

1 ½ cups tomatoes, cubed

1 jalapeno pepper, chopped

10 black olives, sliced

Place the chops, hot sauce, and pickle juice in a bowl and marinate in the fridge for 15 minutes. Preheat your grill to High. Remove the chops from the fridge and grill them for 14 minutes on both sides. Combine dill pickles, tomatoes, jalapeño pepper, roasted peppers, and black olives in a bowl. Serve chops topped with the pickle mixture.

457.   Hot Tender Pork Shoulder

Serves: 4 | Ready in about: 2 hours 10 minutes

3 tbsp olive oil

2 lb pork shoulder

1 onion, chopped

2 tbsp garlic, minced

1 tbsp hot paprika

1 tbsp basil, chopped

1 cup chicken broth

Salt and black pepper to taste

Preheat your oven to 350 F. Heat olive oil in a skillet and brown the pork on all sides for about 8-10 minutes; remove to a baking dish. Add onion and garlic to the skillet and sauté for 3 minutes until softened. Stir in hot paprika, salt, and pepper for 1 minute and pour in chicken broth. Transfer to the baking dish, cover with aluminium foil and bake for 90 minutes. Then remove the foil and continue baking for another 20 minutes until browned on top. Let the pork cool for a few minutes. Slice and sprinkle with basil. Serve topped with the cooking juices.

458.   Chianti Pork Tenderloin

Serves: 4 | Ready in about: 30 minutes

½ cup Chianti red wine

1 tsp Mediterranean seasoning

1 cup red onions, chopped

2 garlic cloves, minced

1 Italian pepper, chopped

2 tbsp olive oil

1 tbsp Dijon mustard

1 ½ lb pork tenderloin

Rub the meat with mustard and Mediterranean seasoning. Heat the olive oil in a skillet over medium heat. Cook the tenderloin steak for 9-10 minutes per side. Sauté the onion, garlic, and Italian pepper for 3 to 4 minutes more until they've softened. Add in red wine to scrape up any browned bits from the bottom of the skillet. Continue to cook until the cooking liquid has thickened and reduced by half. Slice the tenderloin and serve topped with the sauce.

459.   Effortless Pork Meatballs

Serves: 4 | Ready in about: 30 minutes

3 tbsp olive oil

1 lb ground pork

2 tbsp parsley, chopped

2 green onions, chopped

4 garlic cloves, minced

1 red chili, chopped

1 cup veggie stock

2 tbsp hot paprika

Combine the pork, parsley, green onions, garlic, and red chili in a bowl and form medium balls out of the mixture. Warm olive oil in a skillet over medium heat. Sear meatballs for 8 minutes on all sides. Stir in stock and hot paprika and simmer for another 12 minutes. Serve warm.

460.   Simple Pork Stew

Serves: 4 | Ready in about: 50 minutes

1 tbsp avocado oil
1 ½ cups buttermilk
1 ½ lb pork meat, cubed

1 red onion, chopped
1 garlic clove, minced
½ cup chicken stock

2 tbsp hot paprika
Salt and black pepper to taste
1 tbsp cilantro, chopped

Warm avocado oil in a pot over medium heat and sear pork for 5 minutes. Put in onion and garlic and cook for 5 minutes. Stir in stock, paprika, salt, pepper, and buttermilk and bring to a boil; cook for 30 minutes. Top with cilantro.

461.   Olive & Tomato Pork Chops

Serves: 4 | Ready in about: 20 minutes

2 tbsp olive oil
4 pork loin chops, boneless
6 tomatoes, crushed

3 tbsp basil, chopped
10 black olives, halved
1 yellow onion, chopped

1 garlic clove, minced

Warm olive oil in a skillet over medium heat and brown pork chops for 6 minutes on all sides. Share into plates. In the same skillet, stir tomatoes, basil, olives, onion, and garlic and simmer for 4 minutes. Drizzle with tomato sauce.

462.   Saucy Pork Chops

Serves: 4 | Ready in about: 40 minutes

2 tbsp olive oil
4 pork chops

½ cup tomato puree
Salt and black pepper to taste

1 tbsp Italian seasoning
1 tbsp rosemary, chopped

Preheat oven to 380 F. Warm olive oil in a skillet over medium heat. Sear pork. Stir in salt, pepper, tomato purée, Italian seasoning, and rosemary and bake for 20 minutes.

463.   Snow Pea Pork Loin

Serves: 4 | Ready in about: 30 minutes

2 tbsp canola oil
2 carrots, chopped
2 garlic cloves, minced

1 lb pork loin, cubed
4 oz snow peas
¾ cup beef stock

1 onion, chopped
Salt and white pepper to taste

Warm canola oil in a skillet over medium heat and sear pork for 5 minutes. Stir in snow peas, carrots, garlic, stock, onion, salt, and pepper and bring to a boil; cook for 15 minutes.

464.   Herb Pork Sausage with Eggs

Serves: 2 | Ready in about: 20 minutes

2 tbsp olive oil
½ cup leeks, chopped
½ lb pork sausage, crumbled
4 eggs, whisked

1 thyme sprig, chopped
1 tsp habanero pepper, minced
½ tsp dried marjoram
1 tsp garlic puree

½ cup green olives, sliced
Salt and black pepper to taste

Warm olive oil in a skillet over medium heat. Sauté the leeks until they are just tender, about 4 minutes. Add the garlic, habanero pepper, salt, black pepper, and sausage; cook for 8 minutes, stirring frequently. Pour in the eggs and sprinkle with thyme and marjoram. Cook for an additional 4 minutes, stirring with a spoon. Garnish with olives.

465.   Zucchini Pork Chops

Serves: 4 | Ready in about: 40 minutes

2 tbsp olive oil
4 pork loin chops, boneless
1 tsp Italian seasoning
1 zucchini, sliced

1 yellow squash, cubed
10 cherry tomatoes, halved
½ tsp oregano, dried
Salt and black pepper to taste

3 garlic cloves, minced
10 Kalamata olives, halved
¼ cup ricotta cheese, crumbled

Preheat oven to 370 F. Place pork chops, salt, pepper, Italian seasoning, zucchini, squash, tomatoes, oregano, olive oil, garlic, and olives in a roasting pan and bake covered for 30 minutes. Serve topped with ricotta cheese.

466. Cheese & Spinach Stuffed Pork Loin

Serves: 6 | Ready in about: 55 minutes

1 ½ lb pork tenderloin	1 cup mushrooms, sliced	Salt and black pepper to taste
6 slices pancetta, chopped	5 sundried tomatoes, diced	

Place a skillet over medium heat and stir-fry the pancetta for 5 minutes until crispy. Add the mushrooms and sauté for another 4-5 minutes until tender, stirring occasionally. Stir in sundried tomatoes and season with salt and pepper; set aside. Preheat the oven to 350F. Using a sharp knife, cut the pork tenderloin in half lengthwise, leaving about 1-inch border; be careful not to cut through to the other side. Open the tenderloin like a book to form a large rectangle. Flatten it to about ¼-inch thickness with a meat tenderizer. Season the pork generously with salt and pepper. Top all over with pancetta filling. Roll up pork tenderloin and tightly secure with kitchen twine. Place on a greased baking sheet. Bake for 60-75 minutes until the pork is cooked through, depending on the thickness of the pork. Remove from the oven and let rest for 10 minutes at room temperature. Remove the twine and discard. Slice the pork into medallions and serve.

467. Garlicky Pork Chops

Serves: 4 | Ready in about: 45 minutes

1 tbsp olive oil	Salt and black pepper to taste	1 tbsp thyme, chopped
4 pork loin chops, boneless	4 garlic cloves, minced	

Preheat oven to 390 F. Place pork chops, salt, pepper, garlic, thyme, and olive oil in a roasting pan and bake for 10 minutes. Decrease the heat to 360 F and bake for 25 minutes.

468. Mustardy Pork Tenderloin

Serves: 4 | Ready in about: 30 minutes

2 tbsp olive oil	1 tbsp rosemary, chopped	½ chili pepper, minced
1 (1 ½-oz) pork tenderloin	1 tbsp tarragon, chopped	Salt and black pepper to taste
2 garlic cloves, minced	3 tbsp stone-ground mustard	
½ cup fresh parsley, chopped	½ tsp cumin powder	

Preheat your oven to 400 F. In a food processor, blend parsley, tarragon, rosemary, mustard, olive oil, chili pepper, cumin, salt, garlic, and pepper until smooth. Rub the mixture all over the pork and transfer onto a lined baking sheet. Bake in the oven for 20-25 minutes. Slice and serve.

469. Fruity Pork Chops

Serves: 4 | Ready in about: 30 minutes

2 tbsp olive oil	4 pork chops, boneless	1 tbsp thyme, chopped
½ tsp cayenne powder	¼ cup peach preserves	

In a large bowl, mix peach preserves, olive oil, and cayenne powder. Preheat your grill to medium. Rub pork chops with some peach glaze and grill for 10 minutes. Turn the chops, rub more glaze and cook for 10 minutes. Top with thyme.

470. Millet & Pork with Chestnuts

Serves: 4 | Ready in about: 30 minutes

2 cups pork roast, cooked and shredded	
½ cup sour cream	3 oz water chestnuts, sliced
1 cup millet	Salt and white pepper to taste

Place the millet and salted water in a pot over medium heat and cook for 20 minutes. Drain and remove to a bowl to cool. When ready, add in pork, chestnuts, cream, salt, and pepper and mix to combine. Serve.

471. Onion & Bell Pepper Pork Chops

Serves: 4 | Ready in about: 30 minutes

2 tbsp olive oil
4 pork chops
Salt and black pepper to taste
1 tsp fennel seeds

1 red bell pepper, sliced
1 green bell pepper, sliced
1 yellow onion, thinly sliced
2 tsp Italian seasoning

2 garlic cloves, minced
1 tbsp balsamic vinegar

Warm olive oil in a large skillet over medium heat. Season the pork chops with salt and pepper and add them to the skillet. Cook for 6-8 minutes on both sides or until golden brown; reserve. Sauté the garlic, sliced bell peppers, onions, fennel seeds, and herbs in the skillet for 6-8 minutes until tender, stirring occasionally. Return the pork, cover, and lower the heat to low. Cook for another 3 minutes or until the pork is cooked through. Transfer the pork and vegetables to a serving platter. Add the vinegar to the skillet and stir to combine for 1-2 minutes. Drizzle the sauce over the pork.

472. Polpette (Meatballs) in Almond Sauce

Serves: 4 | Ready in about: 30 minutes

3 tbsp olive oil
8 oz ground pork
8 oz ground beef
½ cup finely minced onions
1 large egg, beaten

1 potato, shredded
Salt and black pepper to taste
1 tsp garlic powder
½ tsp oregano
2 tbsp chopped parsley

¼ cup ground almonds
1 cup chicken broth
¼ cup butter

Place the ground beef and pork, onions, egg, potato, salt, garlic powder, pepper, and oregano in a large bowl. Shape the mixture into small meatballs, about 1 inch in diameter, and place them on a plate. Let sit for 10 minutes at room temperature. Warm the olive oil in a skillet over medium heat. Add the meatballs and brown them for 6-8 minutes on all sides; reserve. In the hot skillet, melt the butter and add the almonds and broth. Cook for 3-5 minutes. Add the meatballs to the skillet, cover, and cook for 8-10 minutes. Top with parsley.

473. Sweet Pork Chops

Serves: 4 | Ready in about: 40 minutes

2 tbsp olive oil
½ cup vegetable stock

2 tbsp wholegrain mustard
1 tbsp honey

4 pork loin chops, boneless
Salt and black pepper to taste

Preheat your oven to 380 F. Mix honey, mustard, salt, pepper, paprika, and olive oil in a bowl. Add in the pork and toss to coat. Transfer to a greased baking sheet and pour in the vegetable stock. Bake covered with foil for 30 minutes. Remove the foil and bake for 6-8 minutes until golden brown.

474. Caraway Pork Tenderloin

Serves: 4 | Ready in about: 30 minutes

2 tbsp olive oil
1 lb pork tenderloin, sliced

Salt and black pepper to taste
3 tbsp ground caraway seeds

1/3 cup half-and-half
½ cup dill, chopped

Warm olive oil in a skillet over medium heat and sear pork for 8 minutes on all sides. Stir in salt, pepper, ground caraway seeds, half-and-half, and dill and bring to a boil. Cook for another 12 minutes. Serve warm.

475. Marjoram Pork Shoulder with Pesto

Serves: 4 | Ready in about: 35 minutes

¼ cup olive oil
1 tsp red pepper flakes
2 garlic cloves, minced

2 lb pork shoulder, cubed
2 tsp dried marjoram
¼ cup lemon juice

2 tsp basil pesto
Salt and black pepper to taste

Warm the olive oil in a skillet over medium heat and sear pork for 5 minutes. Stir in marjoram, red pepper flakes, lemon juice, garlic, basil pesto, salt, and pepper and cook for another 20 minutes, stirring often. Serve immediately.

476.   Pork in Oregano Tomato Sauce

Serves: 4 | Ready in about: 50 minutes

2 tbsp olive oil
1 lb pork loin, sliced
3 garlic cloves, chopped
3 carrots, sliced

1 red onion, chopped
Salt and black pepper to taste
3 cups chicken stock
2 tbsp tomato paste

2 tsp turmeric powder
1 tsp dried oregano
2 tbsp parsley, chopped

Preheat oven to 360 F. Warm the olive oil in a pot over medium heat and cook pork, onion, and garlic for 8 minutes. Stir in carrots, salt, pepper, stock, tomato paste, turmeric, and oregano and transfer to a baking dish. Bake for 30 minutes. Serve topped with parsley.

477.   Pork Chops with Cabbage Mix

Serves: 4 | Ready in about: 35 minutes

½ green cabbage head, shredded
2 tbsp olive oil
4 pork chops

4 bell peppers, chopped
1 tsp rosemary
2 tbsp wine vinegar

2 spring onions, chopped
Salt and black pepper to taste

Warm 1 tbsp of olive oil in a skillet over medium heat. Cook spring onions for 3 minutes. Stir in vinegar, cabbage, bell peppers, salt, and pepper and simmer for 10 minutes. Heat off. Preheat the grill over medium heat. Sprinkle pork chops with remaining oil, salt, pepper, and rosemary and grill for 10 minutes on both sides. Share chops into plates with cabbage mixture on the side. Serve immediately.

478.   Tasty Pork Loin

Serves: 4 | Ready in about: 8 hours 10 minutes

1 tbsp olive oil
2 lb pork loin, sliced
1 lb pearl onions

Salt and white pepper to taste
1 tsp Italian seasoning
1 cup vegetable stock

1 tbsp tomato paste
2 bay leaves

Place the pork, olive oil, salt, pepper, pearl onions, Italian seasoning, stock, tomato paste, and bay leaves in your slow cooker. Cover with the lid and cook for 8 hours on Low. Discard the bay leaves and serve.

479.   Mouth-Watering Pork Stew

Serves: 4 | Ready in about: 50 minutes

1 tbsp olive oil
1 lb pork stew meat, cubed
2 shallots, chopped
14 oz canned tomatoes, diced

1 garlic clove, minced
3 cups beef stock
2 tbsp paprika
1 tsp coriander seeds

1 tsp dried thyme
Salt and black pepper to taste
2 tbsp parsley, chopped

Warm olive oil in a pot over medium heat and cook pork meat for 5 minutes until brown, stirring occasionally. Add in shallots and garlic and cook for an additional 3 minutes. Stir in beef stock, tomatoes, paprika, thyme, coriander seeds, salt, and pepper and bring to a boil; cook for 30 minutes. Serve warm topped with parsley.

480.   Easy Pork & Vegetable Gratin

Serves: 4 | Ready in about: 40 minutes

3 tbsp olive oil
1 lb pork chops
½ cup basil leaves, chopped
½ cup mint leaves, chopped

1 tbsp rosemary, chopped
2 garlic cloves, minced
1 eggplant, cubed
2 zucchini, cubed

1 bell pepper, chopped
2 oz mozzarella, crumbled
8 oz cherry tomatoes, halved

Preheat oven to 380 F. Place pork chops, basil, mint, rosemary, garlic, olive oil, eggplant, zucchini, bell pepper, and tomatoes in a roasting pan and bake covered with foil for 27 minutes. Uncover, sprinkle with the mozzarella cheese, and bake for another 5-10 minutes until the cheese melts.

481.   Wine Pork Chops

Serves: 4 | Ready in about: 30 minutes

2 tbsp olive oil
4 pork chops
1 cup red onion, sliced

10 black peppercorns, crushed
¼ cup vegetable stock
¼ cup dry white wine

2 garlic cloves, minced
Salt to taste

Warm olive oil in a skillet over medium heat and sear pork chops for 8 minutes on both sides. Put in onion and garlic and cook for another 2 minutes. Mix in stock, wine, salt, and peppercorns and cook for 10 minutes, stirring often.

482.   Vegetables & Pork Chops

Serves: 4 | Ready in about: 70 minutes

2 tbsp olive oil, divided
½ lb green beans, trimmed
½ lb asparagus spears

½ cup frozen peas, thawed
2 tomatoes, chopped
1 lb pork chops

1 tbsp tomato paste
1 onion, chopped
Salt and black pepper to taste

Warm the olive oil in a saucepan over medium heat. Sprinkle the chops with salt and pepper. Place in the pan and brown for 8 minutes in total; set aside. In the same pan, sauté onion for 2 minutes until soft. In a bowl, whisk the tomato paste and 1 cup of water and pour into the saucepan. Bring to a simmer and scrape any bits from the bottom. Add the chops back and bring to a boil. Then lower the heat and simmer for 40 minutes. Add in green beans, asparagus, peas, tomatoes, salt, and pepper and cook for 10 minutes until the greens are soft.

483.   Pork Stew with Mushrooms

Serves: 4 | Ready in about: 8 hours 10 minutes

2 tbsp olive oil
2 lb pork stew meat, cubed
1 lb mushrooms, chopped
Salt and black pepper to taste

2 cups chicken stock
1 carrot, chopped
1 yellow onion, chopped
2 garlic cloves, minced

2 cups tomatoes, chopped
½ cup parsley, chopped

Place pork cubes, salt, pepper, stock, olive oil, onion, carrot, garlic, mushrooms, and tomatoes in your slow cooker. Cover with the lid and cook for 8 hours on Low. Top with parsley.

484.   Red Pork Stew

Serves: 4 | Ready in about: 50 minutes

3 tbsp olive oil
1 ½ lb pork stew meat, cubed
Salt and black pepper to taste

1 cup red onions, chopped
1 cup dried apricots, chopped
2 garlic cloves, minced

1 cup canned tomatoes, diced
2 tbsp parsley, chopped

Warm the olive oil in a skillet over medium heat. Sear pork meat for 5 minutes. Put in onions and cook for another 5 minutes. Stir in salt, pepper, apricots, garlic, tomatoes, and parsley and bring to a simmer and cook for an additional 30 minutes.

485.   Mixed Mushroom Beef Stew

Serves: 4 | Ready in about: 60 minutes

1 lb cremini mushrooms, sliced
2 tbsp olive oil
2 tbsp tomato paste
1 ½ lb beef meat, cubed

1 carrot, chopped
2 garlic cloves, chopped
1 large onion, chopped
5 cups beef stock

1 tsp thyme, chopped
2 bay leaves
1 oz dried button mushrooms
Salt and black pepper to taste

Soak button mushrooms in water for 10 minutes. Warm the olive oil in a pot over medium heat. Season the beef with salt and pepper and cook for 5 minutes, stirring often. Add in the onion and garlic and cook for another 3 minutes. Stir in carrot, tomato paste, thyme, bay leaves, and mushrooms for 5 minutes. Pour the button mushrooms and beef stock and simmer for 40 minutes. Adjust the seasoning and serve right away.

486.   Parsley Pork Butt with Leeks

Serves: 4 | Ready in about: 1 hour 40 minutes

2 lb boneless pork butt roast, cubed
3 tbsp olive oil
Salt and black pepper to taste
2 lb leeks, sliced

2 garlic cloves, minced
1 (14-oz) can diced tomatoes
1 cup dry white wine
½ cup chicken broth

1 bay leaf
2 tsp chopped fresh parsley

Season the pork cubes with salt and pepper. Warm the oil in a saucepan over medium heat. Brown the pork on all sides, about 8 minutes; transfer to a bowl. Add the leeks, salt, and pepper to the fat left in the saucepan and sauté for 5-7 minutes, stirring occasionally, until softened and lightly browned. Stir in garlic and cook until fragrant, about 30 seconds. Pour in tomatoes and their juice, scraping up any browned bits, and cook until tomato liquid is nearly evaporated, 10-12 minutes. Preheat oven to 325 F. Add the wine, broth, and bay leaf to the saucepan and return the pork with any accumulated juices; bring to a simmer. Cover, transfer to the oven and cook for about 60 minutes until the pork is tender and falls apart when prodded with a fork. Remove and discard the bay leaf. Sprinkle with parsley.

487.   Weeknight Pork Loaf with Fontina Cheese

Serves: 6 | Ready in about: 90 minutes

1 red onion, chopped
2 garlic cloves, minced
2 lb ground pork

2 tbsp milk
¼ cup Fontina cheese, grated
1 egg, whisked

10 black olives, chopped
2 tbsp oregano, chopped
Salt and black pepper to taste

Preheat your oven to 360 F. Combine the onion, garlic, pork, milk, Fontina cheese, egg, olives, oregano, salt, and pepper in a bowl. Press the mixture into a lightly greased loaf pan. Bake for 50-60 minutes. Let cool slightly. Serve sliced.

488.   Pork Loin with Capres & Cheese

Serves: 4 | Ready in about: 70 minutes

2 tbsp olive oil
1 ½ lb pork loin, cubed
2 tbsp marjoram, chopped

1 garlic clove, minced
1 tbsp capers, drained
1 cup chicken stock

Salt and black pepper to taste
½ cup ricotta cheese, crumbled

Warm the olive oil in a skillet over medium heat and sear pork for 5 minutes. Stir in marjoram, garlic, capers, stock, salt, and pepper and bring to a boil. Cook for 30 minutes. Mix in cheese.

489.   Opulent Pork Stew

Serves: 4 | Ready in about: 35 minutes

2 tbsp olive oil
1 lb pork shoulder, cubed
Salt and black pepper to taste

1 onion, chopped
2 garlic cloves, minced
1 tbsp chili paste

2 tbsp balsamic vinegar
¼ cup chicken stock
¼ cup mint, chopped

Warm olive oil in a skillet over medium heat and cook onion for 3 minutes. Put in pork cubes and cook for another 3 minutes. Stir in salt, pepper, garlic, chili paste, vinegar, stock, and mint and cook for an additional 20-25 minutes.

490.   Pizza Burgers

Serves: 4 | Ready in about: 20 minutes

¼ tsp mustard powder
¼ tsp cumin
1 ¼ lb ground beef

½ tsp garlic salt
¼ tsp red pepper flakes
½ tsp Italian seasoning

1 cup passata
8 mozzarella cheese slices

Preheat grill to medium. In a large bowl, lightly mix with your hands the ground beef, mustard powder, cumin, garlic salt, pepper flakes, and Italian seasoning. Shape the mixture into 4 patties. Grill the burgers for about 10 minutes, turning them occasionally to ensure even cooking. In the last 2 minutes of cooking, top each burger with a generous tablespoon of passata and 2 slices of cheese per burger. Remove and let sit for 1–2 minutes before serving.

491. Orecchiette with Mushroom & Sausage

Serves: 2 | Ready in about: 30 minutes

½ cup cremini mushrooms, sliced
1 tbsp olive oil
½ medium onion, diced
2 garlic cloves, minced

4 oz Italian sausage
½ tsp Italian seasoning
8 oz dry orecchiette pasta
2 cups chicken stock

1 cup baby spinach
¼ cup heavy cream
1 tbsp basil, chopped

Warm olive oil in a pan over medium heat. Add the onion, garlic, and mushrooms and sauté for 5 minutes until tender. Remove the sausage from its casing and add it to the pan, breaking it up well. Stir-fry for 5 more minutes or until the sausage is no longer pink. Season with Italian seasoning and add the pasta and chicken stock; bring the mixture to a boil. Lower the heat to medium-low and t simmer for 9-11 minutes or until the pasta is cooked. Remove from the heat. Add the spinach and stir until it wilts, 3 minutes. Stir in the heavy cream. Serve topped with basil, and enjoy!

492. Pork Tenderloin with Apple Sauce

Serves: 4 | Ready in about: 35 minutes

2 tbsp olive oil
1 lb pork tenderloin
Salt and black pepper to taste

¼ cup apple jelly
¼ cup apple juice
2 tbsp wholegrain mustard

3 sprigs fresh thyme
½ tbsp cornstarch
½ tbsp heavy cream

Preheat your oven to 330 F. Warm the oil in a skillet over medium heat. Season the pork with salt and pepper. Sear it for 6-8 minutes on all sides. Transfer to a baking sheet. To the same skillet, add the apple jelly, juice, and mustard and stir for 5 minutes over low heat, stirring often. Top with the pork and thyme sprigs. Place the skillet in the oven and bake for 15-18 minutes, brushing the pork with the apple-mustard sauce every 5 minutes. Remove the pork and let it rest for 15 minutes. Place a small pot over low heat. Blend the cornstarch with heavy cream and cooking juices and pour the mixture into the pot. Stir for 2 minutes until thickens. Drizzle the sauce over the pork. Serve sliced.

493. Beef with Zoodles

Serves: 4 | Ready in about: 20 minutes

2 tbsp olive oil
1 lb beef steaks, sliced
2 zucchini, spiralized

½ cup sweet chili sauce
1 cup carrot, grated
3 tbsp water

Salt and black pepper to taste

Warm olive oil in a skillet over medium heat and brown beef steaks for 8 minutes on both sides; reserve and cover with foil to keep warm. Stir zucchini noodles, chili sauce, carrot, water, salt, and pepper and cook for an additional 3-4 minutes. Remove the foil from the steaks and pour the zucchini mix over to serve.

494. The Best Meatballs Ever

Serves: 4 | Ready in about: 25 minutes

2 tbsp olive oil
1 lb ground beef meat

1 onion, chopped
3 tbsp cilantro, chopped

1 garlic clove, minced
Salt and black pepper to taste

Combine the beef, onion, cilantro, garlic, salt, and pepper in a bowl and form meatballs out of the mixture. Sprinkle with oil. Preheat the grill over medium heat and grill them for 14 minutes on all sides. Serve with salad.

495. Bell Pepper & Beef Bake

Serves: 4 | Ready in about: 1 hour 40 minutes

2 tbsp olive oil
1 lb beef steaks
1 red bell pepper, sliced

1 green bell pepper, sliced
1 yellow bell pepper, sliced
2 tbsp oregano, chopped

4 garlic cloves, minced
½ cup chicken stock
Salt and black pepper to taste

Preheat your oven to 360 F. Warm olive oil in a skillet over medium heat. Sear the beef steaks for 8 minutes on both sides. Stir in bell peppers, oregano, garlic, stock, salt, and pepper and bake for 80 minutes. Serve warm.

496.   Succulent Pork Chops

Serves: 4 | Ready in about: 30 minutes

3 tbsp olive oil
4 pork chops
Salt and black pepper to taste

5 tbsp chicken broth
6 garlic cloves, minced
¼ cup honey

2 tbsp apple cider vinegar
2 tbsp parsley, chopped

Warm olive oil in a large skillet over medium heat. Season the pork chops with salt and pepper and add them to the skillet. Cook for 10 minutes on both sides or until golden brown; reserve. Lower the heat and add 3 tablespoons of broth, scraping the bits and flavors from the bottom of the skillet; cook for 2 minutes until the broth evaporates. Add the garlic and cook for 30 seconds. Stir in honey, vinegar, and the remaining broth. Cook for 3-4 minutes until the sauce thickens slightly. Return the pork chops and cook for 2 minutes. Top with parsley and serve.

497.   Beef Steak in Mushroom Sauce

Serves: 4 | Ready in about: 30 minutes + marinating time

For the steak
2 tbsp olive oil
1 lb beef skirt steak
1 cup red wine
For the mushroom sauce
1 lb mushrooms, sliced
1 tsp dried dill

2 garlic cloves, minced
1 tbsp Worcestershire sauce
1 tbsp dried thyme

2 garlic cloves, minced
1 cup dry red wine

1 tsp yellow mustard

Salt and black pepper to taste

Combine the wine, garlic, Worcestershire sauce, 2 tbsp of olive oil, thyme, and mustard in a bowl. Place in the steak, cover with plastic wrap and let it marinate for at least 3 hours in the refrigerator. Remove the steak and pat dry with paper towels. Warm olive oil in a pan over medium heat and sear steak for 8 minutes on all sides; set aside. In the same pan, sauté mushrooms, dill, salt, and pepper for 6 minutes, stirring periodically. Add in garlic and sauté for 30 seconds. Pour in the wine and scrape off any bits from the bottom. Simmer for 5 minutes until the liquid reduces. Slice the steak and top with the mushroom sauce. Serve hot.

498.   Basic Beef Meatballs

Serves: 4 | Ready in about: 25 minutes

¼ cup fresh mozzarella cheese, crumbled
1 lb ground beef
¼ cup panko breadcrumbs
Salt and black pepper to taste
1 red onion, grated

2 tbsp parsley, chopped
2 garlic cloves, minced
1 lemon, juiced and zested
1 egg

½ tsp ground cumin
½ tsp ground coriander
¼ tsp cinnamon powder

Preheat your oven to 390 F. Line a baking sheet with parchment paper. Combine beef, breadcrumbs, salt, pepper, onion, parsley, garlic, lemon juice, lemon zest, egg, cumin, coriander, cinnamon powder, and fresh mozzarella cheese in a bowl and form balls out of the mixture. Place meatballs on the sheet and bake for 15 minutes. Serve warm.

499.   Savory Beef Stew

Serves: 4 | Ready in about: 80 minutes

3 tbsp olive oil
2 lb beef shoulder, cubed
Salt and black pepper to taste
1 onion, chopped

2 garlic cloves, minced
3 tomatoes, grated
1 tsp red chili flakes
2 cups chicken stock

1 cup couscous
10 green olives, sliced
1 tbsp cilantro, chopped

Warm olive oil in a pot over medium heat and cook beef for 5 minutes until brown, stirring often. Add in onion and garlic and cook for another 5 minutes. Stir in tomatoes, salt, pepper, chicken stock, olives, and red chili flakes. Bring to a boil and simmer for 1 hour. Cover the couscous with boiling water in a bowl, cover, and let sit for 4-5 minutes until the water has been absorbed. Fluff with a fork and season with salt and pepper. Pour the stew over and scatter with cilantro.

500.   Appetizing Beef Meatballs

Serves: 4 | Ready in about: 30 minutes

1 tsp olive oil
¼ cup finely chopped onions
¼ cup raisins, chopped
1 tsp ground cumin

½ tsp ground cinnamon
¼ tsp smoked paprika
¼ tsp nutmeg
1 large egg

1 lb ground beef
⅓ cup panko bread crumbs
1 (28-oz) can diced tomatoes

Place ground beef, bread crumbs, onions, raisins, cumin, cinnamon, nutmeg, smoked paprika, and egg in a bowl and mix gently with your hands. Shape the mixture into 20 meatballs. Warm the olive oil in a large skillet over medium heat. Sear the meatballs for 8 minutes, rolling around every minute or so with a fork to brown them on most sides. Place the meatballs on a paper towel–lined plate. Discard the fat from the pan and wipe it out with paper towels. Add in the meatballs and pour the tomatoes over. Cover and cook until the sauce begins to bubble. Lower the heat to medium, cover partially and cook for 7-8 more minutes. Serve and enjoy!

501.   Stuffed Peppers with Beef

Serves: 4 | Ready in about: 50 minutes

2 tbsp olive oil
2 red bell peppers
1 lb ground beef
1 shallot, finely chopped

2 garlic cloves, minced
2 tbsp fresh sage, chopped
Salt and black pepper to taste
1 tsp ground allspice

½ cup fresh parsley, chopped
½ cup baby arugula leaves
½ cup pine nuts, chopped
1 tbsp orange juice

Warm the olive oil in a large skillet over medium heat. Sauté the beef, garlic, and shallot for 8-10 minutes until the meat is browned and cooked through. Season with sage, allspice, salt, and pepper and remove from the heat to cool slightly. Stir in parsley, arugula, pine nuts, and orange juice and mix. Preheat oven to 390 F. Slice the peppers in half lengthwise and remove the seeds and membranes. Spoon the filling into the pepper halves. Bake in the oven for 25-30 minutes.

502.   Roasted Beef with Kale Slaw & Bell Peppers

Serves: 4 | Ready in about: 35 minutes

2 tsp olive oil
1 lb skirt steak
4 cups kale slaw

1 tbsp garlic powder
Salt and black pepper to taste
1 small red onion, sliced

10 sundried tomatoes, halved
½ red bell pepper, sliced

Preheat your broiler. Brush steak with olive oil, salt, garlic powder, and pepper and place under the broiler for 10 minutes, turning once. Remove to a cutting board and let rest for 10 minutes, then cut the steak diagonally. In the meantime, place sun-dried tomatoes, kale slaw, onion, and bell pepper in a bowl and mix to combine. Transfer to a serving plate and top with steak slices to serve.

503.   Filet Mignon in Mushroom Sauce

Serves: 2 | Ready in about: 25 minutes

8 oz cremini mushrooms, quartered
2 tbsp olive oil
2 filet mignon steaks
1 shallot, minced
2 tsp flour

2 tsp tomato paste
½ cup red wine
1 cup chicken stock
½ tsp dried thyme
1 fresh rosemary sprig

1 tsp herbes de Provence
Salt and black pepper to taste
¼ tsp garlic powder
¼ tsp shallot powder
¼ tsp mustard powder

Warm 1 tbsp of olive oil in a saucepan over medium heat. Add the mushrooms and shallot and stir-fry for 5-8 minutes. Stir in the flour and tomato paste and cook for another 30 seconds. Pour in the wine and scrape up any browned bits from the sauté pan. Add the chicken stock, thyme, and rosemary. Bring it to a boil and cook until the sauce thickens, 2-4 minutes. In a small bowl, mix the herbes de Provence, salt, garlic powder, shallot powder, mustard powder, salt, and pepper. Rub the beef with the herb mixture on both sides. Warm the remaining olive oil in a sauté over medium heat. Sear the beef for 2-3 minutes on each side. Serve topped with mushroom sauce.

504.   Chickpea & Beef Stew

Serves: 4 | Ready in about: 60 minutes

2 tbsp olive oil
½ lb beef stew meat, cubed
1 celery stalk, chopped
1 tsp fennel seeds
1 tsp hot paprika

1 carrot, chopped
1 onion, chopped
Salt and black pepper to taste
2 garlic cloves, chopped
4 cups beef stock

½ tsp dried cilantro
1 tsp dried oregano
14 oz canned tomatoes, diced
2 tbsp parsley, chopped

Warm olive oil in a pot over medium heat and cook beef meat, onion, and garlic for 10 minutes. Stir in celery, carrots, fennel seeds, paprika, salt, pepper, cilantro, and oregano for 3 minutes. Pour in beef stock and tomatoes and bring to a boil. Cook for 40 minutes. Top with parsley.

505.   Beef Ribs

Serves: 4 | Ready in about: 2 hours 10 minutes

2 tbsp olive oil
2 lb beef ribs

2 garlic cloves, minced
1 onion, chopped

½ cup chicken stock
1 tbsp ground fennel seeds

Preheat your oven to 360 F. Mix garlic, onion, stock, olive oil, fennel seeds, and beef ribs in a roasting pan and bake for 2 hours. Serve hot with salad.

506.   Zucchini & Mozzarella Beef

Serves: 6 | Ready in about: 35 minutes

1 tbsp olive oil
1 lb beef shoulder, cubed
1 cup chopped onions
½ cup diced carrots
1 tsp ground cumin

½ tsp ground cinnamon
Salt to taste
4 garlic cloves, minced
2 tbsp tomato paste
½ cup chopped prunes

1 (15-oz) can chickpeas
2 tbsp lemon juice
¼ cup chopped pistachios
2 tbsp fresh thyme, chopped

Warm olive oil in a pot over medium heat. Season the beef cubes with salt and pepper and add them to the skillet. Cook for 4 minutes, stirring often until golden brown; reserve. Add the onions, carrots, cumin, cinnamon, and salt to the pot and cook for 5 minutes until tender. Push the vegetables to the edge of the pot.

Add the garlic and cook for 1 minute. Add the tomato paste and cook for 1 more minute, stirring constantly while blending and mashing the tomato paste into the vegetables. Add the beef back to the pot along with 2 cups of water and prunes. Bring to a boil. Lower the heat and simmer for 5-7 minutes until the stew thickens slightly. Stir in the chickpeas and cook for 1 minute. Remove the stew from the heat, and stir in the lemon juice. Sprinkle the pistachios and thyme on top. Serve.

507.   Pumpkin & Beef Stew

Serves: 6 | Ready in about: 35 minutes

2 tbsp canola oil
2 lb stew beef, cubed
1 cup red wine
1 onion, chopped

1 tsp garlic powder
Salt to taste
3 whole cloves
1 bay leaf

3 carrots, chopped
½ butternut pumpkin, diced
2 tbsp cornstarch
3 tbsp water

Warm canola oil on Sauté mode. Brown the beef for 5 minutes on each side. Deglaze the pot with wine, scraping the bottom to remove any browned beef bits. Add in onion, salt, bay leaf, cloves, and garlic powder. Seal the lid, press Meat/Stew and cook on High for 15 minutes. Release the Pressure quickly.

Add in pumpkin and carrots without stirring. Seal the lid and cook on High Pressure for 5 minutes. Release the Pressure quickly. In a bowl, mix water and cornstarch until cornstarch dissolves completely; mix into the stew. Allow the stew to simmer while uncovered on Keep Warm for 5 minutes until you attain the desired thickness.

508. Paprika & Shallot Beef

Serves: 4 | Ready in about: 50 minutes

2 tbsp olive oil
1 lb beef meat, cubed
1 lb shallots, chopped

1 tbsp sweet paprika
Salt and black pepper to taste
1 ½ cups chicken stock

4 garlic cloves, minced
1 cup balsamic vinegar

Warm olive oil in a pot over medium heat and sauté shallots, balsamic vinegar, salt, and pepper for 10 minutes. Stir in beef, paprika, chicken stock, and garlic and bring to a simmer. Cook for 30 minutes. Serve immediately.

509. Cherry Tomato Beef Pot

Serves: 4 | Ready in about: 30 minutes

3 tbsp olive oil
2 garlic cloves, minced
1 lemon, juiced and zested

1 ½ lb ground beef
Salt and black pepper to taste
1 lb cherry tomatoes, halved

1 red onion, chopped
2 tbsp tomato paste
1 tbsp mint leaves, chopped

Warm olive oil in a skillet over medium heat and cook beef and garlic for 5 minutes. Stir in lemon zest, lemon juice, salt, pepper, cherry tomatoes, onion, tomato paste, and mint and cook for 15 minutes. Serve right away.

510. Beef with Walnuts

Serves: 4 | Ready in about: 30 minutes

3 tbsp olive oil
1 ½ lb beef meat, cubed
2 tbsp lime juice

1 tbsp balsamic vinegar
5 garlic cloves, minced
Salt and black pepper to taste

2 tbsp walnuts, chopped
2 scallions, chopped

Warm olive oil in a skillet over medium heat and sear beef for 8 minutes on both sides. Put in scallions and garlic and cook for another 2 minutes. Stir in lime juice, vinegar, salt, pepper, and walnuts and cook for an additional 10 minutes.

511. Tasty Beef Stew

Serves: 4 | Ready in about: 35 minutes

2 tbsp olive oil
2 pears, peeled and cubed

1 lb beef stew meat, cubed
2 tbsp dill, chopped

2 oz heavy cream
Salt and black pepper to taste

Warm olive oil in a skillet over medium heat and sear beef for 5 minutes. Stir in pears, dill, heavy cream, salt, and pepper and bring to a boil. Simmer for 20 minutes.

512. Lamb with Broccoli

Serves: 4 | Ready in about: 70 minutes

2 tbsp olive oil
1 lb lamb meat, cubed
1 garlic clove, minced

1 onion, chopped
1 tsp rosemary, chopped
1 cup vegetable stock

2 cups broccoli florets
2 tbsp sweet paprika
Salt and black pepper to taste

Warm olive oil in a skillet over medium heat and cook onion and garlic for 5 minutes. Put in lamb meat and cook for another 5-6 minutes. Stir in rosemary, stock, broccoli, paprika, salt, and pepper and cook for 50 minutes. Serve hot.

513. Grapefruit Leg Lamb

Serves: 4 | Ready in about: 7hours 10 minutes

2 cups stewed tomatoes, drained
3 ½ lb leg of lamb, cubed
1 lb small potatoes, cubed

1 grapefruit, zested and juiced
4 garlic cloves, minced
Salt and black pepper to taste

½ cup basil, chopped

Place the potatoes, tomatoes, grapefruit juice, grapefruit zest, garlic, leg of lamb, salt, and pepper in your slow cooker. Cover with lid and cook for 8 hours on Low. Top with basil.

514.　　Thyme Lamb Bake

Serves: 4 | Ready in about: 90 minutes

3 tbsp butter
2 lb leg of lamb, sliced
3 garlic cloves, chopped

2 onions, chopped
3 cups vegetable stock
2 cups dry red wine

2 tbsp tomato paste
1 tsp thyme, chopped
Salt and black pepper to taste

Preheat oven to 360 F. Melt butter in a skillet over medium heat. Sear the lamb for 10 minutes on both sides. Remove to a roasting pan. In the same skillet, add and cook onions and garlic for 5 minutes. Stir in stock, red wine, tomato paste, thyme, salt, and pepper and bring to a boil. Cook for 10 minutes and pour over lamb. Bake for 1 hour.

515.　　Delicious Beef Meal

Serves: 4 | Ready in about: 40 minutes

1 tbsp olive oil
1 lb beef meat, cubed
1 red onion, chopped
1 garlic clove, minced

1 celery stalk, chopped
Salt and black pepper to taste
14 oz canned tomatoes, diced
1 cup vegetable stock

½ tsp ground nutmeg
2 tsp dill, chopped

Warm olive oil in a skillet over medium heat and cook onion and garlic for 5 minutes. Put in beef and cook for 5 more minutes. Stir in celery, salt, pepper, tomatoes, stock, nutmeg, and dill and bring to a boil. Cook for 20 minutes.

516.　　Party Leg of Lamb

Serves: 4 | Ready in about: 2 hours 20 minutes

½ cup butter
2 lb leg of lamb, boneless
2 tbsp tomato paste

2 tbsp yellow mustard
2 tbsp basil, chopped
2 garlic cloves, minced

Salt and black pepper to taste
1 cup white wine
½ cup sour cream

Preheat your oven to 360 F. Warm butter in a skillet over medium heat. Sear leg of lamb for 10 minutes on all sides. Stir in mustard, basil, tomato paste, garlic, salt, pepper, wine, and sour cream and bake for 2 hours. Serve right away.

517.　　Lamb with Eggplant

Serves: 4 | Ready in about: 70 minutes

2 tbsp olive oil
1 cup chicken stock
1 ½ lb lamb meat, cubed

2 eggplants, cubed
2 onions, chopped
2 tbsp tomato paste

2 tbsp parsley, chopped
4 garlic cloves, minced

Warm olive oil in a skillet over medium heat and cook onions and garlic for 4 minutes. Put in lamb and cook for 6 minutes. Stir in eggplants and tomato paste for 5 minutes. Pour in the stock and bring to a boil. Cook for another 50 minutes, stirring often. Serve garnished with parsley.

MEATLESS RECIPES

518.   Braised Carrots

Serves: 4 | Ready in about: 20 minutes

2 tbsp butter
1 lb carrots, cut into sticks
¾ cup water

¼ cup orange juice
1 tbsp honey
Salt and white pepper to taste

1 tsp rosemary leaves

Combine all ingredients, except the carrots and rosemary, in a heavy saucepan over medium heat and bring to a boil. Add carrots and cover. Turn the heat to a simmer and continue to cook for 5–8 minutes until carrots are soft when pierced with a knife. Remove the carrots to a serving plate. Then, increase the heat to high and bring the liquid to a boil. Boil until the liquid has reduced and is syrupy, about 4 minutes. Drizzle the sauce over the carrots and sprinkle with rosemary. Serve warm.

519.   Garlic Buttery Green Beans

Serves: 6 | Ready in about: 25 minutes

2 tbsp butter
1 lb green beans, trimmed
4 cups water

6 garlic cloves, minced
1 shallot, chopped
Celery salt to taste

½ tsp red pepper flakes

Pour the water into a pot over high heat and bring to a boil. Cut the green beans in half crosswise. Reduce the heat and add in the green beans. Simmer for 6-8 minutes until crisp-tender but still vibrant green. Drain beans and set aside. Melt the butter in a pan over medium heat and sauté garlic and shallot for 3 minutes until the garlic is slightly browned and fragrant. Stir in the beans and season with celery salt. Cook for 2–3 minutes. Serve topped with red pepper flakes.

520.   Roasted Artichokes

Serves: 4 | Ready in about: 50 minutes

4 artichokes, stalk trimmed and large leaves removed
2 lemons, freshly squeezed
4 tbsp extra-virgin olive oil

4 cloves garlic, chopped
1 tsp fresh rosemary
1 tsp fresh basil
1 tsp fresh parsley

1 tsp fresh oregano
Salt and black pepper to taste
1 tsp red pepper flakes
1 tsp paprika

Preheat oven to 400 F. In a small bowl, thoroughly combine the garlic with herbs and spices; set aside. Cut the artichokes in half vertically and scoop out the fibrous choke to expose the heart with a teaspoon. Rub the lemon juice all over the entire surface of the artichoke halves. Arrange them on a parchment-lined baking dish, cut side up, and brush them evenly with olive oil. Stuff the cavities with the garlic/herb mixture. Cover them with aluminum foil and bake for 30 minutes. Discard the foil and bake for another 10 minutes until lightly charred.

521.   Eggplant Rollatini with Tomato Sauce

Serves: 4 | Ready in about: 60 minutes

2 tbsp olive oil
1 ½ cups ricotta cheese
2 (14-oz) cans diced tomatoes
1 shallot, finely chopped

2 garlic cloves, minced
1 tbsp Italian seasoning
1 tsp dried oregano
2 eggplants

½ cup grated mozzarella
Salt to taste
¼ tsp red pepper flakes

Preheat your oven to 350 F. Warm olive oil in a pot over medium heat and sauté shallot and garlic for 3 minutes until tender and fragrant. Mix in tomatoes, oregano, Italian seasoning, salt, and red flakes and simmer for 6 minutes. Cut the eggplants lengthwise into 1,5-inch slices and season with salt. Grill them for 2-3 minutes per side until softened.

Place them on a plate and spoon 2 tbsp of ricotta cheese. Wrap them and arrange on a greased baking dish. Pour over the sauce and scatter with the mozzarella cheese. Bake for 15-20 minutes until golden brown and bubbling.

522.   Kale & Mushroom Stir-Fry

Serves: 4 | Ready in about: 10 minutes

1 cup cremini mushrooms, sliced
4 tbsp olive oil
1 small red onion, chopped
2 cloves garlic, thinly sliced

1 ½ lb curly kale
2 tomatoes, chopped
1 tsp dried oregano
1 tsp dried basil

½ tsp dried rosemary
½ tsp dried thyme
Salt and black pepper to taste

Warm olive oil in a saucepan over medium heat. Sauté the onion and garlic for about 3 minutes or until they are softened. Add in the mushrooms, kale, and tomatoes, stirring to promote even cooking. Turn the heat to a simmer, add in the spices and cook for 5-6 minutes until the kale wilt.

523.   Hot Green Beans

Serves: 4 | Ready in about: 25 minutes

2 tbsp olive oil
1 red bell pepper, diced
1 ½ lb green beans
4 garlic cloves, minced

½ tsp mustard seeds
½ tsp fennel seeds
1 tsp dried dill weed
2 tomatoes, chopped

1 cup cream of celery soup
1 tsp Italian herb mix
1 tsp chili powder
Salt and black pepper to taste

Warm olive oil in a saucepan over medium heat. Add and fry the bell pepper and green beans for about 5 minutes, stirring periodically to promote even cooking. Add in the garlic, mustard seeds, fennel seeds, and dill and continue sautéing for an additional 1 minute or until fragrant. Add in the pureed tomatoes, cream of celery soup, Italian herb mix, chili powder, salt, and black pepper. Continue to simmer, covered, for 10-12 minutes until the green beans are tender.

524.   Carrot & Pea Noodles

Serves: 4 | Ready in about: 25 minutes

2 tbsp olive oil
4 carrots, spiralized
1 sweet onion, chopped

2 cups peas
2 garlic cloves, minced
¼ cup chopped fresh parsley

Salt and black pepper to taste

Warm 2 tablespoons of olive oil in a pot over medium heat and sauté the onion and garlic for 3 minutes until just tender and fragrant. Add in spiralized carrots and cook for 4 minutes. Mix in peas, salt, and pepper and cook for 4 minutes. Drizzle with the remaining olive oil and sprinkle with parsley.

525.   Vegetable Skewers

Serves: 4 | Ready in about: 30 minutes

1 cup mushrooms, cut into quarters
6 mixed bell peppers, cut into squares

4 red onions, cut into 6 wedges
4 zucchini, cut into half-moons

2 tomatoes, cut into quarters
3 tbsp herbed oil

Preheat grill to medium-high. Alternate the vegetables onto bamboo skewers. Grill them for 5 minutes on each side until the vegetables begin to char. Remove them from heat and drizzle with herbed oil.

526.   Autenthic Marinara Zoodles

Serves: 4 | Ready in about: 65 minutes

2 (14-oz) cans crushed tomatoes
2 tbsp olive oil
16 oz zucchini noodles
1 (14-oz) can diced tomatoes,

1 onion, chopped
4 garlic cloves, minced
1 tbsp dried Italian seasoning
1 tsp dried oregano

Sea salt to taste
¼ tsp red pepper flakes
¼ cup Romano cheese, grated

Warm the olive oil in a pot over medium heat and sauté onion and garlic for 5 minutes, stirring frequently until fragrant. Pour in tomatoes, oregano, Italian seasoning, salt, and red pepper flakes. Bring just to a boil, then lower the heat, and simmer for 10-15 minutes. Stir in the zucchini noodles and cook for 3-4 minutes until the noodles are slightly softened. Scatter with Romano cheese and serve.

527.   Asparagus & Hazelnut Roast

Serves: 4 | Ready in about: 25 minutes

2 tbsp olive oil
1 lb asparagus, trimmed

¼ cup hazelnuts, chopped
1 lemon, juiced and zested

Salt and black pepper to taste
½ tsp red pepper flakes

Preheat oven to 420 F. Arrange the asparagus on a baking sheet. Combine olive oil, lemon zest, lemon juice, salt, hazelnuts, and black pepper in a bowl and mix well. Pour the mixture over the asparagus. Place in the oven and roast for 15-20 minutes until tender and lightly charred. Serve topped with red pepper flakes.

528.   Lentil & Spinach Stew

Serves: 4 | Ready in about: 40 minutes

2 tbsp olive oil
1 cup dry red lentils, rinsed
1 carrot, chopped
1 celery stalk, chopped
1 red onion, chopped
4 garlic cloves, minced

3 tomatoes, puréed
3 cups vegetable broth
1 tsp cayenne pepper
½ tsp ground cumin
½ tsp thyme
1 tsp turmeric

1 tbsp sweet paprika
1 cup spinach, chopped
1 cup fresh cilantro, chopped
Salt and black pepper to taste

Heat olive oil in a pot over medium heat and sauté the garlic, carrot, celery, and onion until tender, about 4-5 minutes. Stir in cayenne pepper, cumin, thyme, paprika, and turmeric for 1 minute and add tomatoes; cook for 3 more minutes. Pour in vegetable broth and lentils and bring to a boil. Reduce the heat and simmer covered for 15 minutes. Stir in spinach and cook for 5 minutes until wilted. Adjust the seasoning and divide between bowls. Top with cilantro.

529.   Kale with Almonds

Serves: 4 | Ready in about: 25 minutes

2 tbsp olive oil
¼ cup slivered almonds
1 lb chopped kale

¼ cup vegetable broth
1 lemon, juiced and zested
1 garlic clove, minced

1 tbsp red pepper flakes
Salt and black pepper to taste

Warm the olive oil in a pan over medium heat and sauté garlic, kale, salt, and pepper for 8-9 minutes until soft. Add in lemon juice, lemon zest, red pepper flakes, and vegetable broth and continue cooking until the liquid evaporates, about 3-5 minutes. Garnish with almonds and serve.

530.   Caramelized Root Vegetables

Serves: 4 | Ready in about: 40 minutes

1 sweet potato, peeled and cut into chunks
3 tbsp olive oil
2 carrots, peeled

2 beets, peeled
1 turnip, peeled
1 tsp cumin
1 tsp sweet paprika

Salt and black pepper to taste
1 lemon, juiced
2 tbsp parsley, chopped

Preheat your oven to 400 F. Cut the vegetables into chunks and toss them with olive oil and seasonings in a sheet pan. Drizzle with lemon juice and roast for 35-40 minutes until vegetables are tender and golden. Serve topped with parsley.

531.   Mushroom Gratin

Serves: 4 | Ready in about: 25 minutes

2 lb Button mushrooms, cleaned
2 tbsp olive oil
2 tomatoes, sliced
2 tomato paste

½ cup Parmesan cheese, grated
½ cup dry white wine
¼ tsp sweet paprika
½ tsp dried basil

½ tsp dried thyme
Salt and black pepper to taste

Preheat your oven to 360 F. Combine tomatoes, tomato paste, wine, oil, mushrooms, paprika, black pepper, salt, basil, and thyme in a baking dish. Bake for 15 minutes. Top with Parmesan and continue baking for 5 minutes until the cheese melts.

532. Bean & Artichoke Pot

Serves: 4 | Ready in about: 40 minutes

2 tbsp olive oil
10 artichoke hearts, halved
1 onion, sliced
12 whole baby carrots

½ cup chopped celery
1 lemon, juiced
2 tbsp chopped fresh basil
1 red chili, sliced

¾ cup frozen fava beans
Salt and black pepper to taste

Warm the olive oil in a pot over medium heat and sauté onion, carrots, and celery for 7-8 minutes until tender. Stir in lemon juice, butter, and 1 cup of water. Bring to a boil, then lower the heat and simmer for 10-15 minutes. Add in artichokes, fava beans, salt, and pepper and cook for another 10 minutes. Top with basil and red chili, and serve.

533. Veggie Medley

Serves: 4 | Ready in about: 70 minutes

2 tbsp olive oil
½ lb green beans, trimmed
1 tomato, chopped
1 potato, sliced
½ tbsp tomato paste

2 tbsp chopped fresh parsley
1 tsp sweet paprika
1 onion, sliced
1 cup mushrooms, sliced
1 celery stalk, chopped

1 red bell pepper, sliced
1 eggplant, sliced
½ cup vegetable broth
Salt and black pepper to taste

Preheat your oven to 375 F. Warm oil in a skillet over medium heat and sauté onion, bell pepper, celery, and mushrooms for 5 minutes until tender. Stir in paprika and tomato paste for 1 minute. Pour in the vegetable broth and stir. Combine the remaining ingredients in a baking pan and mix in the sautéed vegetable. Bake covered with foil for 40-50 minutes.

534. Roasted Potato with Veggie Mix

Serves: 4 | Ready in about: 45 minutes

4 tbsp olive oil
1 lb potatoes, peeled and diced
2 red bell peppers, halved
1 lb mushrooms, sliced

2 tomatoes, diced
8 garlic cloves, peeled
1 eggplant, sliced
1 yellow onion, quartered

½ tsp dried oregano
¼ tsp caraway seeds
Salt to taste

Preheat oven to 390 F. In a bowl, combine the bell peppers, mushrooms, tomatoes, eggplant, onion, garlic, salt, olive oil, oregano, and caraway seeds. Set aside. Arrange the potatoes on a baking dish and bake for 15 minutes. Top with the veggies mixture and bake for 15-20 minutes until tender.

535. Savory Grilled Vegetables

Serves: 4 | Ready in about: 20 minutes

¼ cup olive oil
4 carrots, cut in half
2 onions, quartered

1 zucchini, cut into rounds
1 eggplant, cut into rounds
1 red bell pepper, chopped

Salt and black pepper to taste
Balsamic vinegar to taste

Heat grill to medium-high. Brush the vegetables lightly with olive oil and season with salt and pepper. Grill the vegetables for 3–4 minutes per side. Transfer to a serving dish and drizzle with balsamic vinegar. Serve and enjoy!

536. Elegant Zucchini Ribbons with Ricotta

Serves: 4 | Ready in about: 10 minutes

3 tbsp olive oil
1 garlic clove, minced
1 tsp lemon zest

1 tbsp lemon juice
4 zucchinis, cut into ribbons
Salt and black pepper to taste

2 tbsp chopped fresh parsley
½ ricotta cheese, crumbled

Whisk 2 tablespoons of oil, garlic, salt, pepper, lemon zest, and lemon juice in a bowl. Warm the remaining olive oil in a skillet over medium heat. Season the zucchini ribbons with salt and pepper and add them to the skillet; cook for 3-4 minutes per side. Transfer to a serving bowl and drizzle with the dressing. Sprinkle with parsley and cheese to serve.

537.   Potato Wedges

Serves: 4 | Ready in about: 30 minutes

1 ½ lb potatoes, peeled and cut into wedges
3 tbsp olive oil
1 tbsp minced fresh rosemary

2 tsp chili powder
3 garlic cloves, minced

Salt and black pepper to taste

Preheat oven to 370 F. Toss the wedges with olive oil, garlic, salt, and pepper. Spread out on a roasting sheet. Roast for 15-20 minutes until browned and crisp at the edges. Remove and sprinkle with chili powder and rosemary.

538.   Mushroom & Asparagus Farro

Serves: 2 | Ready in about: 40 minutes

½ oz dried porcini mushrooms, soaked
2 tbsp olive oil
1 cup hot water
3 cups vegetable stock
½ large onion, minced

1 garlic clove
1 cup fresh mushrooms, sliced
½ cup farro
½ cup dry white wine

½ tsp dried thyme
½ tsp dried marjoram
4 oz asparagus, chopped
2 tbsp grated Parmesan cheese

Drain soaked mushrooms, reserving the liquid, and cut them into slices. Warm the olive oil in a saucepan oven over medium heat. Sauté the onion, garlic, and soaked and fresh mushrooms for 8 minutes. Stir in the farro for 1-2 minutes. Add the wine, thyme, marjoram, reserved mushroom liquid, and a ladleful of stock. Bring it to a boil. Lower the heat and cook for about 20 minutes, stirring occasionally and adding another ladleful of stock, until the farro is cooked through but not overcooked. Stir in the asparagus and the remaining stock. Cook for 3-5 more minutes or until the asparagus is softened. Sprinkle with Parmesan cheese and serve warm.

539.   Rich Baked Honey Acorn Squash

Serves: 4 | Ready in about: 35 minutes

1 acorn squash, cut into wedges
2 tbsp olive oil

2 tbsp honey
2 tbsp rosemary, chopped

2 tbsp walnuts, chopped

Preheat your oven to 400 F. In a bowl, mix honey, rosemary, and olive oil. Lay the squash wedges on a baking sheet and drizzle with the honey mixture. Bake for 30 minutes until squash is tender and slightly caramelized, turning each slice over halfway through. Serve cooled and sprinkled with walnuts.

540.   Turnip with Chickpeas

Serves: 4 | Ready in about: 50 minutes

2 tbsp olive oil
2 onions, chopped
2 red bell peppers, chopped
Salt and black pepper to taste
¼ cup tomato paste

1 jalapeño pepper, minced
5 garlic cloves, minced
¾ tsp ground cumin
¼ tsp cayenne pepper
2 (15-oz) cans chickpeas

12 oz potatoes, chopped
¼ cup chopped fresh parsley
1 lemon, juiced

Warm olive oil in a saucepan oven over medium heat. Sauté the onions, bell peppers, salt, and pepper for 6 minutes until softened and lightly browned. Stir in tomato paste, jalapeño pepper, garlic, cumin, and cayenne pepper and cook for about 30 seconds until fragrant. Stir in chickpeas and their liquid, potatoes, and 1 cup of water. Bring to a simmer and cook for 25-35 minutes until potatoes are tender and the sauce has thickened. Stir in parsley and lemon juice.

541.   Broccoli & Walnuts

Serves: 2 | Ready in about: 10 minutes

1 garlic clove, minced
½ cups walnuts, chopped

3 cups broccoli florets, steamed
1 tbsp mint, chopped

½ lemon, juiced
Salt and black pepper to taste

Mix the walnuts, broccoli, garlic, mint, lemon juice, salt, and pepper in a bowl. Serve chilled.

542.   Roasted Tomatoes

Serves: 2 | Ready in about: 50 minutes

¼ cup olive oil
1 lb mixed cherry tomatoes
10 garlic cloves, minced

Salt to taste
1 fresh rosemary sprig
1 fresh thyme sprig

2 crusty bread slices

Preheat your oven to 350 F. Toss the cherry tomatoes, garlic, olive oil, and salt in a baking dish. Top with the herb sprigs. Roast the tomatoes for about 45 minutes until they are soft and begin to caramelize. Discard the herbs and serve with bread.

543.   Zucchini Boats with Mushroom Filling

Serves: 2 | Ready in about: 50 minutes

2 zucchini, cut in half lengthwise
2 cups button mushrooms, chopped
2 tbsp olive oil

2 cloves garlic, minced
2 tbsp chicken broth
¼ tsp dried thyme

1 tbsp parsley, finely chopped
1 tbsp Italian seasoning
Salt and black pepper to taste

Preheat your oven to 350 F. Warm the olive oil in a large skillet over medium heat and add the olive oil. Sauté the mushrooms and garlic for 4-5 minutes until tender. Pour in the chicken broth and cook for another 3–4 minutes. Add the parsley, oregano, and Italian seasoning and season with salt and pepper. Stir and remove from the heat. Spoon the mixture into the zucchini halves. Place them in a casserole dish and pour 2-3 tbsp of water or broth in the bottom. Cover with foil and bake for 30-40 minutes until zucchini is tender.

544.   Oven-Baked Green Beans

Serves: 6 | Ready in about: 15 minutes

2 tbsp olive oil

2 lb green beans, trimmed

Salt and black pepper to taste

Preheat your oven to 400 F. Toss the green beans with some olive oil, salt, and spread them in a single layer on a greased baking dish. Roast for 8-10 minutes. Transfer green beans to a serving platter and drizzle with the remaining olive oil.

545.   Cheesy Asparagus with Tomatoes

Serves: 6 | Ready in about: 30 minutes

3 tbsp olive oil
2 garlic cloves, minced
12 oz cherry tomatoes, halved

1 tsp dried oregano
10 Kalamata olives, chopped
2 lb asparagus, trimmed

2 tbsp fresh basil, chopped
¼ cup Parmesan cheese, grated
Salt and black pepper to taste

Warm 2 tablespoons of olive oil in a skillet over medium heat sauté the garlic for 1-2 minutes, stirring often, until golden. Add tomatoes, olives, and oregano and cook until tomatoes begin to break down, about 3 minutes; transfer to a bowl. Coat the asparagus with the remaining olive oil and cook in a grill pan over medium heat for about 5 minutes, turning once until crisp-tender. Sprinkle with salt and pepper. Transfer asparagus to a serving platter, top with tomato mixture, and sprinkle with basil and Parmesan cheese. Serve and enjoy!

546.   Oregano Vegetable Stew

Serves: 6 | Ready in about: 70 minutes

1 (14 ½-oz) can diced tomatoes, drained with juice reserved
3 tbsp olive oil
1 onion, chopped
2 tbsp fresh oregano, minced
1 tsp paprika

4 garlic cloves, minced
1 ½ lb green beans, sliced
1 lb Yukon Gold potatoes, peeled and chopped

1 tbsp tomato paste
Salt and black pepper to taste
3 tbsp fresh basil, chopped

Preheat your oven to 360 F. Warm the olive oil in a skillet over medium heat. Sauté onion and garlic for 3 minutes until softened. Stir in oregano and paprika for 30 seconds. Transfer to a baking dish and add green beans, potatoes, tomatoes, tomato paste, salt, pepper, and 1 ½ cups of water; stir well. Bake for 40-50 minutes. Sprinkle with basil.

547.   Olive Zucchini Bake

Serves: 4 | Ready in about: 1 hour 40 minutes

3 tbsp olive oil
1 (28-oz) can tomatoes, diced
2 lb zucchinis, sliced
1 onion, chopped

Salt and black pepper to taste
3 garlic cloves, minced
¼ tsp dried oregano
¼ tsp red pepper flakes

10 Kalamata olives, chopped
2 tbsp fresh parsley, chopped

Preheat your oven to 325 F. Warm the olive oil in a saucepan over medium heat. Sauté zucchini for about 3 minutes per side; transfer to a bowl. Stir-fry the onion and salt in the same saucepan for 3-5 minutes, stirring occasionally until the onion is soft and lightly golden. Stir in garlic, oregano, and pepper flakes and cook until fragrant, about 30 seconds. Add in olives, tomatoes, salt, and pepper, bring to a simmer, and cook for about 10 minutes, stirring occasionally. Return the zucchini, cover, and transfer the pot to the oven. Bake for 10-15 minutes. Sprinkle with parsley and serve.

548.   Stir-Fried Cherry Tomatoes

Serves: 4 | Ready in about: 10 minutes

2 tbsp olive oil
2 lb cherry tomatoes, halved

2 tbsp balsamic glaze
Salt and black pepper to taste

1 garlic clove, minced
2 tbsp fresh basil, torn

Warm olive oil in a skillet over medium heat. Add the cherry tomatoes and cook for 1-2 minutes, stirring occasionally. Stir in garlic, salt, and pepper and cook until fragrant, about 30 seconds. Drizzle with balsamic glaze and decorate with basil. Serve and enjoy!

549.   Mushrooms & Garlic-Parsley Sauté

Serves: 6 | Ready in about: 15 minutes

3 tbsp butter
2 lb cremini mushrooms, sliced

2 tbsp garlic, minced
Salt and black pepper to taste

1 tbsp fresh parsley, chopped

Melt butter in a skillet over medium heat. Cook the garlic for 1-2 minutes until soft. Stir in the mushrooms and season with salt. Sauté for 7-8 minutes, stirring often. Remove to a serving dish. Top with pepper and parsley to serve.

550.   Cauliflower & Mushroom Roast

Serves: 4 | Ready in about: 35 minutes

2 tbsp olive oil
4 cups cauliflower florets
1 celery stalk, chopped

1 cup mushrooms, sliced
10 cherry tomatoes, halved
1 yellow onion, chopped

2 garlic cloves, minced
2 tbsp dill, chopped
Salt and black pepper to taste

Preheat oven to 340 F. Line a baking sheet with parchment paper. Place in cauliflower florets, olive oil, mushrooms, celery, tomatoes, onion, garlic, salt, and pepper and mix to combine. Bake for 25 minutes. Serve topped with dill.

551.   Balsamic Baby Artichoke Antipasto

Serves: 4 | Ready in about: 5 minutes

1 (14-oz) jar roasted red peppers
8 canned artichoke hearts
1 (16-oz) can garbanzo beans

1 cup whole black olives
¼ cup balsamic vinegar
Salt to taste

1 lemon, zested

Slice the red peppers and put them into a large bowl. Cut the artichoke hearts into quarters, and add them to the bowl. Add the garbanzo beans, olives, balsamic vinegar, lemon zest, and salt. Toss all the ingredients together. Serve.

SIDES, SAUCES & SPICES

552.   Stuffed Cherry Tomatoes with Cheese

Serves: 6 | Ready in about: 10 minutes

2 tbsp fresh dill, chopped
30 cherry tomatoes

3 oz cream cheese, softened
¼ cup mayonnaise

2 tbsp roasted garlic paste
3 tbsp grated Parmesan cheese

Cut off the top of the cherry tomatoes. Discard the seeds and core with a small teaspoon. Drain upside down on paper towels. Beat the cream cheese in a small bowl until soft and fluffy. Add mayonnaise, roasted garlic paste, and Parmesan cheese; beat well. Divide the mixture between the cherry tomatoes and sprinkle with dill. Serve.

553.   Spicy Grilled Mushroom Bruschetta

Serves: 4 | Ready in about: 20 minutes

8 thick baguette slices
4 tsp aioli
12 oz mixed mushrooms
2 tbsp butter

¼ tsp dried thyme
¼ tsp dried oregano
½ tsp garlic powder
½ lemon, juiced and zested

Salt and black pepper to taste
1 tbsp fresh parsley, chopped

Melt butter in a heavy skillet over medium heat. Add mushrooms and cook without stirring for 4–5 minutes. Stir in herbs, lemon zest and juice, and garlic powder and cook until accumulating liquid is mostly evaporated. Season with salt and pepper.

Preheat a grill pan over medium heat. Grill the bread until dark brown marks decorate their faces, top, and bottom. Transfer to a serving plate. Spread the aioli onto the toasted bread slices. Spoon the mushrooms onto the bread and top with parsley.

554.   Cheese & Bell Pepper Stuffed Tomatoes

Serves: 2 | Ready in about: 35 minutes

½ lb mixed bell peppers, chopped
1 tbsp olive oil
4 tomatoes
2 garlic cloves, minced

½ cup diced onion
1 tbsp chopped oregano
1 tbsp chopped basil
1 cup shredded mozzarella

1 tbsp grated Parmesan cheese
Salt and black pepper to taste

Preheat your oven to 370 F. Cut the tops of the tomatoes and scoop out the pulp. Chop the pulp and set aside. Arrange the tomatoes on a lined parchment paper baking sheet. Warm the olive oil in a pan over medium heat. Add garlic, onion, basil, bell peppers, and oregano, and cook for 5 minutes. Sprinkle with salt and pepper. Remove from the heat and mix in tomato pulp and mozzarella cheese. Divide the mixture between the tomatoes and top with Parmesan cheese. Bake for 20 minutes or until the cheese melts. Serve.

555.   Bell Peppers Stuffed with Rice

Serves: 4 | Ready in about: 70 minutes

4 red bell peppers, tops and seeds removed
2 tbsp olive oil
1 cup cooked brown rice
4 oz crumbled ricotta cheese
4 cups fresh baby spinach

3 Roma tomatoes, chopped
1 onion, finely chopped
1 cup mushrooms, sliced
2 garlic cloves, minced

1 tsp dried oregano
Salt and black pepper to taste
2 tbsp fresh parsley, chopped

Preheat your oven to 350 F. Warm olive oil in a skillet over medium heat and sauté onion, garlic, and mushrooms for 5 minutes. Stir in tomatoes, spinach, rice, salt, oregano, parsley, and pepper, and cook for 3 minutes until the spinach wilts. Remove from the heat. Stuff the bell peppers with the rice mixture and top with ricotta cheese. Arrange the peppers on a greased baking pan and pour in 1/4 cup of water. Bake covered with aluminum foil for 30 minutes. Then, bake uncovered for another 10 minutes. Serve and enjoy!

556. Simple Roasted Mushrooms

Serves: 4 | Ready in about: 30 minutes + marinating time

6 portobello mushroom caps
1 tsp extra-virgin olive oil

2 tsp balsamic vinegar
Salt and garlic powder to taste

¼ cup fresh thyme, chopped
¼ cup fresh oregano, chopped

Mix all ingredients, except mushrooms, in a large bowl. Add in the mushroom caps, cover with a lid, and refrigerate for at least 2 hours at room temperature. Preheat oven to 400 F. Arrange the mushrooms on a parchment-lined baking sheet. Roast them for 15–20 minutes until cooked. To serve, slice the caps into small wedges.

557. Balsamic Roasted Red Pepper & Olive Spread

Serves: 6 | Ready in about: 10 minutes

¼ tsp dried thyme
1 tbsp capers
½ cup pitted green olives

1 roasted red pepper, chopped
1 tsp balsamic vinegar
2/3 cup soft bread crumbs

2 cloves garlic, minced
½ tsp red pepper flakes
1/3 cup extra-virgin olive oil

Place all ingredients, except olive oil, in a food processor and blend until chunky. With the machine running, slowly pour in the olive oil until well combined. Refrigerate or serve at room temperature.

558. Sautéed Broccoli with Garlic

Serves: 4 | Ready in about: 15 minutes

1 red bell pepper, cut into chunks
3 tbsp olive oil
2 garlic cloves, minced

½ tsp red pepper flakes
½ lb broccoli florets
Salt to taste

2 tsp lemon juice
1 tbsp anchovy paste

Warm olive oil in a skillet over medium heat. Add the broccoli, garlic, and red pepper flakes and stir briefly for 3-4 minutes until the florets turn bright green. Season with salt. Add 2 tbsp of water and let the broccoli cook for another 2–3 minutes. Stir in the red bell pepper, lemon juice, and anchovy paste and cook for 1 more minute. Serve.

559. Sweet Potato Mash

Serves: 4 | Ready in about: 30 minutes

¼ cup mascarpone cheese, softened
¼ cup olive oil

½ tsp ground nutmeg
1 ¼ lb sweet potatoes, cubed

Salt and black pepper to taste
1 tbsp fresh chives, chopped

Place the sweet potatoes in a pot over high heat and cover with water. Bring to a boil, then lower the heat and simmer covered for 20 minutes. Drain the potatoes and back to the pot. Stir in mascarpone, olive oil, nutmeg, salt, and pepper. Mash them with a potato masher until smooth. Sprinkle with chives.

560. Pecorino-Eggplant Casserole

Serves: 4 | Ready in about: 40 minutes

2 tbsp olive oil
1 lb eggplants, sliced
1 onion, sliced

1 cup tomatoes, sliced
4 tbsp Pecorino cheese, grated
1 celery stalk, sliced

4 garlic cloves, crushed
1 tsp Italian seasoning
1 chili pepper, minced

Preheat your oven to 360 F. Arrange the vegetables on a greased baking dish and sprinkle them with spices and olive oil. Roast the vegetables for 18-20 minutes. Scatter the cheese on the top and continue to bake for 10 minutes.

561. Zucchini Marinara

Serves: 4 | Ready in about: 25 minutes

2 tbsp olive oil
1 shallot, chopped
1 garlic clove, minced

1 zucchini, sliced into rounds
Salt and black pepper to taste
1 cup marinara sauce

¼ cup mozzarella, shredded
2 tbsp fresh basil, chopped

Warm olive oil in a skillet over medium heat. Sauté the shallot and garlic for 3 minutes until just tender and fragrant. Add in the zucchini and season with salt and pepper; cook for 4 minutes until lightly browned. Add marinara sauce and bring to a simmer; cook until zucchini is tender, 5-8 minutes. Scatter the mozzarella cheese on top of the zucchini layer and cover; heat for about 3 minutes until the cheese is melted. Sprinkle with basil and serve immediately.

562. Red Onion & Asparagus Side Dish

Serves: 6 | Ready in about: 20 minutes

2 tbsp olive oil
1 ½ lb asparagus spears

1 tsp garlic powder
1 red onion, sliced

Salt and black pepper to taste

Preheat your oven to 390 F. Brush the asparagus with olive oil. Toss with garlic powder, salt, and black pepper. Roast in the oven for about 15 minutes. Top the roasted asparagus with the red onion. Serve and enjoy!

563. Arugula & Zucchini Stuffed Mushrooms

Serves: 4 | Ready in about: 65 minutes

4 portobello mushrooms, stems removed
2 tbsp olive oil
2 cups arugula
¼ cup chopped fresh basil
1 onion, finely chopped

1 zucchini, chopped
¼ tsp dried thyme
⅛ tsp red pepper flakes
2 garlic cloves, minced

½ cup grated Parmesan cheese
Salt and black pepper to taste

Preheat your oven to 350 F. Warm olive oil in a skillet over medium heat and sauté onion, arugula, zucchini, thyme, salt, pepper, and red flakes for 5 minutes. Stir in garlic and sauté for 30 seconds. Turn the heat off. Mix in basil and scoop into the mushroom caps and arrange them on a baking sheet. Top with Parmesan cheese and bake for 30-40 minutes, until mushrooms are nice and soft and the cheese is melted.

564. Cherry Tomato & Fennel Traybake

Serves: 4 | Ready in about: 35 minutes

¼ cup olive oil
20 cherry tomatoes, halved

2 fennel bulbs, cut into wedges
10 black olives, sliced

1 lemon, cut into wedges
Salt and black pepper to taste

Preheat your oven to 425 F. Combine fennel, olive oil, tomatoes, salt, and pepper in a bowl. Place in a baking pan and roast in the oven for about 25 minutes until golden. Top with olives and serve with lemon wedges on the side.

565. Fast Green Bean Stir-Fry

Serves: 4 | Ready in about: 15 minutes

1 tbsp olive oil
1 tbsp butter
1 fennel bulb, sliced

1 red onion, sliced
4 cloves garlic, pressed
1 lb green beans, steamed

½ tsp dried oregano
2 tbsp balsamic vinegar
Salt and black pepper to taste

Heat butter and olive oil in a saucepan over medium heat. Add in the onion and garlic and sauté for 3 minutes. Stir in oregano, fennel, balsamic vinegar, salt, and pepper. Stir-fry for another 6-8 minutes and add the green beans; cook for 2-3 minutes. Adjust the seasoning and serve.

566. Cheesy Zucchini Strips

Serves: 4 | Ready in about: 30 minutes

4 zucchini, quartered lengthwise
2 tbsp olive oil

½ cup grated Pecorino cheese
1 tbsp dried dill

¼ tsp garlic powder
Salt and black pepper to taste

Preheat your oven to 350 F. Combine zucchini and olive oil in a bowl. Mix cheese, salt, garlic powder, dill, and pepper in a bowl. Add in zucchini and toss to combine. Arrange the zucchini fingers on a lined baking sheet and bake for about 20 minutes until golden Set oven to broil and broil for 2 minutes until crispy. Serve and enjoy!

567. Broccoli & Cheese Quiche

Serves: 4 | Ready in about: 45 minutes

1 tsp Mediterranean seasoning
3 eggs
½ cup heavy cream

3 tbsp olive oil
1 red onion, chopped
2 garlic cloves, minced

2 oz mozzarella, shredded
1 lb broccoli, cut into florets

Preheat your oven to 320 F. Warm the oil in a pan over medium heat. Sauté the onion and garlic until just tender and fragrant. Add in the broccoli and continue to cook until crisp-tender for about 4 minutes. Spoon the mixture into a greased casserole dish. Beat the eggs with heavy cream and Mediterranean seasoning. Spoon this mixture over the broccoli layer. Bake for 18-20 minutes. Top with the shredded cheese and broil for 5 to 6 minutes or until hot and bubbly on the top. Serve.

568. Risotto ai Funghi

Serves: 4 | Ready in about: 25 minutes

1 ½ cups mixed mushrooms, sliced
3 tbsp olive oil
1 shallot, chopped

1 cup Arborio rice
4 cups vegetable stock
2 tbsp dry white wine

1 cup grated Parmesan cheese
2 tbsp butter
2 tbsp fresh parsley, chopped

Pour the stock into a small saucepan over low heat and bring to a simmer; then, turn the heat off. Warm the olive oil in a large saucepan over medium heat. Sauté the mushrooms and shallot for 6 minutes until tender. Stir in rice for 3 minutes until opaque. Pour in the wine and stir. Gradually add the hot stock to the rice mixture, about 1 ladleful at a time, stirring until the liquid is absorbed. Remove the saucepan from the heat, stir in butter and 3 tbsp of Parmesan cheese. Cover and leave to rest for 5 minutes. Scatter the remaining cheese and parsley over the risotto and serve in bowls.

569. Clasic Marinara Sauce

Serves: 6 | Ready in about: 50 minutes

2 (14-oz) cans crushed tomatoes with their juices
1 tsp dried oregano
2 tbsp + ¼ cup olive oil

2 tbsp butter
1 small onion, diced
1 red bell pepper, chopped
4 garlic cloves, minced

Salt and black pepper to taste
½ cup thinly sliced basil
2 tbsp chopped rosemary
1 tsp red pepper flakes

Warm 2 tbsp olive oil and butter in a large skillet over medium heat. Add the onion, garlic, and red pepper and sauté for about 5 minutes until tender. Season with salt and pepper. Reduce the heat to low and add the tomatoes and their juices, remaining olive oil, oregano, half of the basil, rosemary, and red pepper flakes. Bring to a simmer and cover. Cook for 50-60 minutes. Blitz the sauce with an immersion blender and sprinkle with the remaining basil.

570. Spiralized Zucchini with Mushroom Sauce

Serves: 4 | Ready in about: 25 minutes

1 lb oyster mushrooms, chopped
2 tbsp olive oil
1 cup chicken broth

1 tsp Mediterranean sauce
1 yellow onion, minced
1 cup pureed tomatoes

2 garlic cloves, minced
2 zucchinis, spiralized

Warm olive oil in a saucepan over medium heat and sauté the zoodles for 1-2 minutes; reserve. Sauté the onion and garlic in the same saucepan for 2-3 minutes. Add in the mushrooms and continue to cook for 2 to 3 minutes until they release liquid. Add in the remaining ingredients and cover the pan; let it simmer for 10 minutes longer until everything is cooked through. Top the zoodles with the prepared mushroom sauce and serve.

571. No-Time Garlic Butter

Serves: 4 | Ready in about: 5 minutes

½ cup butter, softened
1 garlic clove, finely minced

2 tsp fresh rosemary, chopped
1 tsp marjoram, chopped

Salt to taste

Blend butter, garlic, rosemary, marjoram, and salt in your food processor until the mixture is well combined, smooth, and creamy, scraping down the sides as necessary. Scrape the butter mixture with a spatula into a glass container and cover. Store in the refrigerator for up to 30 days.

572.   Garlic Infused Olive Oil

Serves: 4 | Ready in about: 35 minutes

Salt and black pepper to taste
1 cup extra-virgin olive oil

4 large garlic cloves, smashed
4 sprigs rosemary

Warm olive oil in a medium skillet over low heat and sauté garlic and rosemary sprigs for 30-40 minutes, until fragrant and garlic is very tender, stirring occasionally. Don't let the oil get too hot, or the garlic will burn and become bitter. Remove from the heat and leave to cool slightly. Using a slotted spoon, remove the garlic and rosemary and pour the oil into a glass container. Use cooled.

573.   Vegetable Sauce

Serves: 6 | Ready in about: 15 minutes

6 tbsp extra-virgin olive oil
¼ tsp ground fennel seeds
½ tsp ground coriander
¼ tsp ground cumin

¼ tsp ground cardamom
¼ tsp salt
¼ tsp ground cloves
2 tbsp fresh cilantro leaves

2 tbsp fresh parsley leaves
2 green chiles, chopped
2 garlic cloves, minced

Place olive oil, fennel seeds, coriander, cumin, cardamom, salt, and cloves in a microwave-safe bowl. Cover and microwave for about 30 seconds until fragrant. Leave to cool at room temperature.

Blitz the oil-spice mixture, cilantro, parsley, chiles, and garlic in your food processor until coarse paste forms, scraping downsides of the bowl as needed. Store in an airtight container in the refrigerator for up to 2-3 days.

574.   Cremini Mushroom Sauce

Serves: 4 | Ready in about: 15 minutes

1 cup cremini mushrooms, chopped
2 tbsp olive oil
1 small onion, chopped

2 garlic cloves, minced
3 tbsp butter
½ cup white wine

½ cup vegetable broth
1 cup heavy cream
2 tbsp parsley, chopped

Heat olive oil in a pan over medium. Add the onion and garlic and sauté until the onion is translucent, 3 minutes. Add the butter and mushrooms and cook for 5-7 minutes until the mushrooms are tender. Pour in the wine and scrape up any browned bits from the bottom of the pan. Simmer for 3-4 minutes. Add the vegetable broth and simmer for 5 minutes until the sauce reduces by about three-quarters. Add the heavy cream and simmer for 2-3 minutes. Sprinkle with parsley. Serve and enjoy!

DESSERTS

575.   Honey-Berry Sorbet

Serves: 4 | Ready in about: 10 minutes + freezing time

1 tsp lemon juice
¼ cup honey

1 cup fresh strawberries
1 cup fresh raspberries

1 cup fresh blueberries

Bring one cup of water to a boil in a pot over high heat. Stir in honey until dissolved. Remove from the heat and mix in berries and lemon juice; let cool. Once cooled, add the mixture to a food processor and pulse until smooth. Transfer to a shallow glass and freeze for 1 hour. Stir with a fork and freeze for 30 more minutes. Repeat a couple of times. Serve in dessert dishes.

576.   Red Wine Poached Pears

Serves: 4 | Ready in about: 1 hour 35 minutes

4 pears, peeled with stalk intact
2 cups red wine
8 whole cloves

1 cinnamon stick
½ tsp vanilla extract
2 tsp sugar

Creme fraiche for garnish

In a pot over low heat, mix the red wine, cinnamon stick, cloves, vanilla, and sugar and bring to a simmer, stirring often until the sugar is dissolved. Add in the pears, make sure that they are submerged and poach them for 15-20 minutes. Remove the pears to a platter and allow the liquid simmering over medium heat for 15 minutes until reduced by half and syrupy. Remove from the heat and let cool for 10 minutes. Drain to discard the spices, let cool, and pour over the pears. Top with creme fraiche and serve.

577.   Grilled Maple Pineapple

Serves: 4 | Ready in about: 10 minutes

1 pineapple, peeled and cut into wedges
1 tbsp maple syrup

½ tsp ground cinnamon

Preheat grill pan over high heat. Place the fruit in a bowl and drizzle with maple syrup; sprinkle with ground cinnamon. Grill for about 7-8 minutes, turning occasionally until the fruit chars slightly. Serve.

578.   Pistachio Dumplings

Serves: 4 | Ready in about: 25 minutes

1 cup vegetable oil
½ cup warm milk
2 cups flour
2 eggs, beaten

1 tsp sugar
1 ½ oz active dry yeast
1 cup warm water
½ tsp vanilla extract

1 tsp cinnamon
1 orange, zested
4 tbsp honey
2 tbsp pistachios, chopped

In a large bowl, sift the flour and combine it with the cinnamon and orange zest. In another bowl, mix the sugar, yeast, and ½ cup of warm water. Leave to stand until the yeast dissolves. Stir in milk, eggs, vanilla, and flour mixture. Beat with an electric mixer until smooth. Cover the bowl with plastic wrap and let sit to rise in a warm place for at least 1 hour. Pour the vegetable oil into a deep pan or wok to come halfway up the sides and heat the oil. Add some more oil if necessary. Using a teaspoon, form balls, one by one, and drop in the hot oil one after another. Fry the balls on all sides, until golden brown. Remove them with a slotted spoon to paper towels to soak the excess fat. Repeat the process until the dough is exhausted. Drizzle with honey and sprinkle with pistachios.

579.   Watermelon Gelato

Serves: 4 | Ready in about: 10 minutes + freezing time

¼ cup honey
4 cups watermelon cubes

¼ cup lemon juice
12 mint leaves to serve

In a food processor or a blender, blend the watermelon, honey, and lemon juice to form a purée with chunks. Transfer to a freezer-proof container and place in the freezer for 1 hour. Remove the container from and scrape with a fork. Return the to the freezer and repeat the process every half hour until the sorbet is completely frozen, for around 4 hours. Share into bowls, garnish with mint leaves, and serve.

580. Almond-Amaretto Squares

Serves: 4 | Ready in about: 1 hour 10 minutes

1 tsp olive oil	2 cups flour	¼ tsp salt
Zest from 1 lemon	3/4 cup sugar	3 eggs
3/4 cup slivered almonds	1 tsp baking powder	2 tbsp Amaretto liqueur

Preheat your oven to 280 F. Combine flour, baking powder, sugar, lemon zest, salt, and almonds in a bowl and mix well. In another bowl, beat the eggs and amaretto liqueur. Pour into the flour mixture and mix to combine.Grease a baking sheet with olive oil and spread in the dough. Bake for 40-45 minutes. Remove from the oven, let cool for a few minutes, and cut diagonally into slices about ½-inch thick. Place the pieces back on the sheet, cut sides up, and bake for 20 more minutes. Let cool before serving.

581. Baked Cardamom Apple Slices

Serves: 2 | Ready in about: 30 minutes

1 ½ tsp cardamom	4 peeled, cored apples, sliced	2 tbsp milk
½ tsp salt	2 tbsp honey	

Preheat your oven to 390 F. In a bowl, combine apple slices, salt, and ½ tsp of cardamom. Arrange them on a greased baking dish and cook for 20 minutes. Remove to a serving plate. In the meantime, place milk, honey, and remaining cardamom in a pot over medium heat. Cook until simmer. Pour the sauce over the apples and serve immediately.

582. Vanilla Pudding with Kiwii

Serves: 4 | Ready in about: 20 minutes + chilling time

2 kiwi, peeled and sliced	2 ¼ cups milk	1 tsp vanilla extract
1 egg	½ cup honey	3 tbsp cornstarch

In a large bowl, beat the egg with honey. Stir in 2 cups of milk and vanilla. Pour into a pot over medium heat and bring to a boil. Combine cornstarch and remaining milk in a bowl. Pour slowly into the pot and boil for 1 minute until thickened, stirring often. Divide between 4 cups and transfer to the fridge. Top with kiwi and serve.

583. Delightful Coconut-Covered Strawberries

Serves: 4 | Ready in about: 20 minutes + cooling time

1 cup chocolate chips	1 lb strawberries	½ tsp ground nutmeg
¼ cup coconut flakes	½ tsp vanilla extract	¼ tsp salt

Melt the chocolate chips for 30 seconds. Remove and stir in vanilla, nutmeg, and salt. Let cool for 2-3 minutes. Dip strawberries into the chocolate and then into the coconut flakes. Place on a wax paper-lined cookie sheet and let sit for 30 minutes until the chocolate dries. Serve.

584. Almond-Chocolate Cups

Serves: 6 | Ready in about: 10 minutes + freezing time

½ cup butter	2 tbsp cocoa powder	2 tsp maple syrup
½ cup olive oil	1 tsp vanilla extract	
¼ cup ground flaxseed	1 tsp ground cinnamon	

In a large bowl, mix the butter, olive oil, flaxseed, cocoa powder, vanilla, cinnamon, and maple syrup and stir well with a spatula. Pour into 6 mini muffin liners and freeze until solid, at least 2 hours. Serve and enjoy!

585.   Almond-Cherry Bulgur Bowl

Serves: 6 | Ready in about: 20 minutes

1 tbsp vanilla sugar	1 cup water	8 dried figs, chopped
1 ½ cups bulgur	½ tsp ground cinnamon	½ cup almonds, chopped
2 cups milk	2 cups cherries, pitted	¼ cup fresh mint, chopped

Combine vanilla sugar, bulgur, milk, cinnamon, and 1 cup of water in a medium pot and stir to dissolve the sugar. Bring just to a boil. Cover, reduce the heat to medium-low, and simmer for 10 minutes or until the liquid is absorbed. Turn off the heat and stir in the cherries, figs, and almonds. Cover and let the hot bulgur thaw the cherries and partially hydrate the figs. Top with mint. Serve chilled or hot.

586.   Minty Sicilian Almond Granita

Serves: 4 | Ready in about: 5 minutes + freezing time

4 small oranges, chopped	2 tbsp lemon juice	¼ cup honey
½ tsp almond extract	1 cup orange juice	Fresh mint leaves for garnish

In a food processor, mix the oranges, orange juice, honey, almond extract, and lemon juice. Pulse until smooth. Pour in a dip dish and freeze for 1 hour. Mix with a fork and freeze for 30 minutes more. Repeat a couple of times. Pour into dessert glasses and garnish with basil leaves. Serve.

587.   Home-Style Fruit Cups

Serves: 4 | Ready in about: 10 minutes

1 cup orange juice	1 cup chopped cantaloupe	½ tsp ground cinnamon
½ cup watermelon cubes	½ cup cherries, chopped	
1 ½ cups grapes, halved	1 peach, chopped	

Combine the watermelon cubes, grapes, cherries, cantaloupe, and peach in a bowl. Add in the orange juice and mix well. Share into dessert cups, dust with cinnamon, and serve.

588.   Stuffed Baked Apples

Serves: 4 | Ready in about: 55 minutes

2 tbsp brown sugar	¼ cup chopped pecans	¼ tsp ground nutmeg
4 apples, cored	1 tsp ground cinnamon	¼ tsp ground ginger

Preheat your oven to 375 F. Arrange the apples cut-side up on a baking dish. Combine pecans, ginger, cinnamon, brown sugar, and nutmeg in a bowl. Scoop the mixture into the apples and bake for 35-40 minutes until golden brown.

589.   Frangelico Nut Bars

Serves: 4 | Ready in about: 10 minutes

2 tbsp olive oil	½ tsp Amaretto liqueur	¼ cup cocoa powder
¼ cup shredded coconut	1 cup almonds	
1 cup pistachios	2 cups dates, pitted	

In a food processor, blend the pistachios, dates, almonds, olive oil, Amaretto liqueur, and cocoa powder until well minced. Make tablespoon-size balls out of the mixture. Roll the balls in the shredded coconut to coat. Serve chilled.

590.   Blackberry-Orange Pannacotta

Serves: 4 | Ready in about: 15 minutes + chilling time

¾ cup half-and-half	3 tbsp sugar	1 tsp orange extract
1 tsp powdered gelatin	1 tsp orange zest	½ cup fresh blackberries
½ cup heavy cream	1 tbsp orange juice	2 mint leaves

Put ¼ cup of half-and-half in a large bowl. Mix in gelatin powder and set it aside for 10 minutes to hydrate. In a saucepan over medium heat, combine the remaining half-and-half, heavy cream, sugar, orange zest, orange juice, and orange extract. Warm the mixture for 4 minutes. Don't let it come to a full boil.

Remove from the heat. Let cool slightly. Add the gelatin into the cream mixture and whisk until the gelatin melts. Pour the mixture into 2 dessert glasses and refrigerate for at least 2 hours. Serve with fresh berries and garnish with mint leaves.

591. Healthy Pomegranate Blueberry Granita

Serves: 2 | Ready in about: 15 minutes + freezing time

1 cup blueberries
1 cup pomegranate juice

¼ cup sugar
¼ tsp lemon zest

Place blueberries, lemon zest, and pomegranate juice in a saucepan over medium heat and bring to a boil. Simmer for 5 minutes or until the blueberries start to break down. Stir the sugar in ¼ cup of water until the sugar is dissolved. Place the blueberry mixture and the sugar water in your blender and blitz for 1 minute or until the fruit is puréed.

Pour the mixture into a baking pan. The liquid should come about ½ inch up the sides. Let the mixture cool for 30 minutes, and then put it into the freezer. Every 30 minutes for the next 2 hours, scrape the granita with a fork to keep it from freezing solid. Serve it after 2 hours, or store it in a covered container in the freezer.

592. Mango Skewers with Vanilla Labneh

Serves: 4 | Ready in about: 15 minutes + straining time

2 cups plain yogurt
2 tbsp honey

1 tsp vanilla extract
A pinch of salt

2 mangoes, cut into chunks

Place a fine sieve lined with cheesecloth over a bowl and spoon the yogurt into the sieve. Allow the liquid to drain off for 12-24 hours hours. Transfer the strained yogurt to a bowl and mix in the honey, vanilla, and salt. Set it aside.

Heat your grill to medium-high. Thread the fruit onto skewers and grill for 2 minutes on each side until the fruit is softened and has grill marks on each side. Serve with labneh.

593. Quick & Easy Granita

Serves: 4 | Ready in about: 10 minutes + freezing time

¼ cup sugar
1 cup fresh strawberries

1 cup fresh raspberries
1 cup chopped fresh kiwi

1 tsp lemon juice

Bring one cup water to a boil in a small saucepan over high heat. Add the sugar and stir well until dissolved. Remove the pan from the heat, add the fruit and lemon juice, and cool to room temperature.

Once cooled, puree the fruit in a blender until smooth. Pour the puree into a shallow glass baking dish and place in the freezer for 1 hour. Stir with a fork and freeze for 30 minutes, then repeat. Serve and enjoy!

594. Pecan & Cinnamon Pear Oat Crisp

Serves: 4 | Ready in about: 30 minutes

2 tbsp butter, melted
4 fresh pears, mashed
½ lemon, juiced and zested

¼ cup maple syrup
1 cup gluten-free rolled oats
½ cup chopped pecans

½ tsp ground cinnamon
¼ tsp salt

Preheat your oven to 350 F. Combine the pears, lemon juice and zest, and maple syrup in a bowl. Stir to mix well, then spread the mixture on a greased baking dish. Combine the remaining ingredients in a small bowl. Stir to mix well. Pour the mixture over the pear mixture. Bake for 20 minutes or until the oats are golden brown.

595.   Quinoa & Dark Chocolate Barks

Serves: 4 | Ready in about: 20 minutes + freezing time

½ cup quinoa
½ tsp sea salt

1 cup dark chocolate chips
½ tsp mint extract

½ cup pomegranate seeds

Toast the quinoa in a greased saucepan for 3 minutes, stirring frequently. Remove the pan from the stove and mix in the salt. Set aside 2 tablespoons of the toasted quinoa. Microwave the chocolate for 1 minute. Stir until the chocolate is completely melted. Mix the toasted quinoa and mint extract into the melted chocolate.

Line a large, rimmed baking sheet with parchment paper. Spread the chocolate mixture onto the sheet. Sprinkle the remaining 2 tablespoons of quinoa and pomegranate seeds, pressing with a spatula. Freeze the mixture for 10-15 minutes or until set. Remove and break into about 2-inch jagged pieces. Store in the refrigerator until ready to serve.

596.   Raspberries Panna Cotta

Serves: 4 | Ready in about: 15 minutes + chilling time

2 tbsp warm water
2 tsp gelatin powder
2 cups heavy cream

1 cup raspberries
2 tbsp sugar
1 tsp vanilla extract

4 fresh mint leaves

Add 2 tbsp of warm water into a small bowl. Stir in the gelatin to dissolve. Allow the mixture to sit for 10 minutes. In a large bowl, combine the heavy cream, raspberries, sugar, and vanilla. Blend with an immersion blender until the mixture is smooth and the raspberries are well puréed.

Transfer the mixture to a saucepan and heat over medium heat until just below a simmer. Remove from the heat and let cool for 5 minutes. Add in the gelatin mixture, whisking constantly until smooth. Divide the custard between ramekins and refrigerate until set, 4-6 hours. Serve chilled garnished with mint.

597.   Marzipan Balls

Serves: 4 | Ready in about: 10 minutes

½ cup avocado oil
1 ½ cup almond flour

½ cup sugar
2 tsp almond extract

Add almond flour and sugar and pulse to your food processor until the mixture is ground. Add the almond extract and pulse until combined. With the processor running, stream in oil until the mixture starts to form a large ball.

Turn off the food processor. With hands, form the marzipan into six 1-inch diameter balls. Press to hold the mixture together. Store in an airtight container in the refrigerator for up to 14 days.

598.   Cinnamon Cheesecake Squares

Serves: 4 | Ready in about: 55 minutes + chilling time

½ cup butter, melted
1 (12-oz) box butter cake mix
3 large eggs

1 cup maple syrup
1/8 tsp cinnamon
1 cup cream cheese

1 tsp vanilla extract

Preheat your oven to 350 F. In a medium bowl, blend the cake mix, butter, cinnamon, and 1 egg. Then, pour the mixture into a greased baking pan. Mix together maple syrup, cream cheese, the remaining 2 eggs, and vanilla in a separate bowl and pour this gently over the first layer. Bake for 45-50 minutes. Remove and allow to cool. Cut into squares.

599.   Fall Pumpkin Cheesecake

Serves: 4 | Ready in about: 50 minutes + chilling time

½ cup butter, melted
1 cup flour
1 (14-oz) can pumpkin purée

1 ½ cups mascarpone cheese
½ cup sugar
4 large eggs

2 tsp vanilla extract
2 tsp pumpkin pie spice

Preheat your oven to 350 F. In a small bowl, combine the flour and melted butter with a fork until well combined. Press the mixture into the bottom of a greased baking pan. In a large bowl, beat together the pumpkin purée, mascarpone cheese, and sugar using an electric mixer.

Add the eggs, one at a time, beating after each addition. Stir in the vanilla and pumpkin pie spice until just combined. Pour the mixture over the crust and bake until set, 40-45 minutes. Allow to cool to room temperat ure. Refrigerate for at least 6 hours before serving. Serve chilled.

600.　Walnut-Carrot Cake

Serves: 6 | Ready in about: 55 minutes

½ cup vegetable oil
2 tsp vanilla extract
¼ cup maple syrup
6 eggs, beaten

½ cup flour
1 tsp baking powder
1 tsp baking soda
½ tsp ground nutmeg

1 tsp ground cinnamon
½ tsp salt
½ cup chopped walnuts
3 cups finely grated carrots

Preheat your oven to 350 F. Mix the vanilla extract, maple syrup, and oil in a large bowl. Stir to mix well. Add in the eggs and whisk to combine. Set aside. Combine the flour, baking powder, baking soda, nutmeg, cinnamon, and salt in a separate bowl. Stir to combine.

Make a well in the center of the flour mixture, then pour the egg mixture into the well and stir well. Add in the walnuts and carrots and toss to mix well. Pour the mixture into a greased baking dish.

Bake for 35-45 minutes or until puffed and the cake spring back when lightly press with your fingers. Remove the cake from the oven. Allow to cool, then serve.

Printed in Great Britain
by Amazon

34830391R00077